CULTURE
A Survival Guide to Customs and Etiquette

BOLIVIA

Mark Cramer

mc Marshall Cavendish
Editions

Photo Credits:
All photos from the author except pages 3, 22, 24, 52, 58, 69, 76, 201, 202 (Martin Vilela); 176 (Mark McMahon—http://filmtrips.com—author of *Driving to the End of the World*); 32 (courtesy of Fremen Tours). ▪ Cover photo: Photolibrary.com.

All illustrations by TRIGG

First published in 1996.
Copyright © 2006 Marshall Cavendish International (Asia) Private Limited

This edition published in 2006 by:
Marshall Cavendish Limited
119 Wardour Street
London W1F 0UW
E-mail: enquiries@marshallcavendish.co.uk

All rights reserved

No part of this publication may be reproduced, stored in a retrieval system or transmitted, in any form or by any means, electronic, mechanical, photocopying, recording or otherwise, without the prior permission of the copyright owner. Request for permission should be addressed to Marshall Cavendish International (Asia) Private Limited, 1 New Industrial Road, Singapore 536196. Tel: (65) 6213 9300, fax: (65) 6285 4871. E-mail: te@sg.marshallcavendish.com

The publisher makes no representation or warranties with respect to the contents of this book, and specifically disclaims any implied warranties or merchantability or fitness for any particular purpose, and shall in no events be liable for any loss of profit or any other commercial damage, including but not limited to special, incidental, consequential, or other damages.

Other Marshall Cavendish Offices:
Marshall Cavendish International (Asia) Private Limited. 1 New Industrial Road, Singapore 536196 ▪ Marshall Cavendish Corporation. 99 White Plains Road, Tarrytown NY 10591-9001, USA ▪ Marshall Cavendish International (Thailand) Co Ltd. 253 Asoke, 12th Flr, Sukhumvit 21 Road, Klongtoey Nua, Wattana, Bangkok 10110, Thailand ▪ Marshall Cavendish (Malaysia) Sdn Bhd, Times Subang, Lot 46, Subang Hi-Tech Industrial Park, Batu Tiga, 40000 Shah Alam, Selangor Darul Ehsan, Malaysia

Marshall Cavendish is a trademark of Times Publishing Limited

ISBN 10: 0-462-00002-8
ISBN 13: 978-0-462-00002-2

Printed in Singapore by Times Graphics Pte Ltd

ABOUT THE SERIES

Culture shock is a state of disorientation that can come over anyone who has been thrust into unknown surroundings, away from one's comfort zone. *CultureShock!* is a series of trusted and reputed guides which has, for decades, been helping expatriates and long-term visitors to cushion the impact of culture shock whenever they move to a new country.

Written by people who have lived in the country and experienced culture shock themselves, the authors share all the information necessary for anyone to cope with these feelings of disorientation more effectively. The guides are written in a style that is easy to read and covers a range of topics that will arm readers with enough advice, hints and tips to make their lives as normal as possible again.

Each book is structured in the same manner. It begins with the first impressions that visitors will have of that city or country. To understand a culture, one must first understand the people—where they came from, who they are, the values and traditions they live by, as well as their customs and etiquette. This is covered in the first half of the book.

Then on with the practical aspects—how to settle in with the greatest of ease. Authors walk readers through topics such as how to find accommodation, get the utilities and telecommunications up and running, enrol the children in school and keep in the pink of health. But that's not all. Once the essentials are out of the way, venture out and try the food, enjoy more of the culture and travel to other areas. Then be immersed in the language of the country before discovering more about the business side of things.

To round off, snippets of basic information are offered before readers are 'tested' on customs and etiquette of the country. Useful words and phrases, a comprehensive resource guide and list of books for further research are also included for easy reference.

CONTENTS

Introduction vi
Acknowledgements xi
Map of Bolivia xii

Chapter 1
First Impressions 1

Chapter 2
Overview of Land and History 6

Setting 7
Regions: the World in Microcosm 9
Temperature Zones: Keeping it Simple 13
Che Guevara 15
Altitude and the Brazilian Football Team 16
Finding Your Level 18
Human Plants 18
What Goes Down Must Come Up 20
Travel Advisory 21
Exotic Gas 23
Wilderness Challengers 26
Coca and Other Conflicts 26
Foreign Relations and Bolivian Law 28
Economic Realities 29
Class Struggle a la Boliviana 35
The Political Landscape 37
The Chronology of Transformation 38
Culture and Tourism 46

Chapter 3
The Bolivian People 49

Characters 50
The Celebrity Industry 51
Stereotypes and Rivalries 80

Chapter 4
The Social Setting 91

Evolution in First Gear 92

Chapter 5
Settling In 110

Immigration and Customs 111
Health 113
Currency and Money 119
Consumer Goods 120
Hotels 121
Transportation 121
Clothing 123
The Postal System 124
Telecommunications 124
Housing 125
Children 126
Dogs in the 'Hood 128
Crime Time 130
Interiors 130

Chapter 6
The Food of Bolivia 132

Food 133
Drinking and Socialising 138

Chapter 7
Enjoying Bolivia 143

Festivals 144
Getting Involved 154
La Paz: The Great Hole 156
From Highland to Jungle: Alternative Cities 178
High Valley Cities 188
Lowland Cities 196
Bolivia Plays Hard to Get 200
Tours for People who Don't Like Tours 217

Chapter 8
Learning the Language — 230

Spanish Language	231
Language and Titles	237
The Business of Language	238

Chapter 9
Working in Bolivia — 240

Business As Not Usual	241
The Art of Waiting	242
Who Do You Know?	243
Cultivating Contacts	243
Practical Business/Social Tips	244
Titles	245
Business Climate: Exports	245
The Curse of Oil	245
The Raw Reality of Raw Materials	246
Business Climate: Internal Economy	249

Chapter 10
Fast Facts About Bolivia — 252

Famous People	256
Acronyms	257
Country Statistics: Superlative Fact Sheet	260
Culture Quiz	261
Do's and Don'ts	268
Glossary	270
Resource Guide	274
Further Reading	293
About the Author	297
Index	298

INTRODUCTION

'To a wanderer in a snow covered field, a dried up prune or an old crust of bread tasted more delicious than a whole meal here with the prosperous guildsmen'.
—Hermann Hesse

Where is Bolivia? Club Med doesn't know, leaving lush semitropical swimming holes without sleek, manicured tourists. Pop-stars don't care, so Bolivia must be content with centuries-old harmonies and dance steps, as well as its home-grown fusion music, Latin, rock and jazz. Corporate giants and pop culture icons have not yet discovered Bolivia, which means that Bolivia must not exist.

At a Washington DC university Spanish class, I asked my students to write down the names of the countries they knew of in Latin America. None of them named Bolivia. (One wrote down Puerto Vallarta, a beach town in Mexico.)

One Cold War rumour referred to remote Bolivia as the safest place to hide during a nuclear war. Since this country was of no strategic importance, neither side had any reason to blow it to bits.

Today, thanks to immense but largely non-violent uprisings in defence of considerable gas, water and petrol resources against detrimental foreign exploitation, Bolivia is finally eligible for a place on the geopolitical map, beyond the classic war on drugs. In a 1995 threat to 'send US aircraft carriers to the coast of Bolivia' in order to destroy coca leaf production, Indiana Congressman Dan Burton showed just how oblivious people are to Bolivia. As a foreign relations expert, Burton, of all people, should have known that Bolivia has no coast!

Even when a people's rebellion forced the powerful Bechtel corporation to be expelled from the country and even when subsequent indigenous uprisings toppled two presidents because they were not seen as committed to protecting natural gas reserves from multinational plundering, North American and European media attention span was short. The fact that this country has remained so remote from world consciousness may be to her advantage. Without renouncing contemporary innovations such as Internet, third generation mobile phones and designer blood pressure pills, Bolivia remains aloof from modern trends of monotony, like twenty-minute brown-bag lunch periods and single-use zoning. Dense mountain valleys remain so isolated that university expeditions find animal and plant species that are new to science and endemic to the region.

Why go to this remote spot on the globe? Here are ten reasons for visiting or living in this absurdly magnificent country.

- **Native South American cultures**
  As Bolivia proceeds to undo its racist past, through new institutions, campaigns of awareness and indigenous movements, peoples of European descent interact with two major native American cultures and a number of other smaller communities native to South America. In December of 2005, Bolivia elected its first indigenous president, Evo Morales, the result of five years of social protest movements led by the country's indigenous majority.

- **Biodiversity**
  Bolivia is at the core of the most biodiverse region on earth, the Tropical Andes. Most of the world's climates and

ecosystems exist within this one country. In some places, a short bus ride or a robust hike can take you from one climate to another. An abundance of medicinal herbs and nutritious grains attract alternative health researchers, and new animal species are being discovered in Bolivia's chaste, sensual hinterlands.

- **Authenticity**
  Bolivia has unusual tourist attractions, but as yet, no tourist 'schlock'. Neither ancient ruins nor fossilised dinosaur tracks have been converted into theme parks. Vast and stunning national parks and protected areas remain virtually unexplored.
- **Alternative economies**
  Bolivia's economy is wide open. With both orthodox statism and transnational capitalism having failed, minds are open for new economic models. A business person who can produce a value-added export (as opposed to exporting raw materials neo-colonial style) will be considered an asset to the country and new ideas for expanding ecofriendly internal production and consumption are encouraged.
- **Arts**
  Bolivia is a feast for the eyes and the ears, as its arts and music flourish, both indigenous and Euro-indigenous, at home and abroad. Bolivia has a small but dedicated art-cinema industry, the quality of whose product far exceeds the meagre resources. Regional textiles add a colourful complexity to the daily context.
- **Hiking and trekking**
  Throughout this trekkers' paradise are stone paved trails originally used by the Incas over 2,000 years ago. Within this proverbial 'middle of nowhere' one might enter a mining town with a Wild West atmosphere, or an indigenous village with a centuries-old irrigation system that inspires the awe of modern agronomists. Even the day hiker can come across rapids carving through contorted canyons, untouched glaciers and rarely visited ruins.
- **Cost of living**
  Bolivia is among the least expensive countries in the world, especially for basic necessities. A fixed income

inadequate in developed countries will be enough here for relative affluence.

- **Security**
  Bolivia is amongst the safer countries in the world. Petty crime is relatively minimal, given the country's poverty, and violent crime is rare, but it is well advised to not flash a gold necklace in an outdoor market. One would expect the local cocaine issue to explode in violence, as it does in neighbouring Colombia. But in Bolivia, even coca growers, called *cocaleros*, employ Ghandi-style non-violent protests such as hunger strikes and penurious 30-day women's marches to defend their native crop against eradication, in the absence of feasible economic alternatives.

- **An uncharted future**
  Bolivia is a country with grave economic and social problems, inherited from her colonial past. As the structural schemes of the 20th century become discredited and the country's indigenous majority awakens, creative alternatives can no longer be stifled and an uncharted future is laden with surprises.

A decade ago, venerable Trotskyite activist and historian, Guillermo Lora, warned me that, "Bolivia is heading for a great social convulsion." He was right, but spirited non-violent dissent has mitigated the rougher edges of social upheaval.

The statistic listing Bolivia as the third poorest country in the Américas, based on per capita income, does not consider that many of the country's indigenous communities maintain self sufficiency without being part of the money economy. Massive famines do not seem to punish this country and natural disasters are rare, so Bolivia doesn't get anywhere near the publicity of Third World sisters such as Indonesia, Ethiopia or Bangladesh.

After years of coups and revolutions, Bolivia's political system has mellowed out into a democracy of relative tolerance. With the ongoing discrediting of traditional political parties, freedom of expression seems to thrive, especially in community radio, independent newspapers and public assemblies. Not unexpectedly, the frame of discourse on private TV is more blunted and ritual dissent by 'responsible' opinion makers follows the CNN model.

The fact that Bolivia has begun developing tourism, modern motorways and shopping centres so late may ultimately be to her advantage. The Ministry of Sustainable Development is in a position to learn from the mistakes of more accelerated countries and take a proactive stance in favour of a humanised form of progress.

Social and psychic adjustment to such a truly foreign place will not be easy. The purpose of this book is to make the adjustment as fluid as possible, so as to facilitate the enriching experiences that this exciting country has to offer.

This goal is best achieved by refraining from an encyclopaedic approach, seeking instead to decipher what is truly essential. *CultureShock! Bolivia* will be brimming with useful information, but rather than cram every town, plaza and hotel into the text, I have been selective in highlighting what I believe are the most singular customs and alluring places. In this way, the drama of Bolivia will not be interrupted with too many asides. The Resource Guide at the end of the text contains useful information not found in the narration.

Should you decide to visit or settle in Bolivia, you will be in good company. Foreigners who choose such a remote and unpublicised country, by definition are not an ordinary breed. Bolivia seems to attract the most stimulating and enlightened world adventurers. You will meet a few of them in this book.

Let your Bolivian adventure begin right here.

ACKNOWLEDGEMENTS

Thanks to Jonathan Griffiths, the original editor on this project, for his spirited exchange of ideas, as well as current editors Natalie Thompson and Patricia Ng, with special thanks to Trigg. *Muchas gracias* to Martha Sonia Arraya, for having painstakingly reviewed the manuscript to root out false stereotypes and add valuable insights on her native culture. The writers at the former *Bolivian Times* are applauded for their dedication to uncovering the marvels and truths of this remarkable country. And special thanks to the late Walter Solón Romero, artist and alchemist, quixotic world explorer and miner of the Bolivian soul, for having let me explore his workshop and delve into his fertile imagination.

Finally, thanks to the many distinguished Bolivians and perceptive foreign visitors who graciously granted me interviews.

A meticulous effort has been made to ensure that all names of establishments, addresses, phone numbers, websites and other types of factual information are accurate. Inevitably, businesses fold, phone numbers change and even reputable written information sources sometimes contain mistakes. I apologise in advance if the reader should telephone a hotel and end up speaking with a funeral parlour. Welcome to Bolivia, an unpredictable country.

MAP OF BOLIVIA

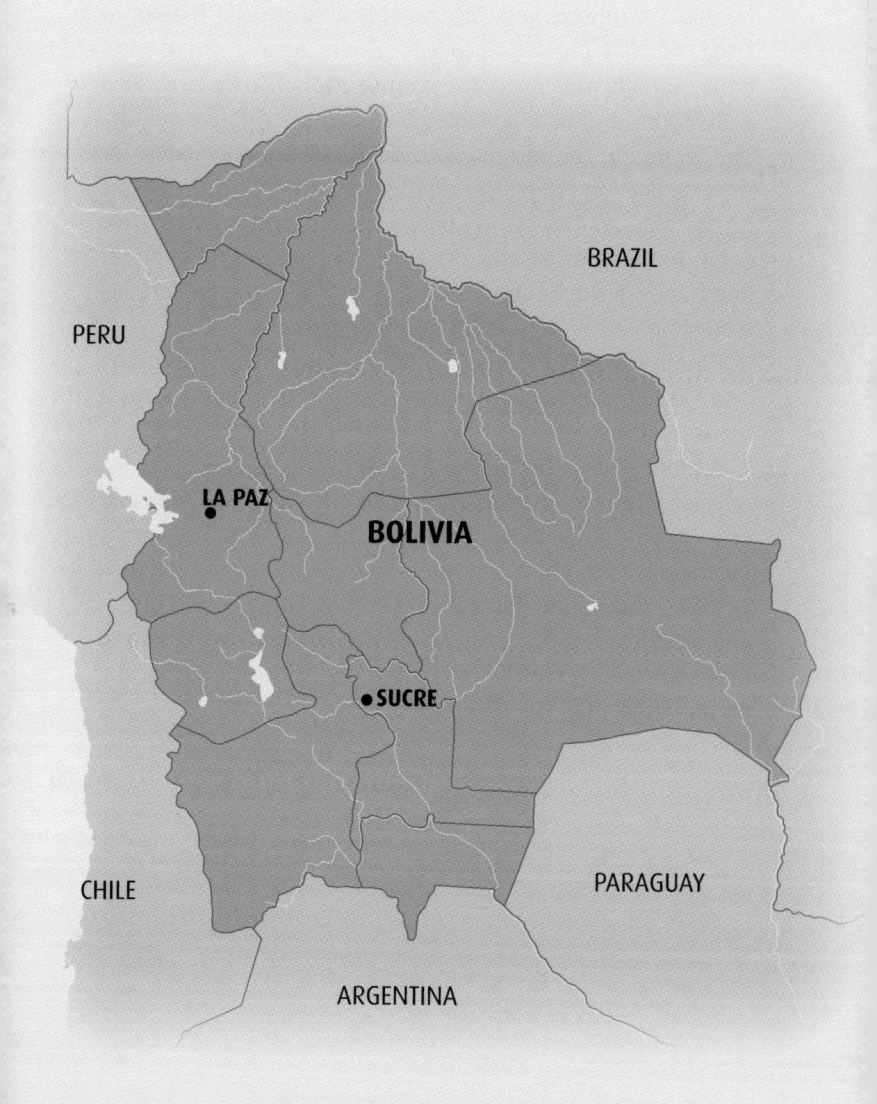

FIRST IMPRESSIONS

CHAPTER 1

THIS IS THE CAPTAIN SPEAKING. WE ARE BEGINNING OUR ASCENT TO LA PAZ AIRPORT...

'I was served coca tea in the first-aid office and quickly recovered my balance and a portion of my self-esteem. I had discovered a country where the unexpected is normal and not a single breath is taken for granted.'
—Author's journal

For my initial arrival in La Paz, the world's highest capital city, I had been working out regularly, and was fit and ready to confront the obscene altitude. We were approaching the only airport in the world where a plane has to go up in order to come down. We glided over the highest navigable lake in the world, the profoundly blue Lake Titicaca, with the snowcapped cordillera real in the background, and then finally descended over the high plane.

My wife and son preceded me down the stairway to the tarmac, 4,100 m (more than 13,000 ft) above sea level. Behind me was a man with a beer belly, a chain smoker who had been counting the seconds for his first light-up after the long flight.

Once in the El Alto airport, on the way to immigration, I felt a silent swell within my chest and head, a shortness of breath and a dizziness that suggested the onset of a major faint. I dumped my two suitcases, not caring the least who might come along and swipe them. I sat in a chair and held my head down between my knees to prevent the loss of consciousness. From the corner of an eye, I glimpsed at Mr Beer Belly, strutting by as if he were on the Olympic fast-walking team. Eventually, my wife sensed I was no longer behind them, found me and called for help.

(Later I would learn from a high altitude medical specialist that physical condition is a poor indicator for adaptation, an opinion corroborated in subsequent years when powerful

Entering La Paz from El Alto, with Mount Huayna Potosí staring upon me.

Brazilian and Argentine football teams would fly up from sea level to La Paz and get roundly defeated by a makeshift Bolivian squad.)

I was served coca tea in the first-aid office, and quickly recovered my balance and a portion of my self-esteem. We were greeted by countless members of my wife's extended family, one of whom, a cheerful brother-in-law, put my two suitcases into his trunk and invited me to sit in the front seat of his car.

The front window became the wide screen of a mind-boggling documentary. Through the streets of the shantytown-turned-city, El Alto, through tangled telephone wires, (facing us) there was the view of Mount Illimani, dressed in brilliant white robes, sitting over the scene judgmentally, imposing a sense of awe.

Suddenly the car came to an edge, and it seemed as if we were going off into a bottomless abyss. They called it 'The Hole'. It was La Paz, twisting and curling far below, an unplanned mixture of colourful highrises and colonial row buildings with a single motorway spiralling down as if into a huge open mine pit, and then temporarily straightening out when it arrived at the city centre, only to begin a new downward spiral, plunging its way to the south zone of the urban labyrinth.

I couldn't see it, but I knew that this hole was virtually bottomless, that there were ancient footpaths that could take me through an unbelievable diversity of ecosystems, to fertile valleys 2,600 m (8,530 ft) above sea level and later as one approached sea level, steamy forests of Amazon tributaries.

I looked back up. There were other footpaths that could lead the hiker into the same cordillera that I had glimpsed at from the plane, and lead me, or so I wished, to view the face of shining glaciers, from a vantage point of 5,000 m (about 17,000 ft) above sea level.

As we entered the city, I could glimpse at the faces in overcrowded streets and not miss the fact that the majority were indigenous, just as I had read. I wondered if there was a correlation between two facts: that the majority population in this country is indigenous and that few places in the world have a comparable degree of biodiversity, for you'd have to search far and wide to find any other country that still maintained 46 per cent of its land as protected forest.

All that oxygen filtering up from Bolivia, helping people breathe in far-off continents, and yet so very little of it was reaching my own lungs! My upward and awkward first steps at an outdoor stairway were interrupted by a gasping for air. A doctor in the family told me that my blood pressure was way above normal, a condition he attributed to the altitude.

I resolved one day to hike with ease at 5,000 m (16,404 ft). But first I had to learn all over again to walk.

Eventually, my first impressions would be reformulated as I went 'down' to the colonial city of Sucre, white stucco façades under orange tile rooftops nestled in a lush green valley, *only* 2,790 m (9,150 ft) above sea level, where I learned first hand the theory of relativity. Suddenly, where people from sea level would be gasping for breath, I was taking in an abundance of oxygen relative to La Paz, in a setting of eternal spring.

From Sucre, I learned to anticipate that every corner of this immense country would offer new surprises: radically different microclimates, changing languages and accents and altered hierarchies of the five senses.

I had discovered a country where the unexpected is normal and not a single breath is taken for granted.

OVERVIEW OF LAND AND HISTORY

CHAPTER 2

'Bolivia is a major part of the Tropical Andes,
the richest and most biodiverse region in the world.
The contradictory settings are remarkably intrusive.
The altitude of La Paz can determine the result of
a football game. The coca leaf catalyzes international
incidents. The downward spiraling road into the dense
Yungas valleys propels 'gravity-assisted' bicyclers.
Abundant rocks along literal 'high' ways allow for road
blockades that contribute to the overthrow of presidents.'
—Author's journal

SETTING

Setting in most places is like stage scenery, a background for the plot of daily life. Though known for its romance, the Eiffel Tower never intervenes in a love affair. The Grand Canyon poses for pictures without enticing its admirers to remain at the rim for weeks and cancel the rest of their holiday.

In Bolivia, the diverse and contradictory settings are much more intrusive and will function as protagonists or antagonists, interacting dynamically with you, the main character.

The altitude of La Paz can intervene to determine the result of a football game. The coca leaf catalyses international incidents. The downward spiralling road into the dense Yungas valleys propels 'gravity-assisted cyclers'. The paucity of highways and the abundance of stones along the way allows for road blockades that can overthrow presidents. The Pachamama (Mother Earth) presides over festivals and joyous occasions. How you get along with these protagonists and antagonists will help determine the plot of your own story.

Fortunately, in Bolivia you may choose your setting. Among the choices, almost every possible world climate and terrain exists, excepting a seacoast. (Bolivia became landlocked following defeat against Chile and British saltpeter interests in the 'Pacific War' (1879–1884), losing the inhospitable but economically strategic sea coast in the most arid desert in the world, the Atacama.)

Bolivians continue to lament this injustice, with largely ineffective diplomatic attempts to regain even a portion of what was taken. In 1979, a meeting of the Organization of American States (OAS) in La Paz was on the verge of passing a breakthrough resolution favouring Bolivia on this issue, until an obscure colonel, Alberto Natusch Busch, chose that precise moment for a bloody military coup, sending OAS representatives scurrying to the airport to flee the city, and leaving the resolution in shreds.

The issue remained in suspended animation until Venezuelan president Hugo Chavez declared, in November of 2003, "I dream of swimming in a Bolivian beach," prompting interest in the issue from Brazilian and Peruvian diplomats, as well as the UN's Kofi Annan.

Regaining their sea coast has been thought of as a partial answer to Bolivia's economic woes, but Chile continues to reject international negotiations, instead calling this a binational issue.

As a consolation, Bolivia's location in the core of South America could one day make her an ideal hub for land-based commerce between any of the five surrounding countries, including industrialised Brazil and Chile.

A more practical infrastructure of paved highways and basic facilities beyond the main routes and cities will help both locals and visitors to travel more comfortably from one place to another. But we're not talking about a system of motorways and fast food restaurants. Bolivia will not lose her status as one of the last frontiers in the world. Dense mountains, compact valleys, virtually impenetrable jungles and vast, sparsely populated expanses will not allow this core of South America to become a nation of strip malls and traffic clover leafs.

By 2005, Bolivia's population exceeded nine million, within a territory that is more than triple the size of Great Britain. Like Australia and Canada, Bolivia has room to take in excess people from overpopulated areas. But where would one put them?

Not too many folks have opted for homesteading in the country's vast, steamy Amazonian region, nor on its chilly, melancholic high plains. In fact, approximately one-sixth of all Bolivians have decided to stay in or go to greater La Paz, which is located in a huge gash in the Andes, referred to as 'The Hole.' La Paz's multi-levelled topography averages 3,600 m (12,000 ft) above sea level.

Easy Money
Looking down on La Paz from snow-covered Mount Illimani 57 km (35 miles) away, you may recall the scene from Rodney Dangerfield's film, *Easy Money*, in which a close-up of a crowded Italian wedding feast shifts to an aerial view: hundreds of people cramped into one tiny back yard, while all the other back yards remain empty.

Why is one-sixth of Bolivia's population crowded into and spilling out of La Paz? Not because of an abundant supply of oxygen, for sure. Nor for a roomy lifestyle.

La Paz is the centre of Bolivian commerce, culture and government. It is here where people with nothing but a hope and a prayer converge—entrepreneurs and indigenous Quechuas with only lemons to sell, recent college graduates and highland Aymara peasants with little formal schooling, international restaurateurs and Cholas, with their dark bowler hats, two long braids of black hair joined together at the end, and bulky embroidered *pollera* skirts, who set up pavement lunch-stands near construction sites.

Central La Paz is not what you would call roomy. Speeding tickets are rare because a slow bus is always in front of you, and contorted streets and anarchistic pedestrians are better than traffic cops at slowing down potential hot-rodders. Bank robberies are unheard of—a quick getaway, on foot or by car, is virtually impossible.

REGIONS: THE WORLD IN MICROCOSM
Bolivia is tucked into a vast territory called the Tropical Andes, the richest and most biodiverse region on earth. One sixth of all the world's plant life is contained in this one per cent of the world's land mass.

Within the dozens of clearly-defined ecological regions and transition zones are at least 100 endemic species of vertebrates alone (meaning that they exist only in this region), and 356 species of mammals, 1,400 of birds, 203 of amphibians, 266 of reptiles and 600 of fish.

There are 14,000 species of native plants with seed, and that excludes ferns, mosses and algae. There are 1,200 species of fern alone. A whopping 3,000 medicinal species are used locally or regionally.

The greatest threats to this biodiversity are deforestation (legal and illegal logging), slash-and-burn agriculture, contamination and human use of this biodiversity which surpasses its productive capability. Imported crops may lead to the loss of variability of agrobiodiversity.

We could fill a section like this with superlatives, but there is also a need for a basic appreciation of more general regions.

Highlands

Much of Bolivia's population, including La Paz, is settled in the cool highlands, between 3,650 and 4,250 m (12,000 and 14,000 ft) above sea level. According to Dr Gustavo Zubieta, who dedicates his medical profession to the study of the effects of high altitude, three-fifths of Bolivia's population live over 2,500 m (8,200 ft) above sea level.

La Paz is the primary highland city, but Potosí (mining), Oruro (folk festivals) and El Alto, a former squatters' settlement and now a protagonist in revolutionary transformations, are other significant highland urban centres.

> **The Lake Makes Waves**
> Lake Titicaca and its pilgrimage town of Copacabana, once the centre of the Inca empire, is a region that exerts cultural and economic influence far beyond its sparse population.

The relative numerous population of the highlands is deceiving. Not far from any urban centre, the hiker or trekker can find a near infinite solitude and a caressing silence. Environmentalists flock to the lowlands but I've found rare species of tiny purple and yellow butterflies above the tree

OVERVIEW OF LAND AND HISTORY 11

line, as well as wading Andean flamingos in hidden wrinkles within the mountains where you don't find the usual llama or alpaca tracks. I was told by one environmentalist that such flamingos are only found in the area of the Laguna Colorado in the south, but I saw them with my own eyes. (Getting lost in the mountains has its advantages, though I wouldn't recommend that anyone go off the trail as I did, for it took me seven hours to find my way out.)

At this altitude are various ecosystems, including the dry puna, and the mossy paramo.

> **The Price of Global Warming**
>
> Perhaps the greatest threat to this region are receding glaciers, a product of global warming. Northern hemisphere oil and automobile culture is one of the primary culprits. One single country, the United States, accounting for less than five per cent of the world's population, consumes 26 per cent of the world's oil.

High Valleys

The second most populated zone, labelled high valleys, offers an eternal spring setting where it's never hot enough to fry an egg on the pavement, nor cold enough to skate on thin ice. The harsh highland terrain has given way to a more tender and green ambience. Both Sucre (the nation's symbolic official capital) and Cochabamba are attractive colonial cities over the challenging 2,500 m (8,200 ft) level, while Tarija, the other major valley city, is lower and warmer. High valley cities are good for eating outdoors in the day and sleeping under a cosy quilt at night.

The river that once flowed through the city of Cochabamba is now a dry bed, and what has been called 'the breadbasket of Bolivia' now suffers periodic droughts.

Tropical Lowlands

The third primary region, the tropical lowlands, occupies two thirds of the land yet only attracts a small percentage of the population, including a large contingent of masochistic foreign trekkers. Here rests the thriving city of Santa Cruz, Bolivia's other economic hub after La Paz with an agro-industrial sector demanding autonomy for the region. Within this vast territory of eastern and northern Bolivia also lie the departments of Beni and Pando, where the melting snows of the Andes have finally matured into full fledged rivers—piranha infested tributaries leading to the Amazon.

Bolivia's tropical lowlands are a haven for people whose professions end with 'ologist.' You'll find ecologists, ethnologists, archaeologists, ornithologists, herbologists and maybe even a tapirologist or a jaguarologist, some of them encountering heretofore undiscovered endemic animal and plant species. The preferred habitat of these 'ologists' is in Bolivia's vast and secluded national parks, set aside to conserve rain and cloud forests and protect small populations of original inhabitants and rising occasionally into a fourth type of region.

Within the tropical lowlands alone are numerous regions and subregions, highlighted by the lowland rainforests (think 'jungle'), the savannah (more grassy and seasonal than the rainforest), and the Chaco, a hot dry land with occasional cold fronts, where the Guarani people have learned to survive, and deeper within, tapirs and jaguar roam.

The rugged landscape of Yungas Choro.

Yungas

A fourth zone, labelled Yungas, might be considered part valley and part lowland. But the Yungas have their own unique characteristic; they are pinched between rugged mountains, nooks and crannies too snug to be called valleys. Yungas towns and roads are perched precariously above luxuriant gorges and ravines sculpted by thundering rivers thousands of feet below. Natural swimming holes abound, untouched by large scale developments. Some of the Yungas contain Bolivia's most popular resort locations, but they retain their unmanicured and primeval sensuality.

Here one finds some of the most impacted ecoregions. Much of Bolivia's plant and animal endemism is sheltered in this region. Somewhere deep within the cloud forest, amidst the dripping ferns, rummages the spectacled bear. The Yungas are home to montane cloud forests, but these humid zones can creep as high as 3,500 m (11,483 ft) at mountain edges or as low as 800 m (2,625 ft) at the edge of the jungle.

TEMPERATURE ZONES: KEEPING IT SIMPLE

Environmentalists can distinguish between 12 broadly defined ecoregions, including thousands of ecosystems and countless microclimates, but for those of us who simply want to know what to wear in the morning, there are three remarkably distinct climate zones; the visitor may choose between:

- Highlands: warm/cool and dry days, cool/cold/frigid nights.
- Valleys: warm, occasional hot days, cool nights.
- Lowlands: steamy hot days, hot/warm nights, sometimes chilly with the surazo winds in the winter dry months.

Seasonal change is minimal in any of these regions but for the fact that with summer (November through March) comes the rainy season. In La Paz, the summer rains turn the surrounding hills into a fuzzy green. In lowlands, the summer rainy season with its syrupy humidity spawns the most dangerous creatures of the jungle, mosquitos and their insect allies, and some roads become motorised canoe channels. But winters, with less rain and humidity, usher in a surprisingly pleasant climate.

Other than variations created by the rainy season, changes in climate in Bolivia are primarily due to altitude. Visitors from most other parts of the world, where weather is a seasonal function linked to latitude, will need to make a psychic adjustment as all of the world's highs and lows are found within Bolivia. On many afternoons in the highlands, it may be necessary to alternately strip down and bundle up as you move between the sun and the shade.

A reprieve from the chill of highland La Paz can be found in the valley cities of Cochabamba and Sucre, or smaller valleys nearer to La Paz.

In La Paz itself, poorer people tend to dwell near the upper rim of 'The Hole' at 3,800 m (12,500 ft) above sea level. The wealthy flock to the lower, warmer areas of the south zone, the only open end of 'The Hole', as far down as 3,120 m (10,200 ft) above sea level. As the affluent see no need to fund the building of sewage systems for the shanty dwellers above, untreated waste trickles down the tributaries and flows into the rich neighbourhoods—their reward for indifference.

OVERVIEW OF LAND AND HISTORY 15

CHE GUEVARA

To understand the deterministic impact of Bolivia's setting, one may analyse the ill-fated expedition of Che Guevara in the late 1960s. After playing a prominent role in Cuba's socialist revolution, Guevara led an expedition into Bolivia, driven by his belief in Latin America as a single economic and cultural entity. His guerilla group was soundly beaten by the Bolivian Army and Guevara himself was captured and killed.

In essence, Guevara was defeated by his failure to consider Bolivia's physical and human geography. His small band of international and Bolivian warriors situated their campaign in the eastern semi-tropics, not the ideal location for El Che's asthma. Furthermore, this region is characterised by its sticky climate and underpopulation.

Here was a corner of Bolivia that had largely eluded the basest forms of exploitation by mine magnates, land barons and the government. The typical inhabitants were rugged individualists with their own lands, poor but self-sufficient. Guevara's strategy involved winning over the inhabitants of the region—equivalent to converting hermit-like Idaho survivalists into socialists.

Had he campaigned nearer to the Altiplano, he would have made contact with the more oppressed sectors of Bolivian society: the miners, whose life expectancy was 40 years, and the peasants, who were given unproductive lands during the agrarian reform of the early 1950s and had no capital or machinery to exploit their crusty terrain.

At the very moment that Che's guerrilla campaign unfolded in isolation, the world famous Domitila Chungara, leader of the Miners' Wives Organisation, was involved in marches and hunger strikes. She said: "When they speak of El Che, a great wound always opens up inside. We were not even aware of his presence in Bolivia!"

Che Guevara remains an icon for various sectors of the university community at Bolivia's national university, but we will never see a Che Guevara School of Geography honouring the fallen hero.

ALTITUDE AND THE BRAZILIAN FOOTBALL TEAM

Che Guevara could have chosen a more hospitable region but didn't. The Brazilian national football team would have made a better choice if given the chance. In the elimination matches leading up to the 1994 World Cup of Soccer, Brazil was obligated to travel up to La Paz to face Bolivia's national team. Brazil, the eventual World Cup champion, was heavily favoured. But in La Paz's Hernán Siles Stadium, Bolivia shut out a fatigued Brazil squad 2–0, virtually clinching a berth in the World Cup. Weeks later, in the steamy Brazilian lowlands, a Bolivian squad that favours cool weather was demolished by the same Brazilian team.

La Paz's altitude allegedly made the difference in the first match, although Bolivians argue that Brazil's brutal 40 plus degree centigrade heat, fuelled by 100 per cent humidity was a compelling impediment against the Andean squad in

OVERVIEW OF LAND AND HISTORY

the rematch. Subsequent Brazilian teams have altered their highland style of play, withdrawing defensively to minimise their huffing and puffing, depending instead on lightning counterattacks, a strategy that has proven optimal.

The World Football Federation issues periodic proclamations, based on medical studies, that football anywhere above 2,500 m (8,200 ft) gives an unfair advantage to the home team. Had this become the law of football, not only would La Paz have been excluded from world competition, but also Cochabamba, at 2,570 m (8,431 ft), and Sucre, at 2,790 m (9,153 ft). The football barons thought they were being nice guys when their ban against high-altitude international competition was 'lifted' to anywhere above 3,000 m (9,900 ft).

The only populous city in the world affected by the ban was La Paz. Bolivians were up in arms. One columnist claimed that geographic discrimination was even worse than racism. Bolivian football officials argued that if La Paz were to be banned, then cities with perilous pollution such as Mexico City or Athens, or those with unbearable heat (most places in the United States in August) should also be banned.

With France as the site for the 1998 World Cup, French president Jacques Chirac defended Bolivia's sovereign right to play World Cup elimination matches in its most important city, a view now endorsed by football's governing body. Even after the 1998 World Cup, the issue of football above 3,000 m (9,900 ft) will continue to inspire controversy.

Why should Bolivia be singled out for its geography? The answer is simple: Bolivia has a singular, incongruous geography that does not just sit around and watch life or football games. It is an exhibitionist, narcissistic geography that continuously calls attention to itself.

FINDING YOUR LEVEL

Those who visit Bolivia have a choice that the Brazilians did not. For climate and physical fitness, the valley cities would rank number one. But as Bolivia's commercial and cultural hub, La Paz has other advantages. Beyond high altitude pathology due to inefficiency of oxygen consumption, which shall be explained in detail in a separate section, high altitude can be beneficial to the health. Hostile microbes and the diminutive creatures that carry them find it much more difficult to survive in the cool, dry climes of the highlands.

Once acclimatised to La Paz, the human being has the joy of hiking around clear blue lagoons in the nearby Cordillera Real above 4,500 m (14,764 ft), face to face with shiny glaciers, looking down over the edge of precipices into deep gashes that spiral down into the green lowlands.

For Europeans, North Americans and Australians accustomed to seasonal changes and cold winters, the coldest 0°C (32°F) winter nights in La Paz are not at all threatening. The outdoors warm up substantially during a sunny day in La Paz, but interiors tend to retain the numbing cold throughout winter days in those rooms without windows facing the sun.

At the Smithsonian Institute's insect zoo on the Washington Mall, insects are referred to as 'the world's most successful creature.' But above 3,000 m (9,900 ft), insects do no better than the Brazilian football team.

HUMAN PLANTS

The three most vital factors in real estate appraisal—location, location, location—are not valid in La Paz, Potosí and other highland cities, where the dictum becomes 'light, light, light.' If the windows in your apartment or house do not face the sun, the cost of your rent or value of your home goes down.

There is a significant temperature difference between the sun and the shade. Even the most modern buildings, with the exception of five-star hotels, do not have central heating and air conditioning. Why should they, if the average daytime high may reach the seventies?

Interior climate in the highlands causes human beings to identify unconsciously with houseplants. Plants bend toward the sunlight. So do we, in La Paz or anywhere on the Altiplano. During the day, we find ourselves drifting toward that room where the windows take in the sun most efficiently. This is not by intellectual design. We do so unconsciously, just like plants.

The prospective buyer or renter should visit the potential home both during the morning and the afternoon. In preferred housing, some windows face the sun in the morning, others in the afternoon. One couple I know decided not to purchase a beautiful condominium at a bargain price simply because, in the future, construction might be initiated that would block their sunlight.

WHAT GOES DOWN MUST COME UP

Verticality is not just a climatic concern. Getting around a multilevelled, contorted city like La Paz requires a clear understanding of the urban geography. A few days after our first arrival, we asked our then six-year-old son how he liked the city.

"I like the downs," he responded, "but not the ups."

During the adjustment stage anywhere above 2,500 m (8,202 ft)—Lake Titicaca, Potosí, La Paz, Sucre and Cochabamba—those who depend upon exercise for their wellbeing may feel thwarted. With every downhill walk, one is condemned to an equal uphill trek. The proverb is reversed; 'What goes down must come up.' Some local doctors believe that the dangers of uphill walking prior to adjustment far exceed the aerobic benefits, in spite of the fact that long distance runners and walkers from Mexico come to the Bolivian highlands to train for a sport they have dominated in international competition. These Mexican athletes come from above-2,000 m (6,561 ft) locations, so they have already been conditioned to altitudes.

For those of us who need exercise to feel good, there is an answer in La Paz. From the upper 'eyebrow' of the city to Humboldt Park in the south section deep below is a nearly 800 m (2,600 ft) drop, with no uphills along the way if you follow the main roads. Half of that distance, beginning at the post office in downtown La Paz, will take about an hour and 15 minutes at a brisk pace. You'll even get to go past the front of the president's house. The magnificent views along the way are not always pretty, but awesome nonetheless.

Watch Your Step

Be careful on pavements; repairmen don't always cover up excavation pits. Such safety measures would be unpatriotic, since Bolivia's charm lies in its unpredictability.

A taxi back up to downtown La Paz costs around US$ 3, while a *micro* (bus) will cost about US$ 0.30.

TRAVEL ADVISORY

This walk is best taken in the afternoon. In La Paz's thin atmosphere, ultraviolet rays are not filtered as much as they would be at sea level and the late afternoon sun is on one's back for most of the trek.

This and other urban walks are more enjoyable during the summer (November through February) when the hills are green, clouds decorate the rich blue sky and frequent showers wash away the nefarious dust. For hikers, winter (May through August) is the best time to get out. Remarkably near the city, rugged trails leading up to the glaciers or down to the tropics are free from treacherous mud and what we call civilisation.

If the highland cities and countryside are more magnificent and comfortable in summer, the lowlands are best visited during the drier winter months, when they are kinder to health and spirit, with fewer mosquitos and other pests. Although temperatures are warm, it is less humid, and there is no need to slosh in mud to cross the street. Even during the winter, should you decide to explore beyond the lowland city limits, be well stocked with mosquito repellent.

The idyllic valleys are comfortable in both winter and summer. You can't go wrong in Cochabamba or Sucre, while lower Tarija may get a little too hot in the thick of summer.

Meanwhile, the Yungas become mosquito infested during the summer rainy season, and mud slides make the hairpin roads quite dangerous.

> ### Easy Riding
> If one plans to visit each and every region of Bolivia, it would not be difficult to schedule trips according to this travel advisory, thus maximising health and comfort. Year in and year out, the weather for each region is quite predictable.

Social movements in 2003 (above) and 2005 (page 24) both forced presidents to resign.

The Andean countries, as well as Mexico and Guatemala, are among the few regions in the world where one can change climate at will. Only the sea is lacking in Bolivia. But from the International Airport in El Alto, an inexpensive plane ride with Bolivia's former flagship (now partly Brazilian owned) Lloyd Airlines will take you to a charming desert-seacoast town in Peru or Chile in less than half an hour.

EXOTIC GAS

The coup d'etat used to be Bolivia's most effective attention-getting device in the world arena. Within today's democratic setting, it loses its greatest claim to fame.

Life without gun-toting dictators could have become boring had it not been for the fact that many Bolivians stubbornly believe that democracy is much more than simply staging an election every four years. Any government policy that becomes a contested issue will bring throngs of demonstrators to the streets.

When political protests by indigenous organisations, union activists, students and civic groups occur in La Paz, the city's geography becomes a main character in the drama.

La Paz is cradled by rugged foothills, with only one main thoroughfare. This avenue draws a reasonably straight line through the city, north to south. Any other path leads to an asymmetrical maze of ups and downs, curves and abrupt turns, considerably adding to the distance and time of a walk or drive. The main avenue thus acts as a receptacle for most business movement, motor vehicle or pedestrian.

Demonstrators can and do effectively paralyse vehicle circulation through the city at places such as the aptly named Villazón 'Knot.' Equivalent knots throughout the country allow for the blocking of traffic over lone roads through dense mountains, effectively paralysing the whole country. Ever since the Aymara anti-colonialist Tupac Katari laid siege on La Paz in 1781, the strategic position of El Alto, the only viable commercial entrance to and exit from La Paz, has allowed for indigenous sieges to blockade the city, as happened in May and June of 2005, in defense of Bolivia's natural resources against opportunistic exploitation by multinationals.

A demonstration in 2005 paralysing the Villazón Knot.

Students, peasants or labour activists usually win concessions through these demonstrations, and presidents are even forced to resign, as was the case in 2003 and 2005, but not without some apparently de rigueur confrontation (almost as if a government minister owned the national tear gas company).

In cities with normal geography, one can coexist with such turmoil without ever coming close to it. But in La Paz, you will inevitably be drawn into contact with these protest confrontations.

Demonstration Réalité

Once, I was interviewing some peasants who had congregated in La Paz. As the street was dangerously narrow, I stood at the back where there was an unimpeded escape route. Suddenly, I heard loud popping sounds and a tangy stench told me that the police had fired tear gas to prevent the 30,000-strong crowd from reaching the government plaza.

I managed to escape downhill just as two peasants were trampled to death. No more than a block away, truant kids were shining shoes, old-timers sat on benches chatting and street vendors continued hawking their wares.

If you are a pedestrian near such action, the best way to gauge the danger level is to look at the people around you. If they continue their chats, or do not pick up their walking pace, nothing is likely to happen. When taking a bus skirting the area of conflict, you will hear the driver asking passengers to close all windows. A taxi becomes the ideal transport in this scenario but during mass demonstrations, many taxi drivers won't drive downtown, fearing a bottleneck on the twisted side streets.

During the first five years of the new century, tear gas was not enough to stop protests in defence of natural gas, and the government of Gonzalo Sánchez de Lozada resorted to real bullets. The cumulative death toll during the entire

> La Paz's bizarre geography and its vulnerable juxtaposition with El Alto maximises the effects of street activism, while the lack of alternative roads in rugged rural areas achieves a similar goal. Ever since Tupak Katari, geography has been a protagonist in social protest.

period was 110 indigenous protesters with 23 killed in one three hour massacre at the impoverished Villa Ingenio in El Alto. The acrid smell of tear gas was relegated to the status of a nostalgic memory.

WILDERNESS CHALLENGERS

How to best coexist with Bolivia's natural setting has been dutifully explained. But many travellers don't give a hoot about peaceful coexistence with Bolivia's awesome topography and would prefer to challenge the setting by climbing the plus 6,000 m (20,000 ft) peaks of the Andes or descending into the depths of the lowlands to mingle with sloths, tapirs, peccaries, crocodiles and other exotic creatures (none of which are nearly as dangerous as the wicked insects.) In later pages, you will have the chance to meet ordinary people who have become extraordinary heroes by venturing where humans are not welcome.

For many visitors, Bolivia's setting, even before the characters are introduced, provides a magnificent adventure. But this country is also the scene of stimulating and contradictory interaction between cultures of European and Amerindian origins, born in the colonial past. In a period of history when 'ethnic cleansing' and religious intolerance are headline stories, Bolivia's awkward experiment in uniting diverse cultures within a context of economic scarcity may one day become a model for other parts of the world.

COCA AND OTHER CONFLICTS
Is Coca Cocaine?

Fidel Flores suspects that the plane sitting on the tarmac at El Alto International Airport is carrying a large shipment of cocaine. It is his job to care for the drug sniffing dogs, to take them into customs rooms, in airport corridors, in cargo holds, to detect cocaine. For this, Flores earns approximately US$ 60 per month, not enough to support a family, for sure, but it's a job he desperately needs.

He lives with his wife and children in the migrant city of El Alto, above La Paz, grown anarchistically into a ramshackle city approaching a million people. Like Fidel, most Alteños are of indigenous origins who dress like poor Westerners and whose culture is a hybrid of ancient and modern customs.

Colonel Alex Alipaz, Fidel's boss, has told him that it will not be necessary to inspect the plane. It is a shipment of artisanry, furniture and statuettes.

Fidel knows his job description: take the dogs to sniff the cargo. He also knows that he has received an order from his superior to not do so; two opposite currents flow through his naive mind.

The first tells him to inspect the cargo anyway, to do his job. There is Law 1008, which automatically imprisons anyone who is suspected of complicity in the drug trade. No due process. No trial required.

The second possibility seems more threatening to him. He has understood, between the lines, during various conversations with superiors, that his life or job would be in danger if he were to disobey orders.

Fidel's limited schooling would not have allowed for analytical nuances required for any possible third, more complex decision, had there been one. He decides to follow his immediate orders, to keep his dogs far from the plane.

The plane takes off, but is later forced to land in Peru, where it is searched. Among the boxes of artisanry, is a shipment of 4,176 kg (9,206 lbs) of cocaine.

Arrested is Luis Amado Pacheco, alias Barbaschoca. Amado Pacheco had been warned in advance, through contacts, that his plane was going to be forced to land in Peru. So confident was he that a customary *coima* (bribe) would provide him protection that he saw no need to hide or escape. But this time, a short circuit in the payoff network leads to his arrest.

Amado Pacheco is a resident of the exclusive south La Paz neighbourhood of Calacoto, an enclave of the oligarchy. Like Fidel Flores, Amado Pacheco is married with children. The difference between his and Fidel's neighbourhood is striking. El Alto is 762 m (2,500 ft) higher than Calacoto. In El Alto: grinding, frigid nights and plumbing out of order. In Calacoto: large, warm mansions equipped with the latest in modern conveniences.

FOREIGN RELATIONS AND BOLIVIAN LAW

The majority of people come from Fidel's Cholo background but even the affluent minority, which includes both Cholo and European origins, is revolted to see him behind bars.

"I was in Congress during the passage of Law 1008," former Senator Leopoldo López told me in an exclusive interview, "and I can assure you that we were all under pressure from the United States Embassy to pass the law."

There is a perception within large segments of Bolivian society, from Calacoto to El Alto, that the Bolivian government takes orders from the United States and world monetary institutions.

Most Bolivians, of all classes and persuasions, look at foreign visitors in a positive light. However, abuses by the US 'War on Drugs' and a US economic policy inflicting an orthodox neoliberal economic theory that has widened the gap between rich and poor, lead many Bolivians to resent the gringo influence. The extent of this resentment could be measured in the 2002 presidential elections when the US ambassador, Manuel Rocha intervened directly in the campaign. If candidate Evo Morales, accused of being a *narco cocalero* (narco coca grower), were to be elected president, the ambassador insinuated that Bolivia could lose its US aid. The ambassador had made an assumption: that Bolivians would automatically rally against anyone and anything associated with coca.

But incidents like the above case of Fidel Flores and the fact that the United States could impose draconian repression, as symbolised by Law 1008, had created a nationalistic backlash among Bolivians.

In the days immediately following Rocha's declaration, his bogeyman Evo Morales zoomed up in the polls and missed first place in the election by a mere two percentage points. It was common to joke that Morales' best campaign support had come from the US Embassy.

Such imagery should not even suggest that Western visitors would be the target of anti-gringo sentiment. There is a pervasive civility in Bolivian culture, a painstaking cordiality, even between opponents.

Nevertheless, if you hang out in bars long enough to get to know folks after they're plastered, you may be privileged to get verbally blasted for the abuses of the gringos. If you are Australian, British or French, you may be labelled as a gringo, even after you've stood up and sung *La Marsaillaise*.

Among the working poor, however, greater resentment is reserved for the local oligarchy. The outpouring of sympathy for Fidel Flores, the airport dog handler, just before the turn of the 20th century, was one of a thousand hidden variables that accumulated in the psyche of a nation and set the stage for the monumental events and transformations of the first decade of the 20th century.

ECONOMIC REALITIES

Economic disparity nurtures the corrupt network of underlings who support white collar drug lords like Amado Pacheco. Exemplifying this disparity is a stunning statistic:

in a nation of over nine million, Bolivia's deposit base is concentrated in the hands of 45,000 people who control 85 per cent of all deposits in the banking system.

In the absence of any viable alternative economy, displaced miners had no choice but to grow the controversial leaf in Chapare, whose production has been considered in excess of the legal needs supplied by Los Yungas producers. Every dollar of coca base and cocaine products requires local inputs of only US$ 0.03, as opposed to agricultural goods requiring US$ 0.13, or other sectors of the economy, which call for up to US$ 0.23. It is cheaper to produce coca, but this product provides far fewer jobs than alternative crops.

The coca growers, the lowest participants in the drug hierarchy, are often the objects of sympathy from upstanding citizens who do not like cocaine traders but who harbour a greater resentment against a failed US anti-drug policy. Bolivia suffered little of the violence associated with the drug trade in places like the US and Colombia. "I don't think our society is violent and never has been," explained René Blattmann, former Minister of Justice.

This aversion to violence in Bolivia led to resentment against the US-trained Bolivian anti-drug forces who have been responsible for the occasional deaths of innocent residents in Cochabamba's Chapare coca producing region, including women and children.

Cocaine: a Western Invention
Further complicating the issue is the fact that the coca leaf was a native product of Bolivia many centuries before cocaine's existence. Cocaine is a Western invention, originating in Germany and made famous by none other than Sigmund Freud.

During the 1990s, in order to meet the US quota for coca eradication, the Bolivian government used aid money to pay coca growers US$ 2,500 per eradicated hectare. But in the absence of markets for alternative produce, many growers simply retreated deeper into the jungle to plant coca.

When former dictator General Hugo Bánzer was elected president, he scrapped the failed coca policy and pledged total eradication of excess Chapare coca by 2002.

By 2001, most coca was eradicated. But promises of markets for alternative products had failed to materialise, and peasants were left with no other viable remunerative activity. Meanwhile, cocaine traffic in the US had not declined, since coca production had merely shifted to Colombia. Before his death from cancer, Bánzer warned the international community that his eradication programme with no parallel economic aid would result in peasants drifting back into coca-growing.

"How can they not understand this phenomenon?" asked former Senator López, referring to both the Bolivian and US governments. "After all, they are pushing for free market economics. Is this not the way the free market functions, on the basis of supply and demand?"

Former senator López agreed with the coca growers' associations that alternative agricultural products with assured markets would greatly reduce the problem.

> Bolivians would love to get the drug monkey off their backs. Statistics prove that benefits from the cocaine trade reach only a small, tightly-knit clan

Throughout the war on drugs in Bolivia, the Western countries that brandished the slogan of 'alternative production' were unwilling to consider removing their own agricultural subsidies so that poor Bolivian peasants could export their farm exports within a framework of fair trade.

Coca or Cocaine?

Bolivians differentiate between coca leaves and cocaine. The coca plant is considered sacred by indigenous Bolivian cultures. To this very day, Indians and highland miners chew a wad of coca leaves in order to combat hunger and fatigue, a custom sometimes adopted by foreign backpackers and aid workers.

The most exotic tea salons in La Paz serve coca tea with pastries. The medicinal benefits of coca leaves are heralded. Coca tea is prescribed for visitors to help combat

In the absence of viable agricultural alternatives, coca growers continue to produce the exploited crop. This grower in Chapare is turning the leaves to ensure even drying.

the symptoms of the *soroche* (altitude sickness). For this reason, some Bolivian tour companies have foreign clients chew coca leaves when descending inhospitable highland mine shafts.

Economists within the Movement Towards Socialism, Evo Morales' coalition, have come up with a creative alternative. Why not industrialise the coca leaf into medicinal and other legitimate products? Rather than exporting a raw material, coca or otherwise, a strategy with few local economic benefits, why not develop added value products? By industrialising prior to export, jobs are created and different economic sectors are bolstered.

The idea is not new. Think of Coca Cola.

The Cocalera March: an Historic Preview of the Dramatic Events between 2000 and 2005

The seventeenth January 1996 was an historic day in the evolution of the coca issue and the enfranchisement of indigenous Bolivians. More than 300 women coca growers, some carrying infants in their colourful shawls, arrived on foot in La Paz after 30 days and more than 500 km (310 miles) of a penurious march that had begun in the most controversial coca growing region, the Chapare. The march was catalysed by escalating skirmishes in which government anti-drug forces attempted to forcibly eradicate coca fields. Three deaths resulted from the confrontations, including that of a child. Several other peasants in the region were maimed in the conflicts.

Knowing that the women *cocaleras* (coca growers) would inspire broad-based sympathy in all sectors of Bolivian society, the government of MNR Gonzalo Sánchez de Lozada (Revolutionary Nationalist Movement) attempted to intercept the march in its incipient stages. (The MNR was the historic consolidator of the 1952 Bolivian revolution and resurfaced in the 1980s to espouse orthodox neoliberal privatisations a la Thatcher.)

The march proceeded, from the lowland tropics into the valleys and Yungas gorges, mainly uphill, under the battering showers of the rainy season. No woman was exempt from various afflictions—from foot blisters to pneumonia—but they trekked on and the nation's attention was riveted on their plight. This media event was oddly juxtaposed in historical period with O J Simpson's famous auto chase; two very different social milestones.

When they finally arrived in the drizzly south suburbs of La Paz, near the end of this pilgrimage, city residents of all social classes lined the roads, offering food and beverages. People observing the march broke down in tears, both men and women, as the marchers laboured by.

The women were interviewed along the way. "This is a march in defence of our right to live ... why should we be forced to cook for the soldiers who had come to eradicate our fields ... we want true alternatives to coca, not just a cow or beautiful words."

These women were compared to the followers of Martin Luther King and Ghandi, and had captured the heart of Bolivia.

One of their demands was a revision of the unconstitutional Law 1008. Prisoners like dog handler Fidel Flores were hoping that this intense national identity with victims of poverty would do something to cut short their time in prison. The march coincided with Minister of Justice Blattmann's campaign to reform the penal system.

"In our country, for centuries freedom hasn't been for everyone," he said, "but rather for certain social and isolated groups. As a result, we can easily state that drug traffickers and white collar workers aren't in our jails today, but poor, humble people are."

A Valid Question
What was clear in the aftermath of the Cocalera March is that the vast majority of Bolivians made a great differentiation between the despised Amado Pachecos and the impoverished bottom rungs of the world cocaine trade.

'The United States wants to decide whether or not to certify the world's countries in their struggle against drugs,' editorialised the now-defunct Jesuit newspaper *Presencia*, 'but who is going to decide if the United States should be certified? No one, of course.'

The *cocaleros* were led by the articulate Evo Morales, and belonged to Bolivia's Labour Confederation (COB). One of their primary demands, ironically, coincided with the stated programme of the US State Department and the Bolivian government: a truly viable alternative economy for the Chapare region. This march helped to build the status of Mr Morales in the realm of creative non-violence, indirectly contributing to his election to the congress in 1997.

CLASS STRUGGLE A LA BOLIVIANA

The massive demonstrations that shut down France in December of 1995 have their 'striking' parallel in Bolivia.

Both the Bolivian Labour Confederation (COB) and the French labour movement coincide in the belief that neoliberal economics lead to cutbacks and impoverishment in social services and diminished purchasing power. Both oppose privatisation of strategic state enterprises. And both commonly take their grievances to the streets.

Historically, the COB has been one of the most militant trade unions in the world. It has remained independent of all international affiliations and once played a central and explicit role in national politics, acting as 'co-government' in the early years of the 1952 revolution.

With the decline in Bolivian mining, COB ranks have been dwindling. The Bolivian government's Education Reform Law between 1994 and 1997 catalysed a new surge in labour militancy. Influenced and endorsed by the World Bank, the Education Reform Law contained clauses which would have disenfranchised the teachers' union and debilitated university autonomy. This hard line government stance, along with human rights abuses by anti-drug forces in the Chapare and the selling off of state assets to foreign companies, had given the COB a new lease of life.

Since then, the COB and its regional associations have continued a process of death and resurrection, but the COB tradition is alive and well in various other militant groups, including the Coordinadora (Committee for the Defense of Water and Life) in Cochabamba, the FEJUVE (Federation of Neighborhood Associations) in El Alto, the

Bolivian women, particularly those who wear the traditional *pollera*, often take on leadership roles in movements of social protests.

CSTBC (Confederation de Peasant Workers of Bolivia), the Movimiento Sin Tierra (The Landless Movement), the Cocaleros and various local unions.

Selling Up or Selling Out?

Another catalyst of the dramatic events of the early 2000s (the water war, the gas war, and other variations) was the Sánchez de Lozada government's 'capitalisation' policy, which sold off half interests and administrative control in strategic enterprises (energy, communications, transportation) to foreign investors. The COB spearheaded the opposition to this process, but failed to rally the middle class. Today, with the failures of these state enterprises to deliver improvements in quality of life and the loss of state revenue for social programmes, the COB's position has been vindicated after the fact.

> ### *TUNUPA* Makes a Point
> Historians and political scientists at the Solón Foundation newsletter, *TUNUPA*, study such issues. In a 2001 newsletter, *TUNUPA* raised several questions: 'After five years of capitalisation, why are the returns from capitalised companies only 3 per cent? [Prior to its privatisation, the Bolivian oil company made significant enough profits to contribute 57 per cent of the government budget.] Why do the capitalised enterprises, as a whole, provide less in tax revenue to the State than they did before they were capitalised? Why are we Bolivians, who own 49 per cent of the shares, not allowed to name our representatives to the boards of directors of the capitalised companies? Why do the Pensión funds issue documents saying that they own these shares when Bolivian citizens are supposedly the owners (of these shares)?'

THE POLITICAL LANDSCAPE

Prior to the time that Nelson Mandela was being elected president of South Africa, Victor Hugo Cárdenas, a full-blooded Aymara Indian who speaks various indigenous and European languages, was elected vice-president, and Remedios Loza, a Chola woman who wears the traditional bowler hat and rounded, ornate skirts of her culture, was elected to parliament. Neither the neoliberal Cardenas nor the populist Loza were sustainable political forces, but they were indicators of an inevitable future.

> It used to be that a white or not-so-white Bolivian would deny any indigenous background. Today, it is typical for most Bolivians of Spanish heritage to proudly affirm that they, like all Bolivians, have Indian blood. But balanced race relations ultimately depend on the sharing of political and economic power. Happy slogans and demagogic public relations campaigns can only go so far. The shift in power inevitably involves conflict, for the privileged do not give up their positions gleefully.

These events signalled a direction in contemporary Bolivia which downgraded the respect attached to assimilating to Creole ways, replacing it with the undigested slogan 'Unity in diversity.' As a rigid economic stratification bordering on a caste system begins to be dismantled, the barriers between Bolivians have been slowly but surely breaking down.

Between 2000 and 2005, six years of indigenous-led conflict, mostly of militant non-violent roots, finally led to a symbolic political transformation. With the election of Evo Morales, perhaps only the second indigenous president in the history of Latin America (Benito Juarez was president of Mexico in the 1860s), Bolivia may never again turn back to its colonial past.

THE CHRONOLOGY OF TRANSFORMATION
The 1990s: Privatisation of Strategic State Enterprises

In the late 1990s, white men did everything they could to retain their aristocracy of power, dividing the spoils between three main political parties, which negotiated their balance of power according to election results but which all espoused the same Thatcherite orthodox neoliberal economics. This economic theory required business to be entirely private, operating without state subsidies. Yet many of the companies that were to privatise Bolivian strategic companies were themselves subsidised by their own governments.

In the political arena, the Condepa (Conciencia de Patria or Conscience of Fatherland) served as a populist contrast with a significant indigenous following under the paternalistic leadership of the 'Compadre' Palenque. Condepa was the only major political party to speak out against privatisations. But Palenque's own hyperpaternalism planted the seeds of the party's demise, and Condepa's willingness to be included as part of the government of former dictator Hugo Bánzer was the final straw that broke the llama's back.

The void left by Condepa meant that no voice from any official party spoke out against the unbridled orthodox free market, all the while that 'free' Bolivian enterprise had no possibility to compete against subsidised foreign competition.

Meanwhile, the other facet of Bolivia's potentially inclusive democracy, the COB (Bolivian Labor Confederation), was also in a state of deterioration, primarily because its base was debilitated with the demise of the mining industry. The COB, far more than Condepa, had represented Bolivia's

OVERVIEW OF LAND AND HISTORY

authentic voice, with a significant indigenous base.

With Condepa gone and the COB in tatters, at the turn of the 20th century there was a near

> One of Bolivia's most impoverished cities, Potosí had supplied gilded Europe with silver, yet in English, something 'worth a Potosí' was priceless.

total political void for the 70 per cent indigenous population. Bolivia's masses were excluded even from being co-opted, since the Popular Participation programme of the previous government was in neglect.

The whitest of all parties was in power, Bánzer's ADN (Democratic Action). Bánzer's government inherited an economically crippled state, with former revenues now subject to the trickle-out-of-the-country effect of the privatisation (labelled 'capitalisation'), a policy inherited from Gonzalo Sánchez de Lozada's MNR (Revolutionary Nationalist Movement). The privatised state enterprises were now incapable or unwilling to significantly finance government social programmes.

The loss of such revenue, especially that of the hydrocarbon industry, led to a situation in which the economy depended almost exclusively on a neo-colonial system of exportation of raw materials. Exporting raw materials before creating any value-added products was hardly a strategy for job creation. Bolivian history documented the results of such an economy; impoverished Bolivians had nourished the world for two centuries with Bolivian silver, saltpeter, and later, tin and gas, and Bolivian intermediaries even expressed a willingness to export water to Chile for a pittance.

A native product, the coca leaf, had always been used for local consumption (tea, medicinal, ceremonial), but excess coca found its way into the Colombian-US cocaine economy. Bolivian producers of excess coca languished at the abject bottom end of this economy, with the real beneficiaries being the Colombian cartels that transformed the coca into an illicit value added powder.

At the behest of the United States Embassy, Bánzer's 'Dignity Plan' sought the massive eradication of all excess coca. With no effective marketing of alternative crops set in place, the 'Dignity Plan' thrilled the United States Embassy but led to even deeper impoverishment of the already poor indigenous growers, many of them former miners who had drifted into coca growing only after having been been laid off from the mines in the 1980s and with no other job alternative.

Social problems in the US sustained a voracious appetite for the forbidden powder at the consumer end, so that eradication at the production end proved useless. Coca growing simply shifted to Colombia.

Thus, at the turn of the 20th century, the political void for Bolivia's indigenous majority was accompanied by the potent pair of economic disenfranchisers: the crushing of coca planting and more significant, the massive crippling of state revenue through the privatisation process.

Through inheriting the policies of Sánchez de Lozada (Goni), President Bánzer was not in a position to lay the blame on Goni, for his ADN had never opposed orthodox 'free' market sacking of the country. Bánzer had dressed himself in a neoliberal straightjacket.

Bolivia's precarious pigmentocracy was presided over mainly by white men who responded to the impositions of other white men from financial institutions like the World Bank and the International Monetary Fund (IMF).

Though government subsidies play a great role in boosting US and European industries, Bolivian business was expected to compete with zero government incentives.

The indigenous majority was left with no voice over the use of their own natural resources, and the power vacuum was confounded when IMF and World Bank loans became contingent on further privatisations, including the essence of life itself: water.

The stage was set for the dramatic events between 2000 and 2005.

2000: El Mallku and Road Blockades

Insurrectional road blockades led by a new indigenous leader, Felipe Quispe (El Mallku), paralyse the country twice during the year. El Mallku is the Secretary General of the CSUTCB (Confederation of Agricultural Workers of Boliva).

The demands are for indigenous autonomy and economic enfranchisement, with a rhetoric reminiscent of the Black Power movement in the USA.

2000: The Cochabamba Water War

The conflict is catalysed by demands of international financial institutions. Either Bolivia privatise its water or it will not receive loans. In October of 1999, Bolivia dutifully legalises water privatisation, with 40-year concession rights given to a consortium whose major shareholder is a Bechtel subsidiary. A law is enacted that requires residents to pay full water costs, satisfying a World Bank demand. The Bechtel-dominated water company, called Aguas del Tunari, hikes water prices to a level that is far beyond the capacity to pay of Cochabamba residents and small growers.

Led by Oscar Olivera, the Coalition for the Defense of Water and Life (La Coordinadora) occupies the main plaza of Cochabamba. Between 4 and 5 February, peaceful marches are met with tear gas and snipers, with 175 protesters injured, two of them blinded.

Only by 8 February does the foreign press get wind of the ongoing drama. Bechtel's role is exposed by The Democracy Center in Cochabamba, and a mass e-mail writing campaign begins, directed at the Bechtel CEO, Riley Bechtel.

Leader Olivera is arrested on 6 March. A State of Siege is declared by the government and a 17-year-old boy is shot dead by a Bolivian army captain (trained at the US School of the Américas). Protests spread, including police mutinies in La Paz and Santa Cruz, with more deaths.

On 10 April, the Bolivian government gives in to the tenacious protesters, ceding control of Cochabamba water to the Coalition (La Coordinadora), with the released Oscar Olivera signing the agreement that expels Bechtel.

Bechtel, the same corporation that later will lobby for the Iraq war and then receive the most lucrative no-bid contract for the reconstruction of Iraq, a corporation whose earnings exceed the combined income of

> In an unofficial March referendum, 96 per cent of Bolivians want the Bánzer government to rescind the contract with Bechtel.

all Bolivians, has been resorting to legal means in an effort to get the Bolivian government to award compensation for the future years of lost profits.

2001: March for Life and Sovereignty

With demands including 'stop land grabs' and 'stop privatisations', but also for aid to flood victims, a two-week foot march from Cochabamba to La Paz begins on 9 April. Though no gains result from the march, it serves to maintain the intensity of Bolivian protest movements. The failure of this protest is exemplified in the 9 November massacre of seven members of the Landless Peasants movement, as they occupied unused land on a large *latifundio* (a large semi-feudal landholding), in a demand for an agrarian reform.

2002: Presidential Election

The coca grower union leader Evo Morales enters the presidential election under the banner of the Movement Towards Socialism (MAS). The US ambassador Manuel Rocha threatens to cut off aid to Bolivia if Morales were to win the election. Following the threat, Morales soars in the polls and nearly wins. Goni becomes president of Bolivia for the second time.

2003: La Paz Police Trigger an Anti-Tax Rebellion

Once more, international financial institutions play a fundamental role in sparking conflict and death. Some called the February mutiny-protest in La Paz 'rage against the IMF'. The IMF adjustment plan required an income tax for Bolivia. In theory, creating a tax base is a good idea, but when subsistence salaried policemen learn that the new tax would more than nullify their salary increase, they go on strike and take to the streets of La Paz on 11 February. Firemen support the action.

Next day, public high school students join the protest. In front of the presidential palace, the students refuse to disband. Military guards fire tear gas into the crowd. Some of the students respond by hurling rocks, then withdrawing to a point protected by the city police.

New waves of demonstrators come to the aid of the students and police, now demanding that the president resign. Protests spread to other cities. Soldiers are sighted on balconies and building tops, as snipers. Deaths follow, including a nurse who was helping the wounded and a man parading a white pacifist flag.

Goni finally backs down, rescinding the tax and firing his cabinet.

2003 September and October: the Gas War

Protesters from El Alto, the most indigenous large city in the Américas, rise up against a pro-multinational government plan that would allow foreign investors to exploit the newly discovered natural gas resources. The plan would have sent the gas through Chile, already a sore point, and the receiving end was to be Mexico and California. Meanwhile, El Alto residents cannot afford their own household gas. One of the companies involved in the deal is Sempra Energy (which has made more than a half billion dollars during the California energy crisis).

The protests spread, blockades are erected throughout the country, oil installations are occupied and a full unarmed insurrection is flaring through the country. Once again Goni, called by *The Economist* 'a pro-American free-marketeer' is willing to use the military in an attempt to quell the disturbances. An estimated 59 people are killed. Following the massacre, Goni and his architect of public order Sánchez Berzain resign and flee to Miami. Goni later claims to BBC radio that druglords are behind the uprising.

Firm Promises

Goni's vice-president, journalist Carlos Mesa, has cautiously distanced himself from the repression. Mesa becomes interim president, promising a referendum on energy exploitation and new elections, and vowing to never use mortal power against his people.

2003 July: Referendum

A referendum is crafted into four ambiguous yes-or-no questions which apparently provide the Bolivian people with the right to determine the fate of their oil and gas but which also seem to give Mr Mesa leeway for negotiating with the impatient foreign corporations. More than 86 per cent of voters support the 'yes' for a new hydrocarbon law, and 92.2 per cent demand the recovery of hydrocarbon property upon its exit from the wells.

Attempting the Impossible
During his temporary presidency, Mr Mesa receives the guarded support of sectors of the opposition and tries to satisfy both the majority of the Bolivian people, who now are demanding nationalisation of gas and oil, and the oil and gas companies who demand that their contracts be fulfilled. Perhaps Mesa will one day write an article telling us if he actually believed it was possible to satisfy both sides at the same time.

2004

With protesters across the country giving Carlos Mesa the benefit of the doubt, an apparent lull settles upon Bolivia.

2005: May and June

A month long blockade begins on 16 May and extends to more than a hundred barricades accross the country. The epicentre is El Alto. As Mesa has promised, there are no deaths. He resigns. Subsequently, one person is killed by repressive forces as he protests in the main plaza of Sucre, where a decision is to be made as to presidential succession.

Following Mesa's resignation, two members of the traditional oligarchy stand in line to take over the presidency. Mesa publicly begs them to put aside their private goals, which would further enflame the nation, and allow the third in line, the non-partisan Supreme Court president, Eduardo Rodríguez, to assume command.

> **One-sided Death Toll**
> At this point it is important to understand that at least 110 protesters have been killed by government forces since this new round of protest movements began in 2000, and yet protesters have not attempted to kill a single human being.

The heavy tension suddenly subsides when the two next in line to the presidency step aside and allow Supreme Court president Eduardo Rodríguez to assume the presidency. Rodríguez promises early elections and blockades are called off.

The country settles into a campaign mode and middle class Bolivians grapple with the possibility of voting for one or two neoliberal candidates from the old order or taking a chance on Evo Morales.

2005: 18 December

Evo Morales becomes the first Bolivian candidate since democracy was renewed in the early 1980s to win a presidential election with a clear majority, over 53 per cent of the votes.

"I thank all the social movements," declares Morales. "Those that struggled to recover our natural resources, those that fought for our rights, and those that struggled to change the course of Bolivian history."

The election results illustrate a geographic-cultural fracture in Bolivia, with Morales carrying the indigenous highlands and valleys while former president Tuto Quiroga gained a majority in Santa Cruz and other lowland regions. Morales' MAS movement has not won complete control of congress.

In the immediate aftermath of the election, it was too early to project whether political change could be parlayed into an economic transformation. The issues that have brought Mr Morales to power, namely defense of natural resources such as hydrocarbons and water and the rights of Bolivia's indigenous majority, will be part of a contentious period. Privileged minorities will inevitably attempt to swap political power in exchange for keeping their economic stranglehold on the country as intermediaries to multinational corporations.

The promised constituent assembly for a new constitution will be a lengthy and embattled process.

Nothing is certain, but Morales is well aware that this is not a personal victory and that Bolivians will continue to demand a new economic model while he will have to deal with foreign financial institutions and multinational corporations with contracts to extract the country's natural resources.

Future conflict is inevitable in the economic realm, though it is hard to imagine that racism could once again pervade the structure of Bolivian society.

Meanwhile, in the immediate aftermath of the election, the image of cultural change flashes through the streets of highland cities, where Bolivian office workers and managers are accustomed to suit-and-tie formalities. President elect Morales has appeared in public in shirtsleeves with no tie, and many Bolivian men are now going to work without a tie.

2006: 1 May

On the symbolic date of 1 May 2006, Evo Morales surprised the nation, announcing the nationalisation of Bolivian gas, by presidential decree, and thereby fulfilling one of his promises to the social movements that had brought him to power.

CULTURE AND TOURISM

This is the dramatic human setting into which the foreign visitor will arrive. Much has been written about the negative effects of tourism upon so-called developing countries. However, for tourists 'with an attitude', Bolivia might as well be Oblivia. It seems that they have not found this place. At the same time the level of awareness and conscience of most visitors to Bolivia is remarkably high. Correspondingly, this author has felt none of the tourist dependency prevalent in so many other developing countries.

Foreigners working for non-governmental organisations often play a positive role in Bolivian society and foreign journalists and human rights activists were instrumental in bringing the water and gas issues to the attention of international sympathisers and opinion makers.

The type of visitor to arrive in Bolivia has probably already been impressed with some aspect of Andean culture. Europeans have heard roving Bolivian, Peruvian and Ecuadorian musicians play in metros and at street fairs. Ethnologists, botanists and linguists have been attracted by the wealth of indigenous customs, traditional forms of social organisation, medicinal plants and health foods, as well as the idiomatic expressions of the Quechuas and Aymaras. Renegade business people outside the multinational milieu are often motivated more by the country's incongruous geography and complex way of life than by a quick profit (or they would have chosen a more mainstream place with fewer obstacles to financial success). Then there is the large contingent of backpackers, usually here to appreciate, and less likely to be upset when things don't go as planned.

Bolivia is far from idyllic. Racism has not vanished even for those Bolivians from impoverished backgrounds who have managed, against all odds, to succeed in business. According to Bolivian economist José Nuñez del Prado, the 'Cholo bourgeoisie' is still not completely accepted by the white business community. A majority of indigenous people find themselves on the lower tier of the two-tiered economy. Rural poverty is frightening, rendered worse due to periodic droughts in Cochabamba, the massive layoffs of miners from Potosí and Oruro back in the 1980s and the demographic paralysis of agrarian reform. Only the informal economy and a low cost of living cushion the effects of a torpid economy.

Petty crime has increased during the past decade but shootings in La Paz are still unheard of.

Crime and Bolivia

If economic hardship were strictly equitable with crime statistics, then Bolivia should be a dangerous place. This country remains safer than most, but on the streets of commercial capital La Paz, street vendors who used to leave their merchandise unattended at lunch time are now attentive to the increase in robberies and muggings.

> Foreign visitors are involved in championing local cultures as sophisticated consumers keenly aware of equitable commerce, as students, and as people who generally interact quite well with the locals.

Unity in diversity seems to be on the rugged path from slogan to reality, making inroads on the public consciousness. A dynamic cadre of young intellectuals, free from the sectarianism of the past, may serve as a bridge between the indigenous majority and the middle class, including vice-president elect Alvaro García Linera, opening economic and social paths that will make the most of Bolivia's natural and human wealth.

Visitors who intend to stay here for several months or longer will have the opportunity for hands-on participation in this dynamic process (as we shall see in later chapters) through non-governmental organisations, volunteer projects, student programmes in agriculture, ecology and the arts, and business investment in sectors that create value added products rather than stripping natural resources and sending them abroad for later industrialisation.

THE BOLIVIAN PEOPLE

CHAPTER 3

'The people [of Bolivia] who rose up in the last several years got riddled with bullets, but they prevented their gas from evaporating into the hands of others, unprivatized their water..., overthrew governments governed from abroad, and said no to the income tax and other wise orders from the International Monetary Fund.'
Eduardo Galeano, internationally esteemed Uruguayan writer, from 'The Second Founding of Bolivia,' *La Jornada* (9 February 2006)

CHARACTERS

On the surface, the people on a Bolivian street form a postcard that broadcasts 'third world country'. People with lighter skin seem to preside over the scene while those with darker faces or more colourful dress seem to be doing most of the heavy labour, which is mainly selling, fixing, cleaning, building, driving and carrying. Between these events, eating takes place. The things being sold range from the exotic to the tacky. The things being fixed are often items which would have gone directly to the city dump in a more prosperous country. The places being cleaned will shine for a half hour and then begin accumulating dust and grime from the street. The places being built have dangerous scaffolds. The things being driven seem to bump and burp, and passengers sometimes bulge from the doors. Some of the things being carried are bending strong backs forwardly. The things being eaten are of great variety, but some of them, in particular *salteñas* (chicken or beef pies) at 11:00 am, are eaten by both those who preside over the scene and those who are hustling and heaving.

There's much more, of course, but this is what tells us that we are near the Plaza San Francisco in hilly La Paz and not in hilly San Francisco, California.

Bolivia becomes more nuanced when we get to know these people, and this chapter will go beyond the faces in the crowd and into their lives and ways of thinking and doing.

In the first edition of this book, I divided the space between people of fame and those who are anonymous. Since that time, a strange thing has happened: most of those famous people have been besieged by scandal and calamity, as if their appearance in this book had been the kiss of death.

That's a metaphor, except for two cases: a famous football player I mentioned committed suicide and a populist TV personality and politician died prematurely of a heart attack following family scandals. Otherwise, the demise of profiled personalities was not marked by the ultimate finality. A jovial senator who was kind enough to give me an exclusive hour in his office was later to fall in disgrace after a truck from his company had a fluke accident and its contraband contents spilled out over the highway. A populist mayor who had been elected term after term with a resounding majority of votes was hustled off the political stage after serious charges of corruption. Two up-and-coming women politicians are now down and out of the political arena following soap opera intrigues. I interviewed a prize-winning film director, and some time after the interview, funding for his next film dried up.

A high-profile banker convicted of violations of banking regulations hosted me in his two-room prison appartment in the 5-star section of La Paz's San Pedro Prison hoping that his published story might help get his sentence reduced. Instead, he languished in jail with no end of the sentence in sight.

I had planned on profiling a dynamic young woman whose youth-oriented TV programme gave high school and college students a free forum to air their opinions of vital issues. It seemed to me like the most exciting trend in TV. But in the absence of commercial sponsors, her show had to be discontinued. Before you consider that my book was somehow a jinx for these people, consider the fragility of Bolivia's celebrity scene.

THE CELEBRITY INDUSTRY

I come from a country where celebrity packaging is one of the top industries. In Bolivia, it seems that would-be celebrities become unravelled before they can assure themselves lifetime

Most of these Bolivians, on their way to school or work, are not dreaming of a vicarious identity with some celebrity. Instead, they are thinking of their participatory role in collective groups: their dance troup, their sandlot football team, their neighbourhood organisation that fights for social justice.

returns from their fame. In a place where power seemed to be monopolised by a few, fame is divvied up among many and may last for 15 days or 15 months but rarely ever 15 years. Those who believe that fame is an illusion will find grist for their mill in Bolivia.

Bolivia has no true celebrities because most film actors, football stars and politicians walk the same streets as the average José. Leading actors stroll on the main avenue and champion football players sit shoulder to shoulder in the stadium with the multitudes.

If asked for an autograph, these surprised headliners never fail to comply. During a period when the celebrity industry is one of the pillars of the US economy, Bolivia's underdevelopment is epitomised by its lack of an autograph industry.

Privacy for Celebrities
I once saw Jorge Ortiz, the star of a prizewinning Bolivian film, *A Question of Faith*, right outside the ticket window, and no one was asking him for an autograph.

The best indicator of Bolivia's evasion of celebrity consciousness is the lack of anyone resembling a gossip columnist.

In this new edition of *CultureShock! Bolivia*, I have resolved to profile people whose future should be more sustainable, using criteria of achievement that transcend simple notoriety. We shall begin, literally, at the top.

Bernardo Guarachi

If altitude determined authority, Bernardo Guarachi would occupy the top echelon, for he was the first and thus far the only Bolivian to have climbed Mount Everest, reaching the peak on 26 May 1998. From rural Patacamaya, Guarachi was the son of pastors who worked as high as 5,000 m (17,000 ft) above sea level. Today he is a mountain climbing guide, famous for his courteousness and inner strength.

Guarachi once responded to an emergency call and carried an injured man heavier than himself down from a perch near the top of snow-covered Huayna Potosí. He has climbed the towering Illimani (outside of La Paz) more than 170 times. He scaled the Chilean Aconcagua, nearly 7,000 m (about 23,000 ft) with no supplementary oxygen.

Guarachi's Everest climb was fraught with obstacles: first financial, then meteorological and even linguistic, since he does not speak the English language used by climbing teams. Once at the peak of Everest, he removed his oxygen mask to place the Bolivian flag.

> **World Record Holder**
> Bernardo Guarachi holds two Everest records: fastest ascent and descent, and longest time spent on top without supplementary oxygen.

Doctors and Pharmacists

Doctors Zubieta (father and son), specialists in high altitude medicine, argue that Guarachi's increased polycythemia, what some would consider an illness, is beneficial against extreme hypoxia, a potentially mortal condition.

The communicative Zubietas represent a type of Bolivian physician-patient relationship which is unencumbered by the typical paternalism of the profession that was targeted by Ivan Illich in his *Medical Nemesis*. Illich criticised the authoritarian relationship of doctor over patient, denouncing that doctors maintained a godlike status by using professional jargon that masked otherwise understandable concepts. Such paternalism requires a doctor's appointment as a prerequisite for the purchase of a medicine which a more actively involved patient may already know is needed.

In Bolivia, pharmacists still assume that adults are discerning enough to handle basic medical information, and traditionally dispense medicines over the counter that require prescriptions in countries with more 'developed' professions, though this custom is disappearing as regulations are tightened.

THE BOLIVIAN PEOPLE

Too Easy?
My own case may prove Illich to be right or wrong. Less than five minutes following a dog bite in La Paz, I decided to zap any potential infection and rushed to the nearest pharmacy, where I was a regular customer. Over the counter they sold me antibiotic pills. I had few illusions but nothing to lose. Was this bad medical practice? Could be. My case might be an argument for stricter regulations.

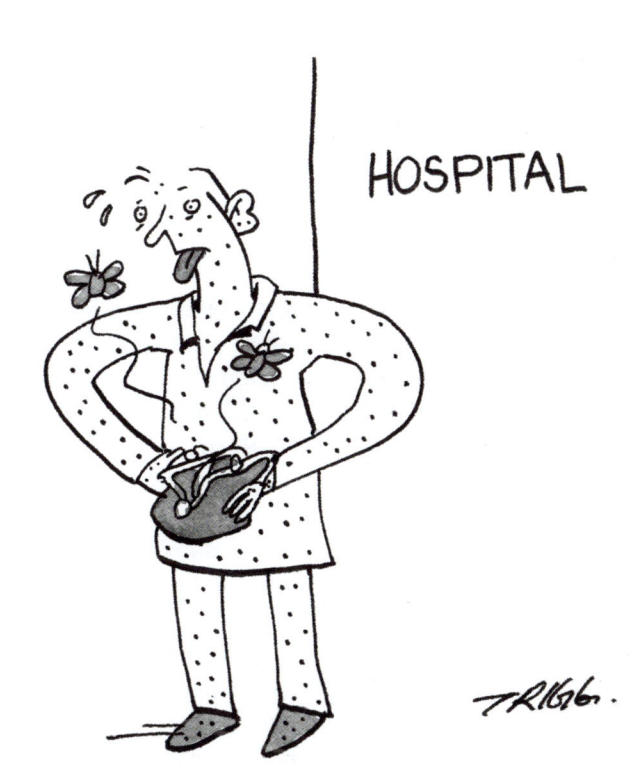

Bolivian doctors are relatively accessible, and I could have found one, even though it was a Sunday. Accessibility comes from supply and demand; there are more doctors than there are patients who want them or can afford their services. The two-tiered nature of health care in Bolivia is one of the reasons for this country's ranking of 126 among 190 nations by the World Health Organization. For example, only 65 per cent of Bolivian births are overseen by skilled attendants. In question is not the availability of health care services but their distribution. Barriers to distribution are primarily financial, but also geographic, linguistic and cultural.

Physicians still make house calls, and visitors staying at a hotel have such service available. Foreign embassies supply lists of approved English-speaking doctors for their nationals.

In the absence of financing for the wobbly state health care system, many doctors do the best they can to plug the gaps by doing volunteer work.

Most of the latest advances in medical technology are available in Bolivia, though most Bolivians do not have access to such technology.

Indigenous Bolivians will often seek the help of alternative practitioners. In some cases, it is simply because Western medicine is unaffordable. The language barrier is another factor, as is a perceived lack of empathy from Spanish speaking doctors. Folk doctors, curanderos and shamans are available even in big cities. Traditional native remedies, some travellers testify, have yielded successful results. Some doctors are more flexible than others in their willingness to incorporate native remedies into their Westernised practice.

Kallawayas

The most famous practitioners of native Bolivian medicine are the Kallawayas. Found in the vast but little know region north of La Paz, in and around towns such as Curva (240 km / 149 miles north of La Paz), Charazani (218 km / 135 miles) and Pelechuco (318 km / 197 miles), the Kallawaya are considered by some as a separate ethnic group with the Puquina language, and by others as Aymara. Kallawayas practice holistic medicine, seeking mind-body equilibrium. Accomplished botanists and pharmacologists, they use as many as 600 herbs in their practice.

Though women are not officially Kallawayas in the medical sense, they participate in reproductive medicine and collect herbs. The Kallawayas are concentrated in a remote region and one would think that they would live an insular existence, but nothing is farther from the truth. In fact, Kallawayas are known as travelling doctors. Kallawayas participated in the 1889 Universal Exposition in Paris, and they use their extensive travel as a way to acquire knowledge of herbs not found in their region.

It takes eight to 10 years for an apprentice Kallawaya to pass a test administered by village elders.

> **Bolivia: Country of Doctors**
> The name Kallawaya was probably derived from the Inca word Kollasuyo, which was the name of present day Bolivia. Kollasuyo means 'Country of Doctors'.

Cholas and Cholos

In 1989, Remedios Loza became the first indigenous woman who wears traditional Aymara dress to sit in the Bolivian Congress. This marked the beginning of what may break the postcard stereotype of the Chola woman selling produce at a market stand or working as a domestic employee.

I once interviewed the then Congresswoman Loza in the new congress building in downtown La Paz. She wears the typical bowler hat, usually black, dark green or brown, that you would have thought, erroneously, had been imported from London.

The Aymara Chola woman's dark hair is braided into two long plaits, joined by wool. The ornate *pollera* skirts are worn over several petticoats, making most women seem overweight.

The outfit includes an embroidered blouse and a *manta* (shawl). Quechua Cholas in the valleys wear a simpler, more streamlined version of this outfit. When in the street, Chola women carry an *ahuayo* on their back, connected with a cloth sling around the neck. This handwoven sack with colourful bands may contain anything from a baby to groceries to goods for sale.

The male counterpart, the Cholo, uses a Western style of dress, and is less distinguishable. Without the symbolism of traditional dress, he encounters greater obstacles in

A Chola with her baby—Bolivia modernises but Chola culture is passed from one generation to another.

maintaining cultural self-esteem. The Cholo and Chola represent a transition between pure indigenous culture and a fusion between these cultures and Western impositions.

Congresswoman Loza's Chola outfit seems to enhance her attractiveness. Her voice is soft and graceful, but her words are braided with steely conviction. I would have liked to ask about her family and cultural background, but I preferred to interview a congresswoman and not a charming relic. By choosing to address national realities rather than picturesque curiosities, Loza is a symbolic influence in assuring that Bolivia chooses a path of true diversity rather than quaint folklore.

Remedios Loza's potentially bright career as a critic of neoliberal economics took a downspin when her party, Condepa, was linked to scandals of corruption, and she herself was involved in a power struggle over the control of a TV programme. The final straw was when her party joined a governmental coalition with an elite party that espoused the very philosophy that the now defunct Condepa had opposed.

Demonstrators and Street Vendors

In the mid 1980s, hyper-inflation threatened to tear the country apart. The programme of invited Harvard consultant, economist Jeffrey Sachs, was free of demagoguery. "If you are brave, if you are gutsy, if you do everything right," he said, "you will end up with a miserable, poor economy with stable prices ... only with stable prices do you have any sort of chance at surviving into the future."

Bolivians understood that such shock treatment would leave massive layoffs and grossly inadequate social services in its wake. But both government and opposition agreed that it had to be done.

Bolivians were bracing themselves for the short-run consequences of the neoliberal shock treatment. Two decades later, with monetary stability a concrete achievement, the short run had become the long-run and unemployment and lack of social services continued to stifle Bolivians, from the working middle class on down. Government representatives were heard rephrasing Jeffrey Sachs' admonishment: "Before we had hyperinflation and misery," they would say.

Two main characters emerged from the orthodox free market austerity experiments—the subsistence street vendor and the political demonstrator. Both of these personages have been present throughout Bolivian history, but today they have evolved into a more tenacious version of themselves.

Both street vendors and demonstrators will be a fundamental part of the visitor's image of Bolivia.

The (Mostly) Peaceful Protester

Grand marches may occupy various parts of a city simultaneously, rendering an accurate crowd count impossible. In rural areas, well-planned roadblocks can paralyse the country. Those vehicles lucky enough to lose themselves from urban bottlenecks, take alternative routes only to encounter another throng. It's even more difficult for truck and bus drivers in rural areas, where no alternative route from the blockaded one may exist. Marches and demonstrations are militant but typically peaceful. Occasionally members of splinter groups heave rocks at police or at vehicles that try to barrel through blockades. I have witnessed episodes in which gas-masked police attacked first; giant green insects with shimmering snouts moving in on the crowd.

In Bolivia, these confrontations are not nearly as menacing as they look. Accompanying the protests are often hunger strikes, and extreme measures include militants having themselves nailed to a cross, as was the case with two prison inmates in 2003, who were protesting lengthy pretrial stays in prison and demanding a speedier justice system.

For the first edition of this book, I wrote that, 'In most countries, a demonstration that chokes the city would be met with far greater forms of repression,' and I still believe that if demonstrators succeeded in paralysing New York City, we'd see a lot of heads getting bashed in. However, I've had to eat my words, as lethal force became a regular response during the second presidency of Gonzalo Sánchez de Lozada. The fact that Goni was eventually discredited and forced to flee the country tells us that mortal repression is no longer a sustainable method of the political elites.

> Tear gas is the preferred method for quelling social disturbance, though in the first five years of the new century, more than 100 protesters were killed by police or by the military. On the other hand, protestors killed no one.

With Bolivia capable of earning an award for the most militant population in the world, it would only be fair to give these protesters a human face by profiling one of their most heroic figures.

Oscar Olivera

Oscar Olivera is one of 10 brothers and sisters. He worked as a child to help support his family. He was diagnosed with a mortal illness that should have left him dead by the age of 22. He worked in various factories, was sometimes fired for his ideals, and went underground between 1980 and 1982 during the García-Meza dictatorship. Since then, he has marched with the *cocaleros* (coca growers) and defended the rights of domestics, shoeshine boys, the unemployed and students.

In 1999, the Bolivian political elites succumbed to 'structural adjustment' demands of the World Bank by privatising the indebted water system of the valley city of Cochabamba. The government granted a 40-year concession to operate the system to a consortium whose dominant players were International Water Limited (an Italian company) and Bechtel, now famous for having advocated war on Iraq and then receiving a lucrative no-bid contract to reconstruct Iraq.

In the Cochabamba consortium some of the 'usual Bolivian suspects' were listed as minority investors, but it was Bechtel's business.

The newly privatised company immediately raised water prices. Earning 1/30 of a European or US salary, Cochabambans were suddenly expected to pay Euro or US level water bills. The poorest citizens faced losing their access to this necessity of life. Oscar Olivera became a leader in the campaign to regain local water control. Thanks to his lucidity and his years of organising experience, he became the spokesperson for the Coalition in Defense of Water and Life, which everyone knows as La Coordinadora.

Militant protests lasted for weeks. A Bolivian army sniper killed one protester while hundreds were injured, and Coalition leaders were arrested. Olivera escaped and then went into hiding. When the protesters refused to give in, the government was obligated to negotiate and Olivera resurfaced.

In April 2000, with massive public support for the protesters, the government had no choice but to cave in and La Coordinadora was given control over of the city's water system, with all the financial encumbrances that such control implied. The unbelievable sequence of events was capped by the Bolivian government's cancellation of the privatisation contract. This was the first significant victory against the global financial community's effort to privatise water resources. Olivera continues to head La Coordinadora's grass roots management while Bechtel continues to seek compensation through world financial bodies where it has much leverage.

Following the Coordinadora victory, Olivera won environmental awards and promptly handed the money over to the Abril Foundation, a new NGO dedicated to research, education and training, under the ideology of economic democracy.

Street Vendors—Opportunity Knocks

As political demonstrations pass by, life goes on. Bystanders either look on with curiosity or go about their chores nonchalantly. But the greatest image-as-message from these scenes focuses on the street vendors who line the march routes. Street vendors would seem to belong on a different channel, a world far removed from political protesters but in Bolivia, hawking one's wares on the street is an act of resistance against the same neoliberal forces that catalyse the demonstrations. The mindset of many street vendors is: 'If there is no employment for me, I'm going to do anything possible to survive.' This 'anything possible' falls short of robbery and burglary precisely because the street outlet is available. As such alternatives diminish, street crime increases.

Knowing that these commercial demonstrations are an act of desperation, the government looks the other way when some vendors cross the line of legality. As a political march passes over El Prado Boulevard, some of the vendors on the fringes are peddling items of dubious legality: pirated video tapes of new films with crude covers (where sometimes you can see a new film before it reaches the theatres), pirated editions of Latin American literature, home-made stew with potatoes and rice which has not met the requirements of the health department, cosmetics, clothing and jewellery, sold with a license but smuggled into the country. (In the Huyustus neighbourhood of La Paz, smuggled VCRs and televisions are sold with a guarantee!) Chilean novelist Isabel Allende should be proud to learn that she is on top of the best-seller list in the category of unremunerated sales.

The government seems to be practising the credo that, 'Fewer laws make fewer offenders.' The freedom of the informal economy may be in part responsible for Bolivia's low crime rate.

Every possible product is sold on the streets of La Paz, from aspirin to blood pressure machines, knick-knacks to

THE BOLIVIAN PEOPLE

In his pavement office, outside City Hall, an independent typist waits for his next assignment. Street vendors are the enterprising face of the Bolivian economy.

works of art. A whole street-based service industry floats among the vendors—plumbers and electricians with tool cases, street-corner typists with old portable Smith-Coronas preparing legal documents.

Street vendors have guilds; political and the commercial street demonstrations overlap when a guild protests against shoddy treatment by government bureaucrats.

Some of these street vending scenes are simultaneously sad and humorous: a woman sits with her preschool daughter under an umbrella, selling plastic bottles of petrol by the litre. This is a 'convenience' petrol station. For a small mark-up, bus drivers low on petrol buy enough to get them through crunch periods. The woman is lucky to make US$ 2 a day.

As they brush the dust from their suits, some city dwellers complain that their streets have been taken over by the masses. But most residents understand the dynamics that caused this situation and learn to live with it, taking advantage of it in the form of either convenient services or lower prices.

> **Reality TV**
> Customs police, captured on live television cameras, raid a house storing smuggled goods. You watch them rush in, expecting them to exit with handcuffed smugglers. Minutes later, they scurry out and are pelted by stones. Bystanders, many of them buyers of contraband goods, cheer. The smugglers have won.
> "We've already paid our bribes at the border," said one woman with ecstatic fury. "If they want to stop the contraband, they should arrest their own officials at the border!"

Independent Labourers

Bolivia's unemployment rate is listed at 8 per cent in urban areas, but the statistic is misleading when considering that 64 per cent live below the poverty line. Joining street vendors in the brigade of insufficient earners are independent labourers. If you rent or buy a house, there is a 95 per cent probability that, sooner or later, you will be in need of a plumber, electrician, bricklayer or roofer. Ground-floor plumbing is laborious as houses do not have crawl space underneath. Tiles and cement must be cracked into.

> **Electricity**
> Electricity is somewhat simpler, but for the fact that both 220 and 110 currents exist, with 110 being phased out. Many older structures have outlets for both 220 and 110. Independent electricians, plumbers and masons do not charge a lot for their services and a generous tip will still leave monetary proof that it is cheaper in Bolivia to get the work done by someone else.

The best method for finding a good technician is through word of mouth, even if the eventual service costs more. In the recent past, many good technicians played hard to get by not having a phone in their shop, and you had to seek them out, but mobile phones are improving communication between people with flooding apartments and on-call plumbers. In emergencies, try street corner repairmen who hang out in strategic neighbourhoods, with their black tool bags marked *plomero* or *electricista*. These renaissance men are also prepared to patch a leaky roof or clean the yard. If they hear you talking about stained glass windows or mosaic tiles, they will jump in and assure you: "I'll take care of that too!"

Their charge is low but there's a catch—just when you're ready to step into a warm bath or write an urgent business letter, the man will tell you he's missing two metres of pipe or six nails, and you'll have to run to the hardware store. Forty-five minutes later, after you have rewarmed the bath water, the man will tell you he needs six tiles to cover up the spot where he broke through the floor. You will then have to hail a taxi and search for a matching tile design.

You are required to see that these independent entrepreneurs are well fed. It's worth it for the low fee they are charging, but don't expect to get any work of your own done while they are around. In the worst case scenario, they will be lacking an important tool for your unique repair problem.

Result: these amiable itinerant repairmen are more than willing to do everything within their limited power to solve your problem. But if you are not hit by an emergency situation, it is best to find the right technician, through word of mouth, from the formal economy. Even then, don't expect everything to work out smoothly; most of these guys do not own a truck, and somewhere during the day, they discover that they must return to their workshop for a tool that they did not anticipate needing.

These men, as well as other service-oriented personnel such as bus and taxi drivers, are addressed as *maestro*, which means master. Having got to know and appreciate several *maestros*, I am further impressed by the luck factor in life. A simple quirk of being born in El Alto, Bolivia instead of Palo Alto, California, makes the difference between US$ 10 a day and US$ 60 an hour, the difference between subsistence and affluence.

Bus Drivers and Unemployed Professionals

Many Bolivian *micros* are old 1950s school buses. For about US$ 0.20, you can ride anywhere in the city, and also to villages beyond. Taller folk may have trouble finding a place for their knees, but at that price, you're not going to get reclining seats.

Like plumbers and electricians, drivers are addressed as *maestro*. Recalling my days in Mexico, I expected that I'd need to board the *micro* with a running jump, or vault off the moving bus at a precise angle defined by the laws of physics for a safe landing. But in Bolivia, most *micro* drivers are franchised or own their own bus, and therefore are paid according to the number of customers. The customer comes first, even if it means stopping for a pick-up in the middle of an intersection. If you are driving behind a *micro*, be prepared!

City planners designate bus stops, to no avail. The phrase to use if you want to get off is '*bajo aquí por favor*' (*baho akee*—I'm getting off here) or '*esquina por favor*' (*eskeena*—corner). Drivers will give change, but it is best to carry coins rather than larger notes. During rush hours, some *micros* are so crowded that people ride hanging out the door, which usually remains open during the trip.

Micro rides are accompanied by radio music of the driver's preference. The serenade is better than lift music but don't expect progressive jazz or Beethoven. If you ride the *micro* enough, you will have memorised the same Number One pop song. And whether you like that song or not, when you arrive home at night, the melody is going to haunt you and taunt you as you attempt to sleep. You may even find yourself unconsciously singing it in the shower next morning. It is no use trying to escape the torturous song by taking a collective taxi for a little more than twice the cost of the *micro*, for the taxi driver happens to like the exact same song.

There is an overabundance of professionals in Bolivian cities. Too many doctors, too many lawyers and too many sociologists. Traditionally, it was degrading for a person with a professional degree to take a lesser job. But these prejudices are becoming ancient history, and some independent labourers may be computer technicians in disguise.

The pay for certain professions is alarmingly low. If one were to include the room and board of a typical house maid as part of her salary, she would be earning more than an entry level public school teacher. The shortage of jobs for college grads has proletarianised many Bolivian professionals. Militant doctors' or teachers' strikes are commonplace.

> **Work Abroad**
> In the past, professional graduates would find work abroad, with the USA as the major absorber. More restrictive immigration laws in the United States have greatly curtailed the brain drain.

Police

In Bolivia, the police department is a path for the most impoverished and under-educated to acquire a degree of respect. In exchange for the uniform, policemen must be willing to accept an obscenely low salary along with occasional abuse.

A foot patrolman tries to stop a wealthy Bolivian driver in a Mercedes for a traffic infraction. The driver shouts an obscenity, pumps on the gas and speeds away.

Law officers are expected to serve the public without the necessary authority or compensation that should come with the job. Members of the police department who seek bribes (called *coimas* in Bolivia) are often motivated by desperation more than greed as the average monthly salary is a mere US$ 80. They are well aware that their higher-ups accept gratuities in exchange for awarding procurement contracts.

On 9 April 2000, when the police were called on to repress massive anti-poverty protests near and in Laz Paz, 800 elite police mutinied and demanded a pay raise. Thousands gathered around police headquarters to show their solidarity.

In February of 2003, as seen in the previous chapter, the La Paz police, followed by police in a few other cities, rebelled against a new income tax. The police were supported by sectors of the population. The military repressed the rebellion, opening wounds of an ancient rivalry between police and the military.

Street Children

Bolivian police tend to refrain from involving children in the law enforcement system.

If child labour laws were enforced in Bolivia, the minimal juvenile crime that now exists might escalate. A World Bank paper notes that 'many children may have to work in order to attend school so abolishing child labor may only hinder their education,' without arriving at the obvious policy recommendation that such abolishment should accompany massive financial support for poor children's education.

A contrapuntal study by Care USA suggests the opposite, that 'mine work prevents children from enrolling and staying in school and hinders learning activities.'

As it is, many orphans and children from poor families are working in a multitude of low-pay occupations. According to the Saranteñani programme, 'there are approximately 400 children ranging from 6 to 18 who live on the streets of La Paz ... with streets being their only means of subsisting.'

In minibus vans, children operate the door for passengers, collect fares and call out the van's destinations through the window.

> Only a lack of finances prevents various church groups, non-governmental organisations and government agencies from providing more assistance and taking in a greater number of child labourers. A number of NGOs provide child workers with scholastic and psychological support as well as drug rehabilitation, receiving funds from international organisations.

This is reminiscent of the medieval Spanish novel *Lazarillo de Tormes*, in which a young rogue, abandoned by his unwed mother, skips from one master to another, receiving minimal support in exchange for exploitative labour. Similarly, many of these minibus workers have been informally adopted by their drivers, in a symbiotic relationship that keeps the children off the streets.

Lustrabotas and Child Miners

Shoeshine boys, called *lustrabotas*, lack paternal guidance during their long hours on the street. Many wear face masks so that school children from their neighbourhood will not recognise them. The basic charge for a shine is

Bs 1 (Boliviano)—less than US$ 0.20. One young boy told me Bs 1, and then after he'd finished, he asked for Bs 2. "I meant Bs 1 for each shoe," he said with a roguish smile.

An older *lustrabotas* named Victor claimed he had graduated high school and was beginning university classes. No other available job, he said, would allow him the time to take classes. "Before," he explained, "there were no kids that did drugs or drank like today. An estimated 10 per cent of *lustrabotas* are alcoholics or use inhalants like *clefa* (a type of glue), petrol or paint thinner."

Dr Javier Pérez of the Good Samaritan Health Centre in La Paz provides free medical assistance to *lustrabotas*. "There is a good chance," says Dr Pérez, "that Victor doesn't attend the university. He just says he does."

"On a good day," says Nestor, another *lustrabotas*, "we can make Bs 10." With pavement meal costs of Bs 1.50–Bs 2, plus bus fares and other items, the expenses total Bs 6.50, leaving him with Bs 3.50 profit per day, about US$ 0.60. "From that we have to buy clothes."

Shoeshine boys use hoods or masks, preferring to work anonymously.

Other boys hop onto *micros* with the permission of the driver to sell *caramelos* (sweets). They begin with a memorised speech saying that, "this job helps me to be productive and not get involved with drugs."

Some of these children are being exploited by a parent and are expected to hand over the money after each day. Others are on their own. Food stands in public markets and on street corners offer healthy lunches for as little as Bs 1.50, so these children do not go hungry. However, the probability of their eventually becoming 'self-made men' is virtually nil. Those without parents or who are not sheltered in special homes may spend nights sniffing glue with companions from their subculture.

If the situation on city streets is grim, child workers in mining regions such as Llallagua and Potosí have even less of a chance for breaking out of the deterministic frame. Care estimates that some 15,000 children are involved in mining, most of them working with their families. This author's wife observed children outside the mines sorting and clearing ore and her guide within the primitive mine was an adolescent.

Most experts agree that the problems of child labourers will not be solved in the absence of a profound economic transformation which would allow the state to finance comprehensive programmes for children. In the meantime, NGOs partly fill the gap, and long-term visitors, the type of people who read this book, are playing an important role.

Sexual Workers

Prostitutes, referred to officially as sexual workers, also receive assistance from non-governmental organisations.

The control of sexually-transmitted diseases is facilitated by the fact that, in Bolivia, the world's oldest profession is legal. In 1995, 1,716 sexual workers registered with the Technical Juridical Police of La Paz. They are required to purchase work permits every three months and must follow government regulations for periodic gynaecological examinations.

But only one third of these women actually attend government clinics as required. The Anti-AIDS Project has an outreach programme that educates sexual workers on the proper use of condoms, and explains the techniques for persuading customers to use them. In this labour intensive industry, it is in the interest of brothel owners to cooperate with educational programmes.

This may partially explain why Bolivia has one of the lowest rates of HIV/AIDS in the world: 0.1 per cent compared to Brazil right next door with 0.7 per cent and Perú with 0.5 per cent. Other sexually transmitted diseases are not being restrained with the same level of success in Bolivia.

Contrary to public perception, Catholic countries tend to be tolerant of prostitution. For this reason, one could live in Bolivia for years without bumping into a streetwalker, something that New Yorkers and Los Angelinos might be surprised to know. With legalised prostitution, there is no need for a Sunset Boulevard in La Paz or Cochabamba. The highest paid sexual workers ply their trade in bars and night clubs, the most picturesque of which is called El Tropezón (The Big Stumble). Next are the women who work in brothels. Any cab driver will take you to a brothel. Finally, the lowest-paid women are the independents.

First class brothels provide drinks and clean, private rooms; the sexual workers in these places have most likely completed high school and wear modern dress. The lowest-class brothels, in La Paz, include women who wear traditional dress and come from the bad dream city of El Alto.

Women called *coperas* work the boîtes essentially to stimulate income from drinks. Doing more serious business with a customer is secondary to the drink income generated. A customers might invite a woman to have a drink for an outrageous price without knowing that the 'rum and coke' has no rum in it.

Like street children, sexual workers are forced into their way of life by poverty and lack of opportunity. Contrary to the viewpoint of many recent popular films, there is nothing romantic about prostitution. In some brothels they put on an uproarious show, but basically we're talking about the business of satisfying needs. Condoms in Bolivia are cheap and readily available in any pharmacy. The best ones are the cheapest, imported from the United States and sold in certain pharmacies for Bs 0.50 (equivalent to US$ 0.10).

Bolivia's liberal attitude toward sexual reality extends even to dogs. Midway between Miraflores and lower La Paz, along the eucalyptus covered Avenida del Libertador, a dog clinic advertises the availability of female dogs to provide sexual satisfaction for your canine macho.

Artists

Street children and sexual workers are forced into their underworlds by a harsh economic reality. Many Bolivian artists may live on the fringe by choice.

Bolivia's rich art scene is laden with poor artists. Since the colonial period, painting has been the most likely medium for an artist to gain international recognition. Corollary professions such as commercial art are not as prevalent or lucrative as they would be in more commercially powerful countries, so Bolivian artists often live and die by their fine arts. A handful of Bolivian painters have acquired worldwide fame, and with it, a degree of fortune. However, the market for high-class painting is limited. Bolivian painters choosing to remain in their country of origin are bucking the odds.

I have read whole books on Bolivian contemporary painting, only to visit galleries the next day and discover great artists who were not included in the books. Styles vary, but much of Bolivian painting is a dynamic hybrid between European art history and traditions, and native popular art.

Notwithstanding a profusion of fine art galleries in La Paz, the best Bolivian gallery may actually be in the valley city of Cochabamba. Housed in a mini-Versailles style mansion built by Bolivia's infamous tin magnate, Simón Patiño, this Cochabamba art museum, referred to as Palacio Portales, offers one of Bolivia's great sensorial experiences. In other salons of the same mansion one can enjoy concerts and lectures. Meanwhile, Casa de la Cultura in Santa Cruz is also prominent in the art scene. Potosí's Casa Real de la Moneda has the country's best collection of colonial art, with a few rooms dedicated to modern artists.

Bolivian art galleries rarely display paintings from beyond Latin America, but the superb local product should satisfy one's passion for great art. Bolivian artists who find success abroad do not cut ties with their native art community. We visited Luis Zilvetti's well equipped studio in Paris, an artist's dream. Zilvetti said that he proudly returns to Bolivia at least once a year for expositions.

A Painter's Viewpoint

One of the more eccentric Bolivian painters, also a fine poet, is Edgar Arandia. As we had tea together at a café on La Paz's El Prado Boulevard, Arandia summed up his background. "I make lots of money in Germany, where I go to paint and exhibit, spend it all in France," he smiled, "then return to Bolivia to paint, write poetry, and help fellow artists who are recovering alcoholics."

Arandia says he's influenced by the Mexican line drawings of José Luis Cuevas, but describes his own contemporary work as 'very classical.' "One always returns to the classics," he contends.

Arandia's first experiences abroad came with exiles stemming from his anti-dictatorship activities. "I received the Bánzer scholarship and the García-Meza scholarship," he explained, referring to two of Bolivia's former military dictators. "I was once wounded in an anti-coup demonstration," he grins, "and lived to hear the announcement of my death over the radio the following day."

Like Arandia, late Bolivian artist Walter Solón Romero was exiled several times. When the García-Meza dictatorship mistook a mural of Bolivia's woman guerrilla independence heroine Juana Azurduy de Padilla for a homage to Che Guevara, he was captured and labelled a subversive. The mural was the work of his students.

"They demanded to know the names of all the art students I'd taught and the teachers I'd studied under, and then they threatened to cut off my hands," he said.

Solón Romero didn't talk. He was finally released thanks to pressure from international human rights organisations.

Many of Solón Romero's fresco murals were destroyed without even a photograph as a reminder, but some 25 still stand in La Paz's San Andrés University (UMSA) and public buildings. Like Arandia, he was influenced by the classics. He was exiled three times but never belonged to a political party. "I went to the Soviet Union twice," he says, "and they tried to convince me, but they never could." Most Bolivian art is not overtly political, with some of Solón Romero's work as a notable exception. More often, Solón's art is humanist, gaining inspiration from Don Quixote and Sancho Panza. As an alchemist, Solón invented new lithographic methods. Like Quixote, Solón was constantly searching past new horizons, and upon his death in 1999, he left a collection of impressive three-dimensional paintings. His work can be seen at the Solón foundation in La Paz (http://www.funsolon.org), and numerous public buildings, especially in Sucre and La Paz, house his murals.

A fine Bolivian original oil painting may be purchased in La Paz or Cochabamba for anywhere from US$ 200 to US$ 1,000; in a New York or Paris gallery, works of equivalent quality would sell for considerably more.

Where to Buy

Bolivian paintings of a more popular culture style may be purchased outdoors at Plaza Humboldt (on Sundays) in La Paz or across the bridge from the Félix Capriles Soccer Stadium in Cochabamba for much lower prices.

Art depends so much on taste, so how can one select the names of a few artists out of hundreds?

Roberto Mamani Mamani, Herminio Pedraza, Patricia Mariaca, María Eugenia Cortés, Angeles Fabbri, Milguer Yapur Daza, Ejti Stih, Hernán Coria, Karine Boulanger, Alfredo de la Placa, Carmen Céspedes and apologies to numerous other quality painters who should have been mentioned.

The sculptures of María Nuñez del Prado and José Antonio Márquez top the list of another genre that thrives in Bolivia, while Mario Sarabia's ceramics mesh ancient and contemporary forms. Edgar Alvarado's watercolours offer an expressionist view of the daily life of Bolivia's common man.

Today, Alfredo La Placa's painting Críptica Andina hangs in front of Café Austria on the first floor of the United Nations in New York City.

Aymaras and Quechuas

Bolivian fine art is influenced by two overlapping cultures that trace their roots to ancient civilisations: the Aymara and Quechua. Approximately 30 per cent of Bolivians are of Quechua origins, with 25 per cent Aymaras. Another 30 per cent are either mestizo (Amerindian with Spanish) or of a minority indigenous culture, and 15 per cent are labelled as white.

The most dominant indigenous influence in Bolivia comes from the Tiahuanaco civilisation. Eventually emerging from the mysterious Tiahuanacos are today's Aymara speakers, extending from southern Perú, Lake Titicaca, La Paz and El Alto (approaching a million inhabitants) all the way to Oruro. The Aymaras have been around for some 2,000 years, resisting colonialism and gaining strength from La Pachamama (Mother Earth). They even have their own flag, the Wiphala, a seven-colour quilt with diagonal checked lines, often seen at political demonstrations.

The Quechuas' language was inherited by the conquering Incas, whose empire lasted only 60 years. Centred in Tiahuanaco, the empire spread from Ecuador to the north, through Perú and Bolivia, to northern Argentina and Chile to the south. It is important to understand that the Quechuas predated the Incas and survived the fall of the Inca empire in 1532. Today's Bolivian Quechuas are primarily located in the regions of Cochabamba, Sucre (Chuquisaca), Potosí and parts of Oruro. The Quechuas built stone roads and bridges, some of which survive today under the label of 'Inca trails'.

Aymaras are proud of their own flag, the Wiphala, which has become a symbol of the new Bolivia.

Both Aymara and Quechua communities and villages have a socio-political structure called the Ayllu, which functions within a system of reciprocity called the Ayni in which collective welfare is supported by a culture of mutual help. For both Aymara and Quechua, the coca leaf has been used in ceremonial contexts for centuries. Both cultures created sophisticated irrigation and food preservation systems.

Thanks to Aymara and Quechua art and music, international awareness of Bolivia is not limited to stereotypes about cocaine. In Europe, roving Altiplano minstrels from Bolivia, Perú and Ecuador play the haunting Andean harmonies, especially the Asian-sounding Huayño that combines major and minor tones.

Typical handmade instruments such as the banjo-like *charango*, the flute-like *quena* and the wind instrument called the *zampoña* (the last two made from reeds of Lake Titicaca), may be purchased in most Bolivian cities.

Continuing Traditions

Today, *ayllu* community structures survive. They were re-enfranchised through the Sánchez de Lozada government's 'Popular Participation' programme, and later, in a more profound way, by the militant movements in the first six years of the new century. Meanwhile, agronomists are tempted to redevelop an indigenous irrigation system that prevents flooding by raising the level of fields and surrounding them with canals, a technique which also served to maintain an even temperature and prevent freezing of crops in the Altiplano regions. According to *The Chronicle of Higher Education*, 'efforts are on to popularise this simple but brilliant method of cultivation.'

Terraced agriculture around Lake Titicaca is another example of Aymara and Inca ingenuity, allowing the Inca socialist theocracy to provide food for all. Indigenous medicinal plants and herbs are today being taken seriously by Western trained medical researchers, and agricultural products original to the Altiplano and nearby valleys, such as the *quinoa* grain, are becoming select exports. Kellog wanted to market a *quinoa* cereal but Bolivian *quinoa* harvests would only meet 15 per cent of the United States market. This leaves *quinoa* under the control of Bolivia's private sector, which markets the supergrain in organic form, in cereals, breads, sweets, instant soups and *pipoca* (popped *quinoa*). *Quinoa* averages 16 per cent protein, compared to wheat's 12 per cent. *Quinoa* also supplies ample amounts of iron, calcium and vitamins B and E.

> For the Tiahuanaco Aymara and Quechua leaders who developed *quinoa* from wild plants, this grain was sacred. The surplus produced enabled the development of great civilisations.

No cursory summary can cover the depth of Aymara and Quechua cultures. In later chapters of this book, the reader will have the opportunity to share experiences of visitors to Bolivia who have interacted with these peoples.

Kollas and Cambas

Borders of Spanish American countries were based on the original Spanish colonial viceroyalties, with little or no attention paid to ethnic considerations. Independent *caudillos* (warrior *políticos*) further contributed to carving out boundaries. The indigenous Aymara nation is split into two by the Bolivia-Perú border. Both Perú and Bolivia have a Quechua and Aymara foundation.

When Bolivian hero Mariscal Andrés de Santa Cruz attempted to create a federation of the two countries shortly after independence, the Lima aristocracy did not trust the Bolivian hillbillies, and Argentina, to the south, feared competition from a potential empire to the north. Politics and not culture determined boundaries.

The most noteworthy cultural rift in Latin America transcends these political considerations. Highlands and lowlands are as different culturally as they are geographically, and only the zones of seasonal change in the Southern Cone of South America and in Northern Mexico are exempt from this phenomenon.

A Mexican from the tropical coast of Vera Cruz may have more in common with a Cuban across the Caribbean than with another Mexican from the highland State of Michoacan. An Ecuadorian from the coastal tropics around Guayaquíl will bond better with a Colombian from tropical Barranquilla than with another Ecuadorian from the highland capital of Quito.

In a similar way, but with its own quirks, Bolivian highlanders, referred to as Kollas, and lowlanders from the Santa Cruz tropics, called Cambas, are as much rivals as they are compatriots.

A relatively insignificant football match was to decide whether the Santa Cruz squad, Blooming, or the La Paz team, Chaco, would gain the final opening in the first division of the football league. Crowd enthusiasm was more spirited for this lesser contest than for other league games with superior teams. It was the Kollas against the Cambas, and never mind that most players on Kolla teams are Cambas anyway.

General Hugo Bánzer's presidency in the 1970s helped to catapult the Camba city of Santa Cruz to a financial position that rivals Kolla La Paz. Today, the Cruceños are widely believed to have become more dynamic capitalists than the Paceños.

The Blame Game

Guillermo Gutiérrez, a Cruceño who had been awaiting trial on charges of violations of Bolivian banking laws, complained to me in a jail cell interview that his imprisonment was the result of a conspiracy of the La Paz bankers club against Santa Cruz banks. Kolla entrepreneurs responded to his charges by alleging that Camba business people were dodging taxes through favourable loopholes created by Bánzer and other politicians.

Upward social mobility for a Kolla in Santa Cruz may be more difficult than for an so-called 'illegal immigrant' in California!

Throughout the Latin American highlands, which in Bolivia would also include the high valley cities of Cochabamba and Sucre as well as La Paz, Potosí and Oruro, the Spanish language is spoken more methodically, with every syllable distinctly pronounced. On the other hand, in the lowlands, from Acapulco to Havana, from El Salvador to Panamá, from Guayaquil on the Ecuador coast to Bolivia's departments of Santa Cruz, Beni and Pando, Spanish is spoken at a faster clip, with final consonants not pronounced and with the 's' aspirated as if it were a quickly breathed 'h.'

Does the weather have something to do with this evolution of the Spanish language? One hypothesis is grounded in the fact that most highland regions in Spanish America retain their indigenous heritage, while African influences predominate in the lowlands, with these distinct cultural influences somehow affecting speech patterns. Another hypothesis with a more objective foundation is that the Spanish colonialists who came from the hot-climate south of Spain tended to drift to the regions of Latin America that most resembled their back-home climates, bringing their regional accents with them.

Further oral evidence of the highland–tropics culture divide comes from the music. Musical styles of the tropics have much in common in their rhythms and harmonies typical of West Africa, the source of many of the Spaniards' African slaves. Although highland music genres vary, they tend to be slower than their tropical counterpart, with harmonies remarkably similar to some music of Asia.

The highland Indians, according to a dominant theory, came to South America via a long migration that began in Asia and crossed the Bering Strait. Our ears tell us that the Asian sound in some Kolla music is more than a coincidence.

STEREOTYPES AND RIVALRIES

Within Bolivia, the highland Kollas have developed stereotypes for the Cambas. Many Kollas believe that Camba women are sexually loose. If a Camba woman does not marry by the time she is 18, she's considered a spinster. Kollas believe that Cambas are arrogant regionalists. Cambas believe that Kollas are slow-witted and backward. Cambas are joyful, while Kollas, they say, are melancholic.

Like most stereotypes, the ones that float around Bolivia are partly true but mostly fictitious, with all human varieties found in each region. Concerned Bolivians who advocate against regionalism should not ignore the fact that the highland–lowland cultural divide is not a uniquely Bolivian phenomenon.

The alarm over the Kolla–Camba split may be exaggerated. With impenetrable geography and poor road and rail connections, the relative isolation of Bolivian regions should have generated a far greater degree of regionalism.

At a Bolivian party or festival, people will be dancing to both tropical and highland music, no matter where they are from. Occasional success of the Bolivian national football team in world competition has also unified lowland Benianos or Cruceños with highland Paceños.

Bolivian tour companies do pioneering work in linking the diverse parts of the country. Many Bolivian non-government organisations have active outreach programmes that know no regional boundaries.

Having lost a plot of seacoast to Chile in 1880 and a large slice of the Chaco region to Paraguay in the 1930s, and other sections to Brazil during different periods, Bolivians are keenly aware today of protecting their most remote regions, which is in the interest of both Kollas and Cambas. I perceive that there is less of a cultural gap between Cambas and Kollas than that which separates African-Americans in South Central Los Angeles from white West LA and Chicano East LA in the single California city.

During the great road blockades led by indigenous highlanders in recent years, reactive calls for Camba autonomy have been led, in part, by the region's agro-industrialists and fomented by the perception that such a large percentage of so-called natural resources are found in the lowlands (see Chapter Nine, Working in Bolivia, page 240).

Both Sides of the Divide

Two images are symbolic of the divide. A group of bikini-attired Camba models called Las Magnificas were referred to as bimbos by some highlanders. Meanwhile, a Camba congressman made racist remarks in congress against the highlanders.

In the end, some Bolivian intellectuals believe that Camba calls for autonomy are a smokescreen that serves to protect the entrenched political class and its privileged position as intermediary of multinational investors. In the January 2005 elections, the 'white man's' candidate won the majority in lowland departments while the indigenous candidate carried the highlands and valleys for a clear majority. However, the highland candidate lost the Department of Santa Cruz with 32 per cent of the vote, which is a significant percentage considering that presidential winners from previous elections gained the presidency with less than 30 per cent of the vote.

Furthermore, candidates from all parties agreed that some form of regional autonomy would be good for Bolivia's future.

Afrobolivianos

Africans were forced into slavery during the Spanish colonial period, labouring in the silver mines at above 4,000 m (14,000 ft). Barbaric working conditions and the drastic change in climate from Africa to Potosí caused an atrocious mortality rate.

Once liberated, the Africans descended to a friendlier altitude. They chose two zones about 110 km (68 miles) north of La Paz in the semi-tropics known as Los Yungas. Today, the two agricultural settlements of Afrobolivianos—Chicaloma (with approximately 100 families) and Tocana (with approximately 300 families)—retain certain African traditions.

In interacting with indigenous communities, many Afrobolivianos learned Aymara, and their dress and diet represent assimilation into the rural indigenous lifestyle. Today, every school child learns to dance the Saya. Another dance featured in carnivals is Los Caporales, which sounds more indigenous than African but is a stylised rendition of the exploitation that Bolivian blacks suffered in the mines. Afrobolivians from the Yungas have also become stars in Bolivia's national football team.

There are no hotels in Chicaloma and Tocana, nor any substantial facilities of comfort. But trekkers can easily reach this region of Afrobolivia by way of breathtaking river gorges and through rich foliage, from the nearby resort towns of Coroico and Chulumani.

A trek to Afrobolivian territory begins in Coroico's village square. Walk downwards to the last house in the village. The path continues, twice crossing the main road to Santa Barbara.

Passing a chapel, Capilla del Carmen, on the left side, you reach the road to Caranavi. Take it for 15 minutes until you cross the Mururata Bridge, where you will be pleasantly distracted by lavish swimming holes. Tocana is another hour and a half downward over a spectacular winding road.

The total trek is only 7 km (4 miles). The highest point is 1,715 m (5627 ft) in Coroico, the lowest is 1,170 m (3839 ft). If you don't relish the uphill return, then continue down the road for 5 km (3 miles) to Santa Barbara and then hitch a ride in a truck back to Coroico. It rains a lot around here, so the best time for the trek is in the May–October dry season, when the mosquito population shrinks.

° La Paz to Yungas was once believed to be Bolivia's most dangerous road. But drivers exercise more caution and are forced to drive more slowly on a hairpin road like this one than on the straight paved La Paz–Oruro Highway, now nicknamed 'The road of death'. The winding La Paz–Yungas road and its breathtaking precipices are featured in the 1995 film, *A Question of Faith*, winner of awards in France, Italy and Puerto Rico.

The new La Paz–Yungas road means that the road of death is no longer an obligatory menace for fearful travellers.

The right time to visit the Afro-Yungas and Coroico is during the alternating six months of dry weather, but most injuries and deaths were due to truck and pickup accidents, although a single bus accident resulted in 36 deaths that year. The improved 1995 safety record for public transportation over this road suggests that the single 1994 bus accident was just a statistical blip.

> Accident statistics along the La Paz–Yungas roads in 1994 showed 102 deaths, 75 of which happened during the six months of wet season. The ratio of deaths to non-fatal injuries suggests a relatively low survival rate in case of accident, with 125 non-fatal injuries, 89 of which occurred in the rainy season.

If you have a phobia about looking down into precipices from moving vehicles, one alternative is the 3-day, cold-to-hot La Cumbre to Coroico trek, which begins in a mountain pass north-east of La Paz, 4,859 m (16,035 ft) high, descending over 3,000 m (9,900 ft). Also travelling to Los Yungas, at a higher arrival point, is the old Inca or Taquesi trail, a walk of about 14 hours over pre-Inca paving.

> **Tips for Trekking**
> Maps for trekking are available in La Paz from Instituto Geográfico Militar (IGM), Calle Juan XXIII 100 and tour agencies specialising in trekking, such as Magri Tourism and Calle Montevideo.

Gravity-Assisted Bicyclers

With a new highway cutting down to Coroico (it separates from the old road not far down from the checkpoint at Unduavi), the old road is less transited and free for adventurers. Anticipating this new function, this author along with his wife and son actually walked from Unduavi at about 3,400 m (11,154 ft) above sea level to Yoloso at 1,100 m (3,608 ft) above sea level, just below Coroico. It took us seven hours.

Several tour companies now specialise in this trip by mountain bike, with solid bikes, accessory equipment and guides furnished, including Gravity Assisted Mountain Biking, (http://gravitybolivia.com). Mainly tourists take the escorted trip but Bolivian youth are apt to do it on their own.

The Guaraní: Cowboys vs Indians

Bolivians travelling to the lowlands rarely get as far as the Chaco, where 125,000 Guaraní are dispersed through the large region of dry, tropical scrubland. More than 30 different indigenous languages and/or cultures survive in today's Bolivia, but the Guaraní grab more attention than their numbers because they live in oil territory.

The Chaco War with Paraguay in the 1930s cost Bolivia most of its Chaco territory but left her with a rich, oil-producing region.

With its hot, flat surface, the Chaco seems to offer little of the geographic awe of the rest of Bolivia. But within its vast territory, giant armadillos roam and wild peanuts grow in a rich ecosystem. Fauna once endemic to the region was first identified in the Guaraní language. As a consequence, Guaraní words were adapted into Western languages, such as jaguar, tapir and piranha. The Guaraní language comes from the vast Arawak family of languages.

For nearly a century and a half, some Guaranís lived in controversial Jesuit reductions, a system rather similar to the California missions. On the one hand, the Jesuit absolute rule benefitted from the indigenous labour. On the other hand, the reductions served as protection against slavery. Some indigenous inhabitants in the Bolivian missions, in the Chiquitos region, ended up as baroque composers and painters whose mestizo work is known today.

Some Guaraní communities gain autonomy using unique methods. Chaco Captain Bonifacio Barrientos was a leader of the Izozog Guaraní community of 5,000 that proposed to make its homeland a protected area. These Guaraní spend most of the year in subsistence economic activities; fruit gathering, hunting wild boar (its meat for consumption and its skin for clothing) and occasional fishing when the rivers are high enough. They travel to work on plantations during the Santa Cruz prime harvest season.

The Izozog inhabitants are very much aware of concepts of ecology and biodiversity. When threatened with an invasion of rats and mice in the early 1980s, the community medicine men decided to prohibit hunting of all natural predators of the rodents, including felines, owls and snakes. The problem was solved within a short period of time.

Alarmed about the encroachment of cattle ranchers, community leader Barrientos and his people published a brochure requesting the creation of a national park to protect their region, a tropical dry-forest. Some environmentalists believe that dry-forests are even more threatened as habitats than rainforests.

During the cowboys vs Indians period of Bolivian history, the army, protecting the interests of cattle ranchers, killed hundreds of Guaraní who opposed the devastation of their habitat. New threats by cattle ranchers earned the Izozog Guaranís the support of Bolivia's Ministry of Sustainable Development and international conservation organisations, but cattle interests induced a bureaucratic snag in the goal for a national park.

In 1994, this Guaraní community became Bolivia's first 'Indigenous Sub-Municipality,' enfranchised by the new 'Popular Participation Law.' The empowerment finally paid off; on 21 September 1995, the Bolivian government declared the Kaa-Iya Gran Chaco a national park. The Indians had, for once, defeated the cowboys.

> **For Love of the Environment**
> Kaa-Iya Gran Chaco is the first Bolivian national park conceived by the inhabitants themselves, who thus became the administrators of the park.

As isolated as the Guaraní seem to be, during the gas 'war' of the early years of the 21st century, groups of Guaraní in proximity with oil corporation installations joined the national movement in defense of gas reserves, going as far as to occupy oil installations of multinational corporations.

Artisans

Bolivia's talented artisans work with materials such as silver, tin, hides, wood, paint and textiles, jewellery, utensils, wallets, musical instruments, clothing, furniture, sculpture, paintings and masks. On Calle Sagárnaga, behind the San Francisco Church in La Paz, a multitude of artisans' shops coalesce into a great street collage.

There seem to be more artisans than tourists to buy their wares. With such keen competition, it is hard to imagine how they manage to make a living.

"The life of an artist is pretty hard," says the master furniture craftsman, Julio Hinojosa, "especially in Bolivia. Most of the time you do it for yourself, for the soul."

THE BOLIVIAN PEOPLE

Hinojosa is one of the lucky ones. Working in mahogany, hand carving furniture, Hinojosa has won over many clients with his intricate woodcarvings.

In fact, a carved relief by Hinojosa has been hanging in Potosí's Casa de la Moneda for nearly two decades. With such a labour-intensive job, he explains, "the most important thing is to work with affection."

Most artisans are not as fortunate as Hinojosa. With exports increasing, perhaps the business of handmade art has some future. But these cultural heroes must compete with neighbouring Perú, whose artisans got a head start in the international arena.

Several of Bolivia's top 100 companies depend on such artistry, including jewellery and textiles.

Truck Drivers and Miners

Bolivian artisans are not wealthy but they get much more recognition than the truck drivers who transport their works.

Yet Bolivian truck drivers are heroes of a sort, navigating some of the most difficult highways in the world. For the driver, Bolivia's incredibly rough terrain is at once more demanding and more captivating than a motorway in Kansas.

In most mountainous countries, drivers expect a pass to get them through the range. Bolivian mountains are so dense that passes must be literally carved out of mountain sides, with room only for one lane. If two vehicles approach, one must move over at the first available ledge.

If your car breaks down on one of these roads, you are guaranteed help. It is in the self-interest of every driver behind you to lend a hand.

Bolivia's commerce depends on the ability of its truck drivers to handle these roads. I once assumed that truck drivers had the most dangerous job in the country, rivalled only by football referees.

Interpretation of statistics from recent years may suggest that truck drivers would win the award for performing the most dangerous job. But if statistics incorporated life expectancy and not just number of accidents, then miners would easily win the honour of having laboured under the most perilous conditions. Visitors to Bolivia may test these statistics in person, by descending mine shafts in Potosí and hitching a ride with a truck driver over the road to Los Yungas.

Highway precipices lined with crosses that pay homage to the victims of fatal accidents provide the type of joyous fright that one experiences on a roller coaster. When death occurs, it is instantaneous. But when you reach your destination unscathed (by far the most probable scenario), you'll have less fear about doing it again.

Both truck drivers and miners stop their work at certain moments to give offerings to La Pachamama. A new vehicle gets sprinkled with alcohol or whisky in what is known as *cha'lla*. Miners offer coca and alcohol to La Pachamama when entering the mine.

The *cha'lla* custom has reached virtually every segment of Bolivian society.

Latin Americans

The cultural gap between middle class, Westernised Bolivians and the Guaraní, is wider than the gap between foreign visitors and Bolivians of Hispanic and other European heritages. At the same time that indigenous Bolivians have been victimised by discrimination from within the country, Westernised Bolivians have been the object of stereotyping from abroad, ever since they were labelled as hillbillies by the Lima aristocracy, following independence in the early 1800s.

Today, well meaning people watch National Geographic documentaries on Amazonian Indians who live in trees (wisely so, in order to avoid insects and vermin) and assume that this is typical South America.

A Sense of Humour Required
I once invited an Ecuadorian friend to speak to a Spanish language class of mine. Following his talk, the students were invited to ask questions. One young man raised his hand and asked if Ecuadorians still live in trees. "Yes we do," said my friend, "but we go up by elevator."

Perhaps the most grotesque stereotype of Bolivia is found in the classic film *Butch Cassidy and the Sundance Kid*. (Adventurers still search for the remains of Butch Cassidy in the Tarija area.)

Near the end of the film, the two American bandits are cornered by the whole Bolivian army. Naturally, the two gringos hide as they shoot. But the stupid Bolivian soldiers stand on top of a wall like shooting-gallery ducks, and are shot down one by one. The film never shows the death of the two bandits, leaving the impression that they might have escaped.

In reality, only a few Bolivian soldiers were required to track down the American bandits, and they were not so foolish as to perch themselves on a wall and announce 'shoot me.'

With Bolivia such a facile target for superficial stereotypes, it is with great care that we have presented a cross section of singular characters from this remote land.

THE SOCIAL SETTING

CHAPTER 4

'The so-called Bolivian nation is not one nation.
We argue that within one nation is another one, Quechua
and Aymara, which we could call an indigenous nation.'
—Peasant leader Felipe Quispe, also known as El Mallku
(the Condor) from an interview in *La Razon*, 22 October 2000

EVOLUTION IN FIRST GEAR

How do Bolivians deal with the extremist geography? They adapt. The blood of altiplano dwellers carries extra red blood corpuscles. The skin of lowland dwellers develops an inherent mosquito repellent. The people in Oruro cope with the melancholy of the Altiplano by staging a joyous and uninhibited Mardi Gras Carnaval, for which they rehearse the whole year.

The visitor's plane will land smoothly in El Alto, but a cultural crash landing is possible unless there's a crash course on rapid adaptation, in order to speed up one's inner evolution.

This chapter will discuss the overall social context that visitors will descend upon, and then jump into real situations that might provoke culture shock.

Festivals

If shock treatment is the preferred strategy, then stepping immediately into a Bolivian festival might help to accomplish the goal of adaptation in record time. The origins of modern Bolivian festivals date back to the Spanish Conquest. Zealous priests, the agents of colonialism, co-opted the religions of the original peoples by infiltrating Catholicism into indigenous festivals: the 'if you can't beat 'em join 'em' strategy.

Imagine an ethnic festival in London with the English members of parliament making a grand entrance performing

Pakistani dances or American Puritans joining a Native American pow wow, dressed in colourful pre-colonial garb.

Such was the initiation of members of Bolivia's declining Creole aristocracy into the world of the native majority. In the late February summer Carnavals of La Paz and Oruro in the 1990s, the grandchildren of racist land owners merged with the descendents of indigenous share croppers in uninhibited street dances. The blend was inconspicuous as the ornate dress for the Diablada, Los Caporales or La Morenada dances includes a surreal mask representing the devil.

Class and Racism

A few decades ago, this scene would have been inconceivable. Bolivia used to be entrenched in a seemingly unbreakable caste system. Society luminaries would take pains for it to be known that they were of Spanish heritage. A few notches down in the pecking order, mestizos, known in the Andes as *cholos*, with vague visions of upward mobility would find overt or subtle ways to proclaim that they were not of indigenous descent, for the few drops of trickle-down colonial power they were allowed.

> Until the middle of the 20th century, a class of indigenous sharecroppers, economically bound for a lifetime to estates called *latifundios*, were called *pongos* because, from the viewpoint of the landowner, their names were insignificant.

The triad of power—landowner, clergyman and political boss—conspired to squeeze the maximum profit from human capital. *Cholos* (a cultural more than racial distinction) were the object of a divide-and-conquer strategy; they were employed by the landowner to police the 'indios'.

Countercurrents of noble efforts to enfranchise the oppressed began with the Jesuit missions in the Chiquitos area of the Oriente lowlands, continuing with Mariscal Antonio José de Sucre, Bolivia's first president, and reaching an artistic peak in anti-racist films of the 1960s and 1970s such as Jorge Sanjinés' *The Blood of the Condor* (*Yawar Mallku*), named by the United Nations as one of the 59 films of greatest social impact in the history of cinema, and the groundbreaking *Chuquiago*, directed by Oscar Soria and Antonio Eguino.

Exacerbating the double domination of class and race was the medieval heritage of the land owners. At a time when Europe was moving from the middle ages to liberal capitalism, Bolivia's Spanish colonisers were a vestige of the Spanish Reconquest against the Moors, rebelling against post-Inquisition reforms that would liberalise society back in Spain.

The economic foundation of the colony was strikingly clear. Spain opened the groin of this rich land and extracted its wealth, without bothering to elaborate value added products prior to exportation. The silver mines in the Cerro Rico (Rich Hill) above Potosí are the shining example of such merciless plundering. With no local economy created, native Bolivians and imported African slaves died in the primitive mines of what became the wealthiest city in the world in the 1700s during a two-century binge of dig and take.

Within the open veins of this landlocked country, in the second quarter of the 20th century, Bolivia's three dominant mining companies, exemplified by tin magnate Simón Patiño, presided over a continuation of the colonial system that had been supposedly terminated with political independence in 1825. The economy of extraction of natural resources was institutionalised. A notable example was *guano*, a bird dung on the Pacific coast which served as rich fertiliser for European farms, over which a war was lost to Chile in 1883 to the benefit of British exporters.

Tin was another example of systematic single-product colonial dependence. Tin was directly exported without even being refined into the simplest of value added exports, (tin cans or roofing material, for example), a process that would have created jobs for the people. During World War II, Bolivia supported the allied effort by selling tin at a tenth of its market value. Then tin collapsed in the world market and the country was left with nothing to show for it.

Later, there was oil and then natural gas, to be extracted from the land and sent abroad, with virtually no job-producing industries at home prior to exportation. Whatever income was derived from taxes of bribes from foreign exploiters went into the deep pockets of a few well-placed intermediaries.

During this time, the country's Creole population, mainly of Spanish descent, was oblivious to the wealth of culture that originated from pre-Inca Aymara, Inca and Quechua cultures. But the languages and customs of resilient Quechuas, Aymaras and other native cultures survived the dehumanising effects of hyperexploitation.

At the time of the Conquest, so highly developed in agriculture, food distribution, architecture and the arts was the Andean culture that it was impossible for the colonisers to simply replace it with their own way of life. Spanish and indigenous customs merged. To this very day, certain collective forms of land ownership and community stemming from the pre-Incas continue to function, such as a vision of extended community called the *ayllu*.

Spaniards who were engaged in commerce were obligated to learn at least rudimentary Quechua or Aymara and a priest who hoped to convert the locals needed to know enough to incorparate their spiritual concepts, such as the Pachamama (Mother Earth) into Catholic ritual.

Revolution and Reform

Independence from the Spaniards was gained by a local Creole class (Spaniards born in the Américas) in 1925, with little changing in the dynamics between the Creole minority and the indigenous and Cholo majority.

In the years leading up to 1952, the simmering discontent within the underclasses seethed into massive resistance. Populist politicians, led by Victor Paz Estenssoro, stepped in to fan the flames, and Paz's Movimiento Nacionalista Revolucionario (MNR) eventually won an election in 1951. When the establishment annulled the election, the insurrection, led by miners, escalated into the Bolivian Revolution, catapulting

The Chaco War

The 1932 Chaco war between Bolivia and Paraguay, partly engineered by rival foreign oil companies, brought indignous peasants, for the first time, into contact with Bolivians beyond their region, stimulating a new national and militant consciousness among the oppressed.

Paz Estenssoro to the presidency in 1952. But the politicians would only manage to legitimise their populist postures by enacting fundamental reforms.

These reforms cushioned a nouveau-riche sector of the dominant class from the wrath that had emerged from centuries of brutal exploitation. Ironically, a segment of the Cholo class was again employed in its old role as enforcer. A poorly conceived agrarian reform enfranchised the indigenous populations. Nationalisation of the irreversibly declining mineral industry enhanced political pride and triggered the growth of a powerful labour movement, whose traditional leaders were the miners. During certain periods, labour was so strong that a system of co-gobierno allowed for sharing of power between the government and the Bolivian Labor Confederation (COB), then under the leadership of Juan Lechín.

Finding a National Identity

In the aftermath of the Revolution, most public facilities were desegregated. Of course, one's race was not objectively measured. To a certain degree, the level of economic affluence determined racial identity, as did choice of dress between Cholos and indigenous Bolivians.

> In the years following the revolution, Bolivia enhanced its reputation as a beacon of instability with a record-breaking number of coup d'etats. So accustomed to such events was the populace that not far from tear gas confrontations, old-timers could be seen chatting leisurely on benches on the La Paz boulevard called El Prado.

Since the 1970s, a Latin Americanist movement opened the eyes of Bolivians of all classes and ideologies to the beauty of indigenous art and music. *Peñas*, unpretentious night clubs featuring national and indigenous music, sprung up throughout Latin America. A dominant highlight in these *peña* programmes was the typical Andean music, which Westerners might remember from the Bolivian song, *El Cóndor Pasa*, recorded by Paul Simon with great respect for original harmonies and using Andean instruments.

Simultaneously, a democratic consciousness emerged, with Bolivians weary of the abuse of military regimes.

When the García-Meza dictatorship, including its nefarious drug connections, was featured in the US television news magazine *Sixty Minutes* in the early 1980s, the whole world momentarily discovered Bolivia, and local advocates for democracy received the international support they had been craving. García-Meza was overthrown in 1981 and democracy was reestablished, in times of economic crisis. Eventually, the Bolivian justice system saw fit to jail García-Meza for life.

Economics and Democracy

Inflation Out of Control
A long bout with hyper-inflation threatened to abort the move towards democracy. My wife recalls an occasion when she was in line to purchase a record album. The salesperson had already quoted the price. By the time the client in front of her had been attended to, a phone call had come in and the price of the record had doubled. In 1985, inflation reached 20,000 per cent!

Bolivia became the proving grounds for free-market shock treatment. This brand of anti-inflationary economics, designed by Harvard professor Jeffrey Sachs, was largely successful in stopping inflation, though Sachs warned at the time that the narrow choice was between poverty with inflation or poverty without it. No one mentioned that the underground cocaine trade might have been at least partly responsible for the post-Sachs improved balance of payments. As Sachs had frankly warned, recession continued. (More recently, Mr Sachs has criticised draconian fiscal adjustment requirements of international financial institutions as they routinely trigger social unrest in Bolivia.)

Although Bolivia is often labelled the second poorest nation in the Américas, "saved from total disgrace by Haiti" said one economist, per capita income information used for this statistic is somewhat misleading. Bolivia's cost of living is low. Within the lower tier of the economy, for example, one can find a full course lunch for US$ 0.50. Healthy items

> Everyone knows that pirated Adidas sweatshirts and smuggled refrigerators do not represent ethical business, but everyone also knows that without this informal economy and in the absence of a viable alternative, the social stability of this country could implode.

such as fruit and vegetables may be purchased at outdoor markets for a minute fraction of what those same items would cost in supermarkets. Meanwhile, a thriving 'underground' economy allows just about anyone to find a spot of pavement and make a subsistence or semisubsistence income, often with contraband or pirated items.

Legitimate Bolivian business people are most hurt by the system, and these are the folks who could be building a new economy. But expedience has caused authorities to look the other way rather than confront the informal economy.

No visitor to Bolivia can escape this reality, and sooner or later choices must be made as a consumer, involving interaction with quasi-legal pirates and smugglers.

Rich Experiences in a Poor Country

One moral advocate asked me how a person with ethical principles could reconcile living a moderately affluent life in a poor country like Bolivia.

Bolivia has no monopoly on destitution. To the east of downtown Los Angeles, California, pedestrians are required to step over passed-out bodies of the homeless, with the crunch of broken glass under their feet. What greater contradiction than homeless people sleeping on heating grates near monuments to democracy in Washington, DC?

The Importance of the Family
A sociologist friend once travelled to South America to research skid rows. He came back with a study on why skid rows were absent. "The extended family acts as a welfare system," he said. Down-and-outers usually have a place to go. In many rural areas, the ancient indigenous community, the *ayllu*, functions as an extended family, with its own self government and welfare system.

The extended family and rural *ayllu* security nets are far from perfect. In Bolivian cities, one encounters abandoned

THE SOCIAL SETTING

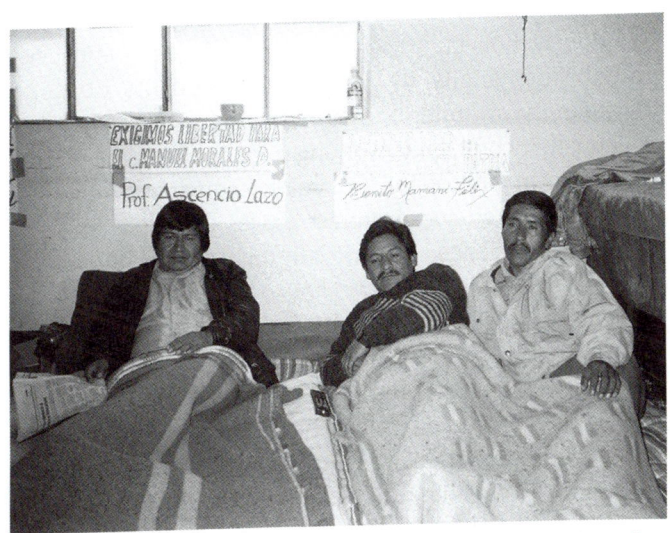

Social dissent is most commonly expressed without violence in Bolivia. The hunger strike, such as this one, in its ninth day, is one of the more common forms of protest.

children living on the streets, many of them glue sniffers, with independent operators of child shelters attempting to cope with the shameful situation.

Poverty and misery are never tolerable, but in Bolivia, there is a certain dignity among the poor, especially the rural poor. Former Vice-president Cárdenas mentions that "Yes, Bolivia is a poor country, but no one here dies of hunger."

As a foreigner, I have found one qualitative difference between Bolivia and some other impoverished lands. Poverty does not breed stoic resignation, for the downtrodden here are quite sophisticated in methods of organising to defend their rights. They can paralyse the country with roadblocks, topple presidents with hunger strikes, and reach a situation in which they become an ad hoc co-gobierno.

Furthermore, poverty in Bolivia, or any other developing country, has much to do with the world economic order. How can Britain, France or the United States offer an ethical escape from the reality of poorer nations when the economies of the developed world continue to derive much benefit from raw materials, cheap labour and a trade imbalance in relation to the Bolivias of the world?

Curiously, Bolivia has a relatively low index of antisocial violence especially when one considers its obscene unemployment/underemployment rate and the grossly inadequate income of its working poor. But then the dignity factor kicks in, philosophies of creative nonviolence abound, and sophisticated social protest proves that Bolivia is one of the most advanced countries in the world in humanistic grass roots organising.

Bolivia can thus be considered a point of hope for foreign visitors involved in socially oriented non-governmental organisations, job-creating businesses and organisations that work with ecology, culture and human rights.

Many Bolivians admit that their country is behind others in the realm of tourism, trade and infrastructure. But the more optimistic ones call this an advantage. Bolivia is still a 'green' country, not by design but simply because her exploiters have not got around to making theme parks out of vast tropical forests and hidden valleys.

Bolivia remains relatively untouched by the symbols of unsustainable modern culture, such as automobile dependency, tacky tourist icons and bland single-use zoning. She finds herself in a position to learn from the wrong turns of other countries and make healthy and judicious choices at the many crossroads that lie ahead.

The existence of an internal cultural gap between cosmopolitan and rural indigenous means that any culture shock we may feel will simply be part of the overall context of Bolivian diversity.

> The fact that Bolivia is a poor country should not discourage the appreciation of its marvels. Culture shock for the visitor to Bolivia will be cushioned by involvement in issues or events of universal proportion; a concert by the music group Altiplano, a peasant march in the tradition of Gandhi and Martin Luther King or a non-governmental environmental organisation lobbying for a new national park.

Postscript: Surrealism a la Boliviana

At the five-star Radisson Hotel in La Paz in 1997, former president Gonzalo Sánchez de Lozada (Goni) received an award from the *Latin Trade* magazine, an international business publication.

The magazine was applauding Goni's 'captalisation' scheme, his special recipe for privatisation between 1995 and 1997. This scheme directed revenue from Bolivia's remaining shares of state enterprises into retirement funds run by private foreign companies, and indirectly phased out state responsibility toward social welfare. Fifty-one per cent of the former state companies were acquired by foreign owners, while the 49 per cent counterpart funds were transferred by the government in the form of stock shares to two foreign Pensión fund managers.

When Latin Trade scheduled the grand event, they didn't know there would be a massive protest nearby against the imminent 'capitalisation' of Bolivia's most strategic industry—Yacimientos Petrolíferos Fiscales Bolivianos (YPFB), the Bolivian oil company.

The state-run YPFB contributed 57 per cent of its profits to the National Treasury. Even after deducting for corruption, the YPFB was Bolivia's primary source of revenue. Capitalisation was lauded by the government as a way for YPFB to finance the potentially lucrative gas pipeline to Brazil and rid Bolivia of corruption.

The protesters disagreed, insisting that this huge loss of revenue would cripple Bolivia's meager but functioning support system for health and education, and that Goni was simply obeying the dictates of global financial institutions.

Giving People a Chance

In a question-and-answer period following the award, a journalist asked Goni why Bolivians were not permitted to buy shares of YPFB, thereby financing the Brazil gas pipeline and avoiding handing administrative control and strategic revenue to foreign companies. "Bolivians would not be interested," was Goni's gruff reply, despite suggestions presented by 20,000 protestors within walking distance.

Goni is now gone, and other defeatists have been discredited. New leaders have taken his place, and these are people who believe that Bolivia has the human, cultural and natural resources to thrive.

These new leaders inherit a mangled economy but with a resilient people. If they were to become co-opted by Bolivia's history of dependency, the road blocks and hunger strikes would be back.

The above context will serve as a background for illustrating specific Bolivian social situations in which the visitor must learn to manoeuvre.

Bolivian Time Frames

Beginning with an exception, I refer to my Bolivian brother-in-law, Alfonso, who always arrives on time. No German or Englishman is any more punctual than Alfonso. But the general rule in Bolivia is to arrive at least a half hour after the hour listed on the invitation.

As a journalist, I was invited to La Paz's Plaza Hotel for a working dinner on election coverage. The invitation said 7:00 pm. I got to the hotel at 7:00 pm. A sign posted for the journalists said 7:30 pm. The actual meeting didn't begin until 8:15 pm. Each time you arrive on time, behaviour modification takes place. For the second invitation, your subconscious will still nag you to arrive on time, and again you will arrive and wait. Sooner or later, the psychological clock will get the message and begin ticking to a different rhythm.

Six weeks later, I had learned my lesson. Proudly I showed up a half hour late to the signing ceremony for a trade agreement between Bolivia and France at the Radisson Hotel. Some 45 minutes later, then Vice President Cárdenas arrived and the ceremony began.

> **Words of Wisdom**
> "Careful before you jump to conclusions about Bolivia," I am reminded by a Bolivian friend, "your ex-president Clinton was late all the time, and the Pope leaves throngs of people waiting in public squares for hours until he arrives."

I once reminded my wife that she was late for her tea invitation. Her answer: it's a social faux-pas to arrive early (meaning to arrive on time).

This Salvador Dali melting-clock solution is neither unique nor original to Bolivia. Evidence suggests that Bolivia's indigenous cultures were quite precise in matters of time.

But in Bolivia today, this elasticity of time extends even to television programmes, which sometimes begin later than the hour they are scheduled. One particular news programme sometimes began at 7:35 pm as scheduled, sometimes at 7:41 pm or 7:43 pm. They must have been waiting for a scoop.

Attending a Social Function

Now let's assume that you've learned to mould time like a piece of clay, and know when to reach your destination. What do you do when you get there?

When you arrive at a social event, you don't just say 'Hi' to everyone. If you already know the guests; you go around the room, shaking hands with each man, and kissing each woman on the left cheek while shaking her hand.

If these people are close friends or family, you shake hands, embrace, then shake hands again with the men and with the women, you may kiss them on the left cheek alone, or left cheek–right cheek.

There are no practice sessions to learn these procedures, and "experience is the worst teacher", as Vernon Law once said, "because it gives you the test before the lesson."

Children are expected to follow the same procedure, and male children are also kissed on the cheek by adults. It gets complicated if there are 26 people in the room and you must make the rounds, embracing each man and kissing each woman one by one, especially if, at the same time, they are moving around and you might miss one.

My solution: commit the faux-pas of arriving first. This will allow you to be the object of the greeting process rather than the subject. Using the same logic in reverse, when leaving be the last.

The Fiesta

If you are uneasy about language subtleties, you will be relieved if the social situation is labelled a party. At parties, you are unlikely to get to know anyone you don't already know. The uninterrupted dancing rarely allows for what we know as a conversation. People of all social classes in Bolivia live an intense social life. They find a time and place for conversation, but a fiesta is usually reserved for dancing.

My wife and I were invited to a New Year's Eve party at a social club. The host said that I would have much in common with his friend and he looked forward to our meeting each other. During the whole night, the incessant music thumped on, and the only words exchanged were, "Would you like another drink?"

From the opposite cultural perspective, a Bolivian acquaintance at a party in Washington DC expressed his dismay to me: "They said this was going to be a party, but everyone is talking and no one is dancing?" He was experiencing culture shock USA.

The fiesta and its lesser cousin the *parrillada* (barbecue), where the art of conversation remains alive, are institutions in which both sexes participate. In the dynamics between same sex versus mixed sex reunions, Bolivia finds itself somewhere between two extremes.

The traditional extreme exalted same sex companionship, with marriage companionship as a secondary part of one's communicative life. In his book, *The Great Good Place*, sociologist Ray Oldenburg refers to the research of Frenchwoman Lucienne Roubin, 'who was able to account for almost every square foot of 'female' and 'male' space' in the villages of Provence, finding that none of the territory was neutral ground, all of it carved up into either male or female terrain.

The modern opposite, at least in the United States, is based on the suburban ideology of what Oldenburg calls 'companionate marriage.' With the loss of neighbourhood hangouts in suburbia there are the 'stresses and strains of an over-insulated togetherness.' 'Companionate marriage,' writes Oldenburg, 'imposes more togetherness than many couples are capable of either utilising or enjoying, while inhibiting stimulating contacts with other adults.' In a balanced situation, time out for same sex companionship is likely to strengthen a marriage.

Marriage and Companionship

In contemporary Bolivia, regular outlets for same sex companionships coexist with increasingly companionate marriages. Men once had the regular *viernes de soltero* (bachelors' Friday) at the tavern, but the custom is disappearing. Male space is conserved at Saturday afternoon ritual games, including a dice game called *cacho*, and get-togethers at the football stadium. Female space survives at teas, an afternoon ritual inherited from the English mining colonisers, but teas may also be mixed-gender occasions. Rummy-canasta card games remain women's afternoon affairs within a home setting. Teas sometimes take place in public eating places specifically designed for such occasions, but most women's get-togethers are at-home events.

Oldenburg suggests that in the West, the strain of a marriage ideology in which couples are supposed to do everything together may be one reason for such a high rate of extramarital affairs. But in Bolivia, where both men and women alike have ample same sex outlets beyond the home, extramarital affairs are no less common.

The Bolivian *farra* (a night of hard drinking) may lead to an extramarital affair for the man. But Bolivian women do not accept this custom with stereotypical submissiveness or resignation. For every man with a mistress, there is probably a woman with a lover outside of marriage.

For these affairs to take place, Bolivian cities provide what is called the 'motel,' which has nothing to do with a motor trip. Cars parked at motels are hidden by curtains. There is an hourly rate, varying according to the quality of the motel. I used to live next to a motel called redundantly Moteles Inn. As I crossed the street for groceries, I observed a car leaving the motel; a woman inside indiscreetly covered her face with *El Diario*, La Paz's largest broadsheet newspaper. Wealthier men avoid these moments of embarrassment by purchasing automobiles with dark, tinted windows.

An occasional scandal may erupt outside motels when the slighted mate discovers the illicit affair. The name-calling described by neighbours who witnessed a motel scandal on my block is not repeatable in these pages.

Name Calling

In Bolivia, name calling is not always intended as a put-down. The art of name calling is a social custom in most of Latin America. In fact, people are often nicknamed affectionately according to their physical differences or oddities—a social taboo in many other countries.

A chubby friend of mine was referred to as Gordito, a superb example of how literal translations may connote the opposite of their original intention. *Gordito*, for example, is a term of affection in Spanish literally meaning 'Fatty,' a disparaging term in English. I've been referred to as Flaquito, with obvious fondness, yet I would not be so pleased to be called 'Skinny' in English.

Try calling a dark skinned person 'Blackie' in the United States. You'll end up in court and receiving front page coverage in the *New York Post*. Yet the equivalent Spanish nickname Negrito is simply construed as a recognition of what one is. When the crafty Afrobolivian football forward, Demetrio Angola, scored a goal against Argentina in the 1995 America Cup football tournament, the nation's football commentators fell in love with El Bonbón (The Chocolate Candy).

El Gringo

In politics, the term 'gringo' often carries a negative connotation. Yet a blonde Bolivian friend of mine is known as El Gringo. When both of us were introduced to a third party one afternoon, it sounded quite bizarre:

"Let me introduce you to The Gringo," said my brother-in-law, referring to our Bolivian friend. And then, looking at me, he said, "and here is the real gringo."

'While other societies have been cultivating taboos on crude references to ethnic origin on race or sex,' writes Latin American specialist, Calvin Sims, 'Latin culture is still surprisingly straightforward about these things. Latin Americans,' adds Sims, 'say this makes them more direct and honest than North Americans, who even while struggling to make their own society speak more tolerantly, still tend to lump all Latin Americans in one stereotypical mass.'

Latin American Stereotypes

It is not frowned upon for different Latin American peoples to stereotype each other. 'Bolivians think of themselves (and are thought of by many other Latin Americans) as a kindhearted nation,' Sims writes.

But between Bolivia and Chile, for example, not so kindhearted things are said. Bolivians view Chile as an expansionist country, not only from having lost their coastline to Chilean occupation in 1880 but because a Chilean company bought up a Bolivian railroad system within the framework of the 1990s privatisation and capitalisation policies of the Bolivian government.

In an important America's Cup football match between Chile and Bolivia, Chilean fans were heard to yell that no country with a standard of living equal to Uganda could beat them. (Bolivia needed a tie to eliminate Chile from the tournament. Losing 2-0 midway through the second half, Bolivia scored two goals to earn the tie.)

Of all the Latin American stereotypes, Argentine arrogance is a prime target. Sims writes that, 'Argentines are seen by other Latin Americans as haughty. And they're proud of it.'

A Chilean sociologist, Hernán Godoy, theorises that Chileans stereotype Peruvians and Bolivians as backwoods peasants with no sophistication in order to compensate for feelings of inferiority in reference to the Argentines. "We Chileans feel that Argentines are whiter, blonder and more secure," he said. "But on the other hand, the Chileans feel blonder and whiter than Peruvians and Bolivians."

Meanwhile, within Bolivia, some Chapacos of the southern city of Tarija are proud to be accused of considering themselves more Argentine than Bolivian. The Chapacos are supposedly descended from Argentine gauchos who ironically were once scorned by the Argentine gentry.

Just where honourable recognition of physical and national traits ends and negative stereotyping begins is hard to say. At a Bolivian social function, I was once moved to defend

Chileans, pointing out that there is a great difference between the militaristic policies of various Chilean governments and the Chilean people. In the United States, where distinctions between different Latins are blurred, I have witnessed great solidarity between Chileans and Bolivians.

Today, a large portion of the cheap contraband that makes its way to Bolivian outdoor markets comes from Chile. The same Bolivian who makes a disparaging remark about the Chileans may, at that very moment, be drinking a fine Chilean wine.

We have now visited part of the landscape of social customs, within a broader historical context. The next step is to settle in.

SETTLING IN

CHAPTER 5

'To expect the unexpected shows
a thoroughly modern intellect.'
—Oscar Wilde

'Be realistic. Try the impossible.'
—Che Guevara

No amount of planning will totally elude the chaos factor, which exerts a greater impact in underdeveloped countries like Bolivia. Bolivia's remoteness from world consciousness makes it a land for adventure and eco tourists, and if you don't look for adventure it may find you anyway. But adventure does not have to be chaos. The better the advance planning, the less likely that you will become a victim of misfortune.

We now go through the important steps that will lead to a satisfying stay, prior to and after arrival, in rough chronological order.

IMMIGRATION AND CUSTOMS

Visa requirements are in constant transition. The best strategy is to visit or call the Bolivian Consulate in your country of origin. In my numerous entries to Bolivia, I have never been asked to prove economic solvency nor have I had any difficulty with other bureaucratic procedures that are supposedly in force.

Indeed, prior to my long term visa, I was able to enter with a fax machine, laptop computer, printer and other household appliances, simply by explaining to the customs official that all items in my suitcases were for *uso personal* (personal use).

There is no guarantee that you will be as fortunate. The best way to get through customs is, upon arriving at the baggage claim area, immediately enlist the services of a porter, who will guide you through the process for US$ 1 per suitcase, to be paid after you have passed through customs. Items officially exempted from customs taxes include clothing, used articles, two cameras and accessories, one video recorder, one tape recorder, one portable typewriter, one set of golf clubs, one portable radio, one bottle of alcohol, 100 cigarettes, 25 cigars and new articles, the total value of which does not exceed US$ 300 (that's what it says), and which may not be sold in Bolivia. Customs laws change periodically, so double-check with the consulate if you fear a customs problem.

> **Business Travellers**
> If travelling on business, there may be other immigration requirements, possibly including a guarantee from your employer. This will be explained at your local Bolivian Consulate.

In the lowland regions, where drug enforcement is more essential and prevalent, document checks are more likely.

If you're staying for a longer period, bring an authenticated birth certificate and a letter verifying a clean record from your local police department; these are currently key documents for securing long term residency. Permanent residence paperwork costs approximately US$ 600.

The cost of various types of long-term residencies may be reduced or waived if you can prove you are here for a project that benefits the country, and you can provide a letter from an important dignitary in the Bolivian government who will corroborate your project.

Upon entering the country, there is no written requirement as to the length of validity of a passport for travellers from certain countries, but some airlines may require at least six months of remaining validity, and the six-month standard is recommended as a peace-of-mind precaution. Tourist visas are granted for 30 days upon entry, or for 90 days through special agreements with certain countries.

Nationals from the USA, UK, Ireland, Canada, Australia and New Zealand are not required to have a tourist visa for stays of 90 days or less, and are granted between 30 and 90 days upon arrival. If they give you 30 days and you want more, they will tell you at that moment where to go prior to the end of the 30 days in order to extend your stay, for no charge. Travellers from any other country should consult their local Bolivian consulate.

HEALTH

Whether you plan to stay in the lowlands, valleys or highlands, the abrupt change in climate, environment and altitude is bound to affect you physically in one way or another. The best defence is an offence: get yourself into good physical condition prior to your trip, with procedures that work best for you on the advice of your physician.

If all the things that might go wrong were listed here, no one would ever travel anywhere beyond one's native borders. The most likely occurrence is a case of what is known in Mexico as Moctezuma's Revenge. To treat this, diarrhoea, kaolin and pectin products are available in Bolivian pharmacies. If some other product has worked wonders for you in the past, take it with you.

With the usual case of *turista*, unless you are on the road and need immediate relief, the best tactic is to let your natural defences learn to adapt to this new territory. Prevent dehydration by following standard medical practices. The best liquid to prevent dehydration and soothe the stomach is *mate de manzanilla* (camomile tea). *Mate* (pronounced 'mahtey,' is the word for herb tea, as opposed to black tea which is *té*. *Mate de anis* (anise tea) is also a popular stomach remedy, especially for altitude-related gas problems. *Trimate*, often served in restaurants after lunch, combines coca, manzanilla and anise teas, has an appealing taste and many Bolivians swear by it as a digestion aid. If the problem does not go away within two days, consult a physician.

Cholera is an exotic disease that pops up often in newspapers, but even when the disease was on the danger list in South America way back in 1991, Bolivia was less affected than neighbouring Peru. Cholera is generally a poor peoples' disease due to unsanitary living conditions. Although tap water in most major Bolivian cities is treated, boiling all drinking water for five minutes is recommended even when no cholera is reported. Bottled water is an alternative.

If cholera reports emerge during your stay, drink bottled water, eat only cooked vegetables and avoid any fish that might have come from affected regions. Avoid the uncooked *cebiche* (raw fish with diced onion and herbs cooked in lemon), and follow standard sanitary procedures you learned in elementary school.

> Also beware of empty restaurants and snack bars. When you see lots of clients, you can guess that food is not being cooled and reheated. Snack food shouldn't be languishing under the sun before it is eaten.

A more exotic poverty disease, contracted by an alarming number of Bolivians, is *chagas*. The disease is caused by a parasite residing in the vinchuca beetle, in the lowlands and valleys but not found in the highlands. *Chagas* is fatal, although curable if caught early. Taking years to gestate, it affects blood vessels and other organs. The vinchucas live in thatched roofing and the cracks in adobe walls, so try not to sleep in such places that are below 2,800 m (9,186 ft) in altitude. It takes six weeks after a bite for a blood test to detect the disease. When in doubt, do not scratch an entry path for the parasite.

If you are prone to high blood pressure, have your pressure monitored at high altitudes by neighbourhood clinics which charge Bs 3 (about US$ 0.60). Most contemporary blood pressure pills are available here, usually costing much less than they would back home. According to one cardiologist I interviewed, the concept for the synthetic ace inhibitors came from a Bolivian snake whose bite caused a quick death because of a rapid drop in blood pressure.

> **Better to Be Safe**
> For up-to-date country-by-country health information, visit the World Health Organization website: http://www.who.int.

Bugs and insects that usually plague third world countries are absent from most of western Bolivian highlands and high valleys. The fact that so many nasty pests do not survive and thrive about 2,500 m (8,202 ft) of altitude might be adequate compensation for the usual tribulations of high altitude adaptation.

Altitude Ailments

Ongoing research is proceeding in La Paz over the effects of high altitude, at the national university and the friendly Instituto de Patología de la Altura (Institute of Altitude Pathology), on Avenida Saavedra 2302 in the Miraflores neighbourhood of La Paz.

The problems of high altitude are due to the change in barometric pressure. Under less pressure, air molecules expand and take up 50 per cent more volume than they would at sea level. Thus, one needs one and a half breaths of air, rather just one at sea level. Even some natives of La Paz have mentioned that they 'feel the altitude' when returning to La Paz after having stayed in lower altitudes for several days.

This sounds scary, especially with the shortening of breath and heart pounding that one may feel upon arrival when walking uphill. But eventually, almost everyone adapts to the altitude. "One's lungs may grow a little," explained Dr Zubieta Jr, "but increased efficiency actually comes from using parts of the lungs that have been lazy or resting."

Other Bolivian doctors say that a condition they call polyglobulia, (an increase in red blood cells), provides additional oxygen capacity. But while some doctors say polyglobulia is a sickness, others insist that the body is simply compensating for oxygen deficiency.

Reliable statistics show that altitude diminishes the performance of low altitude football teams. But there are numerous examples of lowland teams that win international tournaments in La Paz.

The Bolivian University's Institute of Altitude Biology (IBBA) has since found that the loss of aerobic power due to altitude of the visiting team was not enough to give the local team a significant advantage.

Bolivia's record in international competition is considerably better at home in La Paz than away at lower altitudes. However, home team advantage is a significant factor in sports competition even when altitude is not a variable.

Visitors who are already in good physical shape (athletes for example) may adjust more efficiently to the altitude, but this is not always the case. Following a successful adjustment, only the most fortunate visitors reach more than 95 per cent of their sea level capacity.

During the days prior to your flight to highland Bolivia, eat lightly. Upon arrival, two days rest, with smaller than normal and lighter meals, and plenty of liquid (without ice) is recommended.

Some people arrive at this top of the Américas and seem to feel no effects whatsoever.

Give it Time
The parents of an acquaintance flew in for a visit and were active from the get-go, with no consequences. For me, regular afternoon naps have been the best medicine. In the beginning, I thought that adjustment would be impossible. In the end, I was hiking at 5,000 m (17,000 ft) with no exceptional difficulty.

The term for the normal case of altitude sickness is *sorojche*, a condition of discomfort which is effectively tamed with rest, in most cases. But there is the stronger Acute Mountain Sickness, which can affect the blood flow in the brain.

Anyone planning on mountain climbing or skiing on the slopes of Chacaltaya, should see a physician before accepting the challenge. When walking or climbing at a high altitude, the best way to alleviate mountain sickness is to descend.

Another danger of high altitude is the easy penetration of ultraviolet rays in combination with the alleged widening of the ozone hole in the southernmost part of South America. If you plan to do a lot of hiking at higher altitudes, sunscreen is an absolute must.

With so much talk of high altitude in the Andes, the fact is, considering the pros and cons, high altitudes have a net positive effect on health, and greater dangers exist in Bolivia's tropical areas. Yellow Fever vaccination may be recommended for travel in the tropics. Protection lasts 10 years. Typhoid protection lasts three years and is recommended for those who are intending to remain for lengthy periods in rural, tropical areas. Insect repellent, water purification tablets, antihistamine, antiseptics and calamine lotion should be the friends of jungle trekkers.

Insuring Your Health

Let's not hype all the bad things that might happen but that probably will not. It's not so difficult to stay healthy in Bolivia. Nevertheless, the traveller should contact one of the various agencies that provide updates and comprehensive information on preventive measures.

Health and Safety Contacts
- In the United States, request health and safety information from the Bureau of Consular Affairs Office, State Department, Washington, DC 20520.
- In the UK, write to the Medical Advisory Services for Travellers Abroad (MASTA), Keppel Street, London WCIE 7HT.
- In Australia, contact the Traveller's Medical and Vaccination Centre in either Sydney or Melbourne.

Each country has its own travel health insurance plans. Less expensive, if you are staying for a longer period, is to purchase health insurance right here in Bolivia. If you remain covered by insurance from your homeland, prior to departure make sure you bring all the required forms, in case of a claim.

The United States and British embassies in La Paz will have an updated list of recommended physicians who speak English or specialise in tourist related ailments. The United States Embassy is located on Avenida Arce 2780. The quainter embassy of the United Kingdom is right next door at Arce 2732, and also serves those Commonwealth countries that do not have an embassy in Bolivia. The numbers of these and other embassies may be obtained from any telephone directory.

CURRENCY AND MONEY

When you speak with your Bolivian consulate, you can also find out the latest exchange rate. At this writing, the Boliviano (Bs) has glided up well above 8 per dollar, and if the pattern continues, will reach a 9:1 ratio to the US dollar at some point in the not-so-far future.

Casas de cambio (currency exchanges) are found easily in all larger cities, and will exchange money at the current rate. Money changers on downtown street corners will do the same for a minimal commission. Protect your wallet after changing your money.

The official currency is the Boliviano, but many items and services may be secured with US dollars (US$). Real estate property, automobiles and other large ticket items are advertised in dollars. Should you decide to pay in Bolivianos, it will be at the official exchange rate. Many businesses will exchange dollars and Bolivianos for customers, including travel agencies, hotels, restaurants, supermarkets and many grocery shops, as well as some street vendors.

What happens if you find yourself low on cash? The most effective method for me in large cities of foreign countries is to make my payments at supermarkets, some restaurants and larger ticket items from major shops with a Visa or Mastercard. (It is quite difficult to cash a foreign cheque in Bolivia.) By maintaining a current account (checking account) in your country of origin and making prompt payments to your credit card provider by cheque, you thus avoid the interest charge. Or, you may use your ATM card to withdraw cash from your account, if they do not accept your credit card. In Bolivia, many businesses, especially small ones, do not accept credit cards.

Certain banks, such as Banco Nacional, will allow foreigners holding long-stay visas to open an account in US dollars. This is practical for those receiving a salary from abroad or doing business globally. The catch—it takes 15 working days for a cheque to clear.

The Bolivian banking system weathered a few storms between 1994 and 1995. This included a fraudulent offshore Banco Boliviano Americano Internacional, that falsely led its depositors to believe that their money was in Florida and insured by the United States government. The bank went belly up and it turned out that its Miami office was a front. Thanks to these scandals, a government fund was created for fortifying banks and forceful banking regulators rectified, at least temporarily, the banking predicament. A good source for rankings of banks is the excellent weekly *Nueva Economía*.

Tipping and Bargaining

Normally, 10 per cent is an acceptable tip in a restaurant, but it is my custom to go beyond this minimum since waiters and waitresses are not making enough. Tips are not required for radio-taxi drivers, but taxi fares are low by Western standards and cab driver salaries are low and a tip is appreciated. In congested cities where the driver has done some extraordinary manoeuvring to get you where you need to go, he deserves a generous tip. I say 'he' because it is rare to find a woman driving a cab. Bargaining, as was mentioned in our discussion of open air markets, is a custom in most countries in the world, and Bolivia is no exception. However, in most formal shops and shopping centres, the custom is extinct.

If you are uncomfortable about bargaining, the vendor will make it easy for you. After you've asked '*cuánto cuesta?*' if you suspect the price is too high, just say '*gracias*' and begin to walk away. A willing vendor will call out to you, saying: 'I can give it to you for X Bolivianos!' ('*Se lo doy en X Bolivianos.*')

CONSUMER GOODS

A few upscale supermarkets and shopping centres offer imported products from your country of origin. However, expect to pay as much or more for the same thing as you would have paid back home. Either decide to do as the locals do 100 per cent, or take with you to Bolivia what you cannot do without. It's your choice. Junk food for the kids (not this author's recommendation), a new generation pharmaceutical product or a special toiletry item. If you're staying for a long time, have visiting friends and family bring care packages from home. Our family's sole import was Mexican tortillas from Los Angeles, California. Buying locally is the best policy, and it's ecological!

HOTELS

Less expensive family owned hotels are much more conducive for getting a feel for the country than the more expensive and generic chains.

In a family hotel, all rooms will probably differ. You might find a hard bed in one room, a soft bed in another; a large colour television in one, a small television with 'snow' on the screen in another; a spartan bathroom in one, a beautiful mosaic bath in another.

> If various rooms are available, ask to see them first before making your choice. Unless you are arriving in Oruro the day of Carnaval, rooms are frequently available without reservation.

TRANSPORTATION

Within cities, *micros* (buses) are the cheapest collective transport, about US$ 0.15 per ride. Slightly more expensive but still only about US$ 0.20 to US$ 0.30 depending on the distance is the minibus—a van. The newcomer learns through behaviour modification, after the first hard thump on the head, to watch his or her head when descending from the minibus.

Next in line is the collective, fixed-route taxi labelled *trufi*, and regular taxis without a fixed route, whose base fare for reasonable distances is double the minibus, or only US$ 0.40. Radio-taxis (the ones with a company emblem on top) also have a fixed rate, between US$ 1.00 and US$ 2.00 depending on the length of the trip. With fixed rates, tourists need not be concerned about crooked taximeters.

The above description provides a handy frame of reference for rates, always subject to change. The cost of rides to more distant zones on any mode of public transport will rise accordingly. Public transportation is cheaper and easier on the nerves than driving. An automobile becomes expedient only if you live in the south zone of La Paz or in the spread out city of Santa Cruz.

Pedestrians should not expect an oncoming automobile to turn or not turn based on its turning signals. Too many drivers simply do not use their signals. At corners in hilly cities, the driver moving uphill has the right of way.

For travel beyond the city, Bolivia has a relatively efficient network of bus companies, called *flotas*. Two major 1990s *flota* accidents, one on the La Paz–Yungas road and the other on the La Paz–Oruro Highway, both resulting in more than 30 deaths, may be cause for future concerns. However, given the high volume of *flota* usage, the safety record is respectable, especially when one considers the narrowness straight away of some sleep provoking stretches or the blood boiling hairpin turns on others.

From my own driving experience in various Latin American countries, I find the greatest danger coming from stray animals, especially donkeys, sometimes cows and pigs, that dart across the road from unfenced farming areas.

Let's be honest, Bolivia's road safety record, although improving, does not measure up statistically to many other countries. In my family, we have decided that the rewards of travelling in Bolivia more than compensate for the slightly greater risk, but this is a personal decision that I would not impose on others.

The quality of service with Lloyd Airlines of Bolivia (LAB) seemed to decline following its privatisation by a then bankrupt Brazilian airline. LAB's on-time rate is imperfect, but this has more to do with Bolivia's weather and geography than any inefficiency on the part of the company. One flight may depend on the arrival of another which has been delayed because of poor weather conditions. Lloyd's safety record remains admirable.

In difficult airports, notably Sucre's, where planes skirt the hills to land, flights are delayed or postponed if the visibility is not completely acceptable. Lateness is preferred to a potential fatal accident. To Sucre's credit, its airport has never experienced an accident involving takeoff or landing.

Enjoy the Unpredictability
My wife and I were once obligated to remain in Sucre an extra day when all flights were cancelled because of poor visibility. Our added time in that exquisite city was greatly appreciated. We knew when we came here that the unpredictability index in Bolivia is higher than in the United States or Europe.

Smaller lowland airports may be closed from one moment to the next during the rainy season due to floods, so take a few extra pairs of underwear just in case.

CLOTHING
Choice of clothing based on the weather should be made according to the travel advisory section in Chapter One. Dressing in layers is especially practical for the highland climate where the temperature varies so much from day to night, from sunlight to shade, and from one level of an urban area to another.

If you expect to cavort with business or social elites, some formal attire will be necessary. Highland cities are more likely to require formal dress. In birthday gatherings of middle class families, men often wear ties. Weekends are the time for casual dress. Following his December 2005 election as president of Bolivia, Evo Morales made a world tour to visit presidents with whose countries Bolivia had ongoing issues.

In Paris, he became perhaps one of the few foreign presidents in history to meet the French president while wearing a sportshirt and leather jacket, with no tie. It has become difficult to project the trends of Bolivian fashion. At the outset of 2006, Evo-style pullovers were becoming trendy.

THE POSTAL SYSTEM

The post office is the most dependable and quickest place to receive post. If you are intending to stay for a lengthy period, apply for a PO Box, called *casilla*.

You don't need a PO Box to receive post. There is a general delivery service called *poste restante* or *lista de correos*, located on the second floor of La Paz's main post office. Letters addressed to you should state Poste Restante, Correo Central, with the name of the city and country on the bottom line.

In order to pick up your post at the *lista de correos* counter, have your passport with you to verify your identity. Some consulates also receive post for citizens of their country.

TELECOMMUNICATIONS

Until the turn of the century, the only way to own a telephone was to purchase stock in the phone company, which was a public cooperative. The whole process took about two weeks, and the cost was about US$ 1,500, paid in full or in monthly instalments. Phones were also available for rent for about US$ 30–50 a month.

Since privatisation and with the profusion of mobile phones and phone cards, the telecommunications terrain has offered many more options, and the scene is changing too rapidly to etch in a text. Once ENTEL lost its temporary monopoly on 28 November 2001, the field was wide open.

Prices dropped but confusion rose. At this time of writing, five other companies entered the market, each with a different strategy. For example, AES, now changed to AXS, invested heavily in infrastructure such as its own fibre optic network. Boliviatel adopted the opposite strategy, initially saving millions by using (and paying for the use of) existing infrastructure. Boliviatel got the jump on AXS, but the bigger investor may regain the edge in the future, unless the fibre optic system is replaced by a more state-of-the-art technology. Dialling methods have changed along the way, and may still change, in an anarchic situation, so there's no use giving advance instructions for making a phone call.

For the visitor, the simplest way to secure an operating telephone is by renting an apartment that already has one. The second simplest way is to purchase a mobile phone. Using the Internet, either from a hotel or Internet café, may turn out the least expensive and most practical, especially for long distance, with voice-over-Internet-protocol looming in the near future.

Standard long distance rates abroad tend to be more expensive from Bolivia than they are from most Western countries to Bolivia, but phone cards have eased the stress, and the Internet has been and is the most popular international communication device for visitors from abroad. Internet cafés abound and they are remarkably cheap compared to their Western counterparts.

Public telephones may still be found in larger cities at sweet stands and in small grocery shops, but the most practical method is to find a child with a mobile phone whose business is to charge you Bs 1 to make a call. Long distance calls and faxes may be made from the offices of various Bolivian phone companies, including ENTEL, the original one.

HOUSING

Older attractive hotels, with colonial-style architecture, are quite inexpensive by Western standards.

There is the *pensión* (boarding house) alternative, where one fair price gets you room and home cooking.

The larger the city, the easier it is to find an apartment with a telephone, furnished or unfurnished. Most apartment ads are run by agencies that may charge you a full month's rent and/or a finder's fee. Look for ads not run by an agency that say *sin intermediario*. Even better, in La Paz, place your own ad in the newspaper *El Diario*, stating that you wish to rent an apartment or house *sin intermediarios*.

In La Paz, where rents are highest, you should be able to secure an attractive and comfortable two bedroom apartment for US$ 200 or less (furnished for US$ 300 or less) in the best neighbourhoods, and around 25 per cent less than that amount in the livelier Miraflores or San Pedro neighbourhoods. Rooms where foreigners stay may be found for approximately for US$ 100 per month or less.

If you plan to purchase a house, expect to pay in full. Interest rates are too high and the loan process too Byzantine to do it any other way. The good news is that prices are low, especially for more stylish older houses. With fewer of the add-on costs associated with house buying in more complicated countries, you should invest a portion of the savings in a contract lawyer. Transfer fees are 3 per cent of purchase price.

> **Tips for Renting**
>
> In Bolivia there is a way to live rent free. It is called '*contrato anticrético*.' The renter lends money to the owner for one year, or two, with a contract stating that all the money you put out will be returned to you when you vacate the property at the end of the contract period. If you have US$ 20,000 laying around, you might consider an apartment in *anticrético*. Should you be bold enough to try this strategy, there is a minor risk involved, and it is advised that you hire a lawyer, through your embassy, to maximise your probabilities.

CHILDREN

Parents planning an extended stay may choose from a large menu of private bilingual schools, in English, French, German and even Hebrew. The tuition at most of these fine schools will be considerably less than comparable tuitions in Europe or North America. The higher the child's grade level, the more Spanish will be filtered in.

Private schools run by foreigners must follow core requirements of both Bolivia's Ministry of Education and the education system of the country of origin. Pre-teens will pick up Spanish through playground communication with other children and via television.

However, the two-tiered education system fosters an enclave mentality, a type of 'gated community', and some children more sensitive to elitism and prejudice have been turned off by a type of caste-system mentality. Even in such schools where the teachers are remarkably in tune with concepts of social justice, the daily image of segregation is more powerful than so much verbiage of equality.

A ranking of the major variables of potential culture shock for children includes (1) adjusting to the altitude; (2) the radical change in eating habits, for even something basic such as milk tastes quite different, and having soup to start a meal seems to be a universal problem for children of many cultures; (3) and language adaptation. Among the private school options, parents may choose either total immersion in an all Spanish-language programme (the kids will easily maintain their English at home) or bilingual education, where English is one of the two languages of primary instruction.

Endless Language Possibilities

Our son was subjected to double total immersion, having had to rediscover his forgotten French and put together the dispersed pieces of his limited Spanish-language background at the Colegio Franco-Boliviano. He had no problem remembering his English. With the help of TV (finally a practical use for this apparatus!), the Spanish came relatively fast. Whichever the language option, adults should not impose their language learning phobias on their children.

If language is a long-term project, food can be a nagging daily tribulation. Certain transition foods may help with adjustment, such as *marraqueta*, the crusty Bolivian bread, *pasankalla* (sweet popcorn), cold cuts and *choclo* (white corn). Certain spices, some tropical fruits such as papaya and *chuño* (dried potato) seem to be the greatest culinary encumbrances.

Other potential adjustment difficulties might be social, getting used to the kissing, embracing and handshake routines ("It's horrible having my face painted by the ladies' lipstick," said one American child) and folk dancing (more of a problem for boys than girls).

Each year our son had to perform a different Bolivian folk dance, for example La Morenada, for a school festival. He emerged unscathed from the experience.

In the end, culture shock Bolivia is much less shocking for children than it is for adults, though the teenage years can be difficult anywhere in the world. One of the best mechanisms for a young person's integration is the sport of football.

There are few if any travel bargains for children who occupy a seat when travelling, but for lodging you can negotiate a reduced cost for kids at most family-run hotels.

Let's not forget the great advantage from travelling with children. As foreigners, you are seen to be more like the locals when you are a family, and our own experience validates the observation of Bolivian expert Alan Murphy that 'even thieves and pickpockets seem to have the traditional respect for families'.

DOGS IN THE 'HOOD

With a child, the issue of household pets may arise. Of the 150,000 dogs in La Paz, 15,000 roam the streets without an owner. A significant number of family dogs are left in the street during the day to join the strays.

One would expect that the pavements would be littered with dog poop, but this is not the case. With less formal education, Bolivian dogs are more respectful than their pampered French counterparts, who go out on a leash and do their duty right on the pavement. On any given morning in most residential neighbourhoods in Bolivian cities, dogs are released from the captivity of their homes for their daily reunion. One morning, I counted 16 dogs on a corner lot as I walked my son to the school bus. (That must have been an important dog occasion because I have not seen that many since then.)

My social conscience told me that we should train our puppy as a house dog and not unleash him in the streets. But his first impressions of the city's canine society made him feel cooped up at home. Once he had had his shots and learned to stop jumping on people, I let him roam. After all, he had earned the right by accepting a typical Bolivian dog diet—leftovers.

With Bolivia's canine liberation, it should be dangerous to walk the streets. But La Paz former health director José Guillermo Prudencio once explained that most complaints come from neighbours in reference to dogs owned by families rather than strays. The most dangerous dogs in La Paz are those that have received formal training to protect houses.

Some dog neighbourhoods are more dangerous than others. In general, the more affluent the neighbourhood,

> As a lone uphill jogger in La Paz's hilly streets, I learned (from a dog bite on the leg) to brandish a visible stone in my right hand. Strays and semi-strays have learned to respect the stone-in-hand signals.

the lower the rate of dog bites. If there is a dog bite, victims as well as their attackers are observed for 10 days, and all medical care is free.

CRIME TIME

The preferred crimes are pickpocketing and auto parts thefts from newer four-wheel drive vehicles. Hijackings are rare, so we're not trying to sensationalise by mentioning that a US citizen was murdered in November 2003 during an attempted carjacking in Santa Cruz.

Bolivia is not a crime-ridden country, but it doesn't hurt to take precautions anyway. If a disagreeable substance is suddenly present on your backpack or handbag, do NOT accept an offer of a good samaritan to clean it. Nor should you become distracted if water is sprayed on your neck, lest you find after drying your neck that your wallet is missing. Some thieves even pose as policemen. If a cop asks you to accompany him in a taxi to the police station, tell him you'd prefer to flag down another policeman in a real squad car.

The United States Embassy is good at reporting such crimes, since they are among the first to receive complaints from tourists. If you compare US Embassy reports from Bolivia with embassy reports from other nations, even developed countries, it would appear that Bolivia is a relatively calm place to be, but since the first edition of this book, crime has suddenly become a topic and certain neighbourhoods hire their own private police.

INTERIORS

Once you get through the basics of settling in, you can begin to see Bolivia from the inside. The interior gardens, courtyards and backstreets are a metaphor for delving into the urban secrets of this extraordinary country, discovering the most authentic lodes of a different way of life. In Bolivian Spanish, the 'interior' also means those parts of the country that are more remote (in space or in spirit), including traditional rural villages and a most challenging geography.

The custom of walling-in dwellings and using thick façades for public buildings conceals some of the prettier parts of every town—the interiors. When exploring for aesthetic sights, by all means enter public buildings and peek into private driveways as doors are being opened. You will be treated to some of the best scenes in Bolivia: lush interior gardens and elaborately designed mosaic patios with stone fountains and archways. If you get lucky, you'll discover some great historic mural painting. And when in any Bolivian city, you are within an hour, sometimes within minutes, of unadulterated natural splendour.

These are some of the things you will need to know to settle down in Bolivia. If one phrase could summarise the whole settling in process, it would be to 'expect the unexpected' and keep yourself in an improvise mode, never losing track of the basic harmony.

THE FOOD OF BOLIVIA

CHAPTER 6

'In South America there are meat, vegetable or cheese pasties of every possible filling but our Bolivian *salteña* is the only one that contains a seductive sauce, as if invented by Circe, the sorceress who seduced Odysseus with secret and forbidden delicacies.'
—Ramon Rocha Monroy, Bolivian novelist and Epicurean, from 'Let's Nationalize the Salteña,' *El Juguete Rabioso*, 19 February 2005.

THE FOOD OF BOLIVIA

FOOD

Bolivia offers attractive diet options, from indigenous health foods to Hispanic cholesterol. If you don't wish to cook, most neighbourhood family restaurants will allow non-boarders to eat regularly for a fee.

It is advised to boil drinking water and cook vegetables to avoid cholera and lesser disorders, though some seasoned travellers have resisted such precautions and are still around. If you need your fresh lettuce, supermarkets sell the safest organic lettuce grown in greenhouses. In high altitudes, cooking takes longer. In La Paz, we used a pressure cooker purchased economically in the Huyustus.

Restaurants are cheap by Western standards, but if you look for those that look like the ones back home, the prices will also be closer to those back home. Lunch is the main meal, and a good, hearty Bolivian lunch, including appetiser, soup, *segundo* (main course), a small dessert (fresh fruit, jello or flan pudding) and tea or coffee costs anywhere from Bs 5 (about US$ 0.60) in small, family restaurants, to Bs 20 (approaching US$ 3.00) in more glossy eateries.

Knowledge of ingredients of typical Bolivian dishes will help you make your choices. Soup haters will discover the soup-loving self within when trying

> The trick is to order the fixed price *almuerzo*, and not a la carte. The best of the least expensive restaurants are often found in the areas surrounding universities, but most neighbourhoods have such quaint or quirky restaurants.

Bolivian soups based on nutritious and tasty grains such as *quinoa* and whole wheat or vegetables.

Bolivian cuisine is extensive, which is no surprise given the variety of agricultural regions. Whole volumes could be written with recipes of indigenous and Creole dishes. Rumours that the potato dominates Bolivian cooking are false, although at least one of this region's approximate 112 varieties of potato is included in most dishes, even when rice or corn are part of the combination. Agribusiness and modern food distribution methods have dented biodiversity, and many varieties of potato, for example, are now hard to find.

Bolivian main dishes may be bathed in a spicy sauce, with hot or bell peppers and cumin as mainstays in the mixture. Bolivian sauces are pungent but not gooey; they won't add cholesterol to the formula since they are not cream based. One of the more pungent native herbs, *quirquiña*, is a crafty salad enhancer.

There are five main varieties of Bolivian hot peppers. *Ají* is long and thin, similar to the Mexican chile serrano, in red or yellow. The *locoto* is fat, round and raspberry sized, green, yellow or orange in colour, and not as hot as the *ají*. A smaller orange *locoto* has a sweet-hot taste. A fat, avocado shaped, egg-sized *locoto* is dark green and bitter. The *ulupica*, is a tiny, pea sized pepper which burns the whole mouth. These peppers are not merely piquant; they have distinct flavours. Once diluted in a sauce, they function as a tasty condiment.

The most typical hot sauce is called *llajua*, made by mixing ground *locotos*, tomatoes, *quirquiña* and salt if desired. A Cochabamba variation is called *k'allu* or *soltero*, made with chopped *locotos*, onions, tomatoes and a local home-made cheese. A hot sauce with fresh, crusty proletarian bread of medieval texture called *marraqueta*, is a treat in itself.

Bolivia is not without its unique types of fast food. During late mornings, a truly delicious meat pie called the *salteña* is a favourite of Bolivians and foreigners alike. *Santeñas* are stuffed with either chicken or beef, and usually include onions, peas, potato, an olive and a slice of egg, all this in a spicy sauce.

Afternoon snacks include less spicy *empanadas* (small cheese pies), *humintas* which are similar to Mexican *tamales* but use fresh corn rather than cornmeal, and *cuñapés*, a mixture of yuca meal and melted cheese.

Soups

Bolivian soups precede the main dish for lunch, but are nutritious enough to constitute a meal in themselves. *Quinoa* (the Bolivian supergrain), *trigo* (wheat) and *maní* (ground raw white peanuts) and an array of vegetables are the base foods for incredibly savoury soups which will not depend on an acquired taste to appreciate.

> **Jaconta**
>
> Jaconta is a soup made with knots of the lamb spine, cooked with rice, whole chuños (small black dried potatoes), chunks of cabbage, a few slices of carrot, diced onions, oregano and *sal*.

Fish

Pejerrey (kingfish) is a delicious white fish from Lake Titicaca, a product of forced migration from Canada. One method of preparing it is to bread it and lightly pan fry. *Pejerrey a la romana* is dipped in batter with garlic, pepper and salt, fried, then served with broiled potato and cooked vegetables and/or green salad with tomatoes.

Other popular fish dishes are huge trouts and *surubí* (brought from Beni area rivers). Trout is either pink or white. *Surubí* has the texture of chicken breast with a fishy flavour. Both can be cooked and served the same as *pejerrey*.

There are other trout recipes, broiled, grilled or oven-cooked, with various sauces. *Surubí* is just as tasty when oven cooked. *Ispi*, only from Lake Titicaca, is a tiny fish that used to be a primary source of protein for the Incas. *Ispi* is deep fried in oil or dried in brine.

Chicken

Chicken *escabeche* is a personal favourite, with a sauce of onions, carrots, green peppers or *locotos* (if you like it hot) and sometimes cauliflower, sautéed in oil and then boiled in vinegar.

Sajta de pollo is standard home cooking and a mainstay of family restaurants. The sauce that smothers the cooked chicken is comprised of ground yellow *ají*, chopped onion and parsley, peas, cumin, garlic and salt. Accompanying the chicken is boiled potato and *tunta* (dried white potato) or rice, topped with a *sarsa* (a salad of finely diced tomato, onion and green *locoto*).

Vegetarian

Plato Paceño dates back to before the Spanish conquest, with slices of white farmers' cheese a post-conquest addition. It consists of chewy white corn on the cob (called *choclo*), fava beans in their pods and potatoes. Half the fun of eating this dish involves the use of hands, peeling off the bean pods and picking out large ears of corn. The kicker is the hot sauce, with *locoto ají*, red tomato and *quirquiña*.

> **Vegetarian Delights**
> The vegetarian restaurant at Hotel Gloria in La Paz, a favourite of locals and foreigners alike, uses tofu to imitate meat dishes.

Beef

Saice is most fashionable for lunch menus. Beef is cut in little chunks and cooked in red *ají* sauce with chopped tomatoes and onions, peas and cumin. Potato and rice or *chuño* are served on the side of the same plate, with a garnish of finely sliced tomatoes and onions.

Charcoal steaks are popular in restaurants called *rodizios* accompanied with various other kinds of meats *al carbón* including sausage and innards, salad and fried potatoes.

Pork

If you don't have a cast iron stomach, you might wish to avoid these delicious pork dishes unless the healthy origin of the animal is documented.

Fricasé is a pork soup, quite similar to the Mexican *pozole*, including hominy and seasoned with garlic and ground yellow *ají*. The *ají* makes the difference.

Chicharrón is pork fried in its own juice with a distinct crispy taste served with *hominy*.

If you enjoy the crunchy *chicharrón* but need to avoid pork, there is the chicken substitute called *chicharrón de pollo*. *Chicharrón* in the Andean countries should not be confused with a Mexican food of the same name consisting of pork skin.

Lechón is a baked suckling pig, seasoned Bolivian style with red *ají*, garlic and cumin, and served with white potatoes, sweet potatoes and bananas, all baked, and accompanied with thinly cut lettuce, tomato and *llajua*.

The adventurous eater also finds various tongue and lamb dishes with distinctive sauces. Animal innards are used in various typical dishes. My favourite is *panza* (stomach) cooked with yellow *ají* sauce, although in restaurants, *panza a la romana* is more popular. *Panza* may be purchased pre-cooked in markets. Otherwise, it takes hours to boil.

Especially popular in warmer climates, as sides to meat dishes, are *yuca* (a tuber) and cooked or fried banana.

> **Wine**
>
> Wine does not usually accompany food. Those few Bolivians who take wine with a meal often sacrifice their principles and allow a superb Chilean wine on their dinner table. In blindfolded wine tasting tests, Bolivian wines from the Tarija area perform at a higher level than their expectation, and I've even served the Tarija product to demanding French wine lovers, who were rather pleased.

There's not much to be disappointed about when it comes to Bolivian food, though sweetbread hedonists may long for a Euro pastry that melts in their mouth.

These are but a few representative Bolivian dishes, part of a surprisingly inventive and varied cuisine. Bolivia's legendary biodiversity works in her favour for providing fresh and nutritious foods for people of all budgets, and even the makeshift meals you see on construction sites or in public market stalls have something attractive to offer.

Coffee or Tea?

Gourmet coffee lovers will not find much in the way of rich, savoury coffee in Bolivia. Freshly brewed decaf is hard to come by so I bring my own coffee beans from abroad and grind them here. An after lunch substitute for coffee is any of the three *mate* (MAH-tay) teas: coca, *manzanilla* (camomile) or anise, all of which seem to have a positive effect on digestion according to anecdotal evidence. *Trimate* (TREE-mah-tay) is a brew combining these three herbs.

DRINKING AND SOCIALISING

Customs of etiquette for dinner and social invitations have been covered in Chapter Four, The Social Setting. Most important is to not arrive 'on time' to a dinner invitation (at least a half hour later than the indicated time) and to greet each and every person in the room upon arrival and likewise show the same respect upon leaving, as a collective 'goodbye' is frowned upon.

Of special interest is how eating and drinking blend with social interaction.

The simplest social occasion in most of Bolivia is centred around the *salteña*, the mildly sweet and pungent meat/chicken pastry with a juicy sauce inside the doughy wrap. The usual time to gather for *salteñas* is the midmorning work break.

> Employees from offices, labourers and neighbours will show up at a stand or small restaurant and sit or stand around eating their *salteña* while they get in a few minutes of chatting.

The *salteña* may also become the star of a birthday party, especially for children. Around noon, parents pick up a large batch of these tasty meat or chicken pies and this becomes the lunch treat for the kids (with parents and family members partaking as well.) Such an event is called a *salteñada*.

If the *salteña* occupies the morning break, tea or herbal brews are the centre of the late afternoon break. Teatime

Too bad that the most congenial bars, like this one in Sucre, don't get going until late evening, rarely serving as day-long neighbourhood hangouts.

seems to have been inherited as a highland Bolivian custom from British miners. The custom has spread to most other regions of Bolivia, and prime time is between 4:30 pm and 5:30 pm. Coffee is also a choice but this is still the hour for tea. Accompanying the tea or herbal brews are sweet breads, regular bread or crusty *marraqueta* with rustic farm cheese, butter and jam. More elaborate teatime includes pastries.

Several possible scenarios avail themselves for this period of animated conversation. This could be the work break, the home or an establishment (tea salon or club). Office or worksite tea hour offers a means for employees or labourers to talk shop or socialise when the workday is winding down. In cool highland areas, a hot brew satisfies a biological need as well, and the mixture of warmth and socialising does not seem a coincidence.

Tea hours at home could involve different groupings. Housewives from more affluent sectors may take turns offering their homes for tea and pastry, possibly accompanied by a rummy game that may involve low-scale gambling. More frequently, the tea hour is a way where extended families can sustain their social ties, and this could mean three or even four generations present. Milk is available for the children. The table setting may be relatively elaborate, as an image of family unity. Unity does not mean blandness and polemics relating to the lives of the family or the external social situation could trigger lively discussion and even debate.

The tea hour at salons or clubs may involve either family or friends. When more formalised, a tea time may also be the setting for a charity event, with money raised through a rummy game or other mechanism.

Among certain indigenous groups and those who identify with them, an informal gathering may include the chewing of coca leaves. Hippie expats and backpackers may choose this type of gathering rather than a tea hour. However, tea hour is by no means limited to affluent classes, with labourers partaking of the custom as well.

Beverage customs at lunch and dinner hours are less elaborate. Lunch may be accompanied by a fruit drink, or soda, with Coca Cola and other soft drink companies exercising their hegemony. In this country where healthy natural fruit drinks were a staple, the soft drink industry has muscled its way into the consciousness of Bolivians and Latin Americans in general.

Coca in Coca Cola
Curiously, in a country where the native coca leaf has been demonised by Western elites, Coca Cola, which allegedly contains coca, has escaped such criticism.

This may not be exclusively a question of palate, since soft drinks which are basically water, sugar and artificial flavouring are less expensive than fresh fruit beverages. Europeans accustomed to drinking wine with lunch will sometimes be disappointed. However, wine is often made available, and Bolivian wines from the Tarija region, as well as Argentine and Chilean wines, are of good quality.

In the battleground of alcoholic beverages for accompanying meals, beer is the leader by many lengths. Like so many 'third world' countries, Bolivia has a thriving beer industry, and foreigners are rarely disappointed with the local array of beers. At high altitudes, visitors should be aware that alcohol and altitude can have a powerful effect. Those who are most affected by this *potent exacta* shouldn't be far away from a napping place.

At dinner, drinking customs are more elaborate. When dinner invitations are tendered, the guest may decided to take a bottle of wine or whiskey to the host, but flowers or chocolates are of equal value as an offering. Pre-dinner appetisers and cocktails may include the national hard drink called Singani or locally made whiskey. For accompanying the dinner, soft drinks, beer, or to a lesser extent, wine, are usually available.

After dinner conversation is usually accompanied by drinking, with liqueurs added to the above array of drinks as an option.

Outside the home, drinking venues in Bolivia may be a culture shock for European continentals. In Europe, the café-bar remains open day and night, and social drinking may occur at various hours of day, evening or night. The doors of Bolivian *whiskerias* remain closed until after dinner time. As for cafés, the lower the altitude the more likely that these venues may be used as gathering places with outdoor facilities.

In Britain, it has been discovered that police problems linked to consumption of beer and alcoholic beverages have been reduced by making opening and closing hours of pubs more flexible, thereby discouraging binge drinking and harmonising with continental European drinking customs. The restricted business hours of Bolivian *whiskeries* may actually stimulate binge drinking, and no one denies that heavy drinking may be a social problem, especially among youth.

Numerous expat bars with upscale appearance are magnets for visitors. Long-stay visitors, especially Europeans, usually stake out their favourite drinking turf and become regulars. Expat bars often become speciality venues. You may find anything from poets' bars and geologists' bars to football bars. Only word of mouth can tell you the specialities of such bars.

Darkened bars may be a venue for *coperas*, occasional prostitutes whose principle livelihood is hanging around the counter or tables and stimulating male guests to imbibe and to invite. For some of these women, drinking on the job is a no-no. How can this be possible? The gullible male believes he is ordering an expensive mixed drink for the sexy woman. Instead, she is served a mere soft drink, and her apparent carnal desires are inextricably connected to the surge of cash.

When all is said and done, drinking of any kind is linked to socialising. In urban Bolivia, the extended family is the dominant social structure for tippling in a group. In rural indigenous Bolivia, the community is the focus, with the local annual festival as the scene of optimum imbibing.

ENJOYING BOLIVIA

CHAPTER 7

'You can take a walk from one climate
to another, from the cold highlands to the
hot lowlands, stripping layers along the way.'
—Author's journal

THE DIFFERENCE BETWEEN TOURISM AND TRAVEL is the difference between seeing and being. If there is no real engagement with local people and geography, the visitor will take home only photographs and trinkets. But if communication with people or communion with geography are achieved, the image of place will remain vibrant within the traveller long after the photos have faded.

What follows is a narrative menu of ways to engage with Bolivian culture and commune with the unbelievable settings that nurture this culture.

FESTIVALS

It may be bad timing for a visitor to arrive on the eve of a festival. There will have been no time for a way of life to sink in, and the visitor may remain an outsider. However, visitors who can follow rhythms may join in the dance and come out with a visceral imprint.

Dominating Bolivia's history is a series of colonial and neo-colonial relationships, beginning with Inca invasions, followed by 300 years of Spanish colonialism and continuing through today, with Bolivian capitalists dependent on foreign enterprises and banks. Of all

> The names of festivals may change from Mexico to Bolivia, but the frenzy of drinking and dancing is similar. Missing in Bolivia are the gunshots you hear at the more spirited Mexican festivals. In both countries, indigenous folk will spend their year's savings on one annual event. When the delirium is over, the new cycle begins.

these periods, the Spanish colony has had the most lasting effect on social customs.

Most festivals are a hybrid of Spanish Catholicism superimposed over indigenous religious ceremonies, an expedient method for Catholicism to make inroads into Bolivian social structures. Many indigenous customs have survived under a cloak of Catholicism.

Bolivia's festivals reconcile two contradictory world views. But the festival, throughout Latin America, also functions as an escape from the drudgery of oppression and thwarted livelihoods. Mexican Nobel Prize winner Octavio Paz addressed this issue in *The Labyrinth of Solitude*, where he explains that the excesses of the fiesta are a type of purging of frustrations born out of historical rape.

El Presterío

In some communities, the custom of El Presterío still exists. *El preste* is the man who is appointed to pay for the whole party, including drinks, food and musicians. Prior to his appointment, he may have been the wealthiest person in town. In the aftermath of the fiesta, he is down to the level of everyone else.

Originally, this custom was the great redistributor of wealth, the social equaliser. But the custom has been diluted in those villages least isolated from contemporary life. Now, villagers are expected to make their contribution to the *preste*.

As the fiesta loses a measure of its democratic traits in rural Bolivia, it democratises in urban areas. A typical festival once had two scenarios: the clubs for the elites and the streets for the masses. But as class structures are loosened, the fiesta is polarised no longer. *Comparsas* (dance troupes) formed by 'elites' swirl down the streets in the same dance chain as Cholos and Indians.

Affluent Bolivians now participate in street festivals, because that's where the real excitement lies. Meanwhile, as indigenous communities become more politicised, fewer folk are likely to blow a whole year's savings on a few days of exuberance and excess.

A Festival Calendar

Virtually every town and even neighbourhood has its own annual festival. This section concludes with a selected list of the most noteworthy annual fiestas.

January

- 6 January—Reyes Magos. Various provinces in the Beni celebrate the arrival of the three kings with dramatic processions.
- 24 January—Alasitas. La Paz hosts a grand artisan fair of realistic miniatures, in tribute to El Ekeko, the god of abundance. People buy miniature representations of all the things they expect to need during the year.

February

- 2 February—Virgen de la Candelaria. Rural communities re-enact the pre-Columbian potato ritual, offering *ch'allas* (sprinkling of alcoholic beverages) to venerate La Pachamama (Mother Earth God). Catholics make a pilgrimage to Copacabana, on the banks of Lake Titicaca. In Santa Cruz, there are processions and traditional music.
- Near the end of the month—Carnaval. Bolivia's equivalent of the Mardi Gras carnival. The city of Oruro is famous for its Carnaval, but most Bolivian cities now create their own version of the Oruro festival. In rural communities, Carnaval may be combined with a fertility celebration, where pairs of llamas and sheep are symbolically partnered and decorated with images of serpents.

  The highlight of Carnaval is Oruro's Saturday Entrada, a day-long procession with thousands of dancers in ornate costumes. La Diablada (Dance of the Devils) and La Morenada, symbolising the tribulations of black slaves in Bolivia, are featured dances. La Paz's Sunday Entrada is only three hours away, for those who have not had enough. In the lowlands, the Entrada in Santa Cruz most resembles the Brazilian counterpart.

  Following the Entrada, dancers continue the revelry in clubs and bars, the bedlam continues in the streets, and

Two generations of Bolivian elite prepare to dance La Diablada in Oruro.

drinks flow freely, with beer and the fermented maize drink, *chicha* or *garapiña*, the favourite brews in Oruro.

For children, Carnaval means great water fights lasting the whole week, with water filled balloons hurled at each other and at passersby. An alternative weapon is the spray can containing billowing white foam, an improvement over the less efficient pie-in-the-face routine.

My son's first orgy of water fights was one of the highlights of his childhood. But if you don't like getting wet or blasted with white foam, steer clear of children, and especially watch out for men and women who are reclaiming their adolescence. Male chivalry is forgotten as women become more likely targets.

One of the most literal examples of culture shock befell a US colleague, a young man who was clobbered in the eye by a water balloon which evidently contained ice. Even as his eye was blackening, he was locating the pickup truck, Hardy Boy style, from which the deadly balloon was hurled.

He entered the house where the truck was parked and located the aggressor, who turned out to be about the

Foam and water fights during Carnaval—sooner or later everyone joins in.

same age and size. With his fists, the avenger struck. The original aggressor-turned-victim soon apologised.

My colleague refuses to believe that his Carnaval experience was an anomaly; as unpredictable as the firecracker that exploded next to my right ear at Place Bastille at a Bastille night concert, compelling me to listen to the concert with my left ear. This colleague of mine now stays home and watches television during Carnaval.

The balloons are not supposed to be filled with ice, and a Bolivian victimised by an ice filled balloon probably would have taken the same reprisal as my colleague. The difference is that the Bolivian would be out on the streets for next year's Carnaval.

On my first trip to Oruro's Carnaval, I splurged for a balcony seat at the Nikkei Plaza Hotel in order to reduce the probability of my getting hit with a water balloon or sprayed with foam. As the parade passed by, I'd go downstairs to take photographs. On my first foray, I was happy that I had eluded the foam from spray-can armies that roamed the street. But on my second descent, I began to feel left out. Why were they not including me in their war? Then, I got splotched with white foam on the back of my head; suddenly I belonged. Watch the folks when a water balloon hits them in a sensitive place by surprise. The initial shock lasts a few seconds, and then a great smile breaks out.

As the war went on and the balloon and spray can arms manufacturers got rich, my maturity level decreased by years and by decades. I found that I was taking more photographs of the revelry than the parade. People from the bleachers that lined the streets joined in with the dancers and revellers only casually acquainted were suddenly arm in arm.

The most inhibited among us will shed their social façades at Carnaval in Oruro. There is something very special when the sombre mining town of Oruro is aroused into sublime joy for three days in late February.

"My only saddening thought," commented Daniel Clinch, a British colleague who went to Oruro, "was that a country like England with such a rich history of tradition and culture had nothing to match, not even a patch, on Carnaval in Oruro.

"In England, the combination of alcohol, lots of people and an abundant supply of water balloons would be a catastrophe. As the day progressed, the standard of behaviour would deteriorate and as the evening unfurled, a mass brawl would undoubtedly ensue."

Clinch remained in Oruro for the whole shebang. The anarchy escalated, but the good spirits of the occasion never diminished. "It's a memory that will last forever," he says with a radiant glow in his eyes.

March

- 12 March—Pujjllay. In Tarabuco, near Sucre. Commemorates a local victory over Spanish troops prior to independence. More than 10,000 local villagers from 68 communities arrive in their finest clothes, adorned with fruits of the earth. Lots of eating, drinking and dancing.
- 19 March—San José. A three-day festival just outside of Oruro at the San José mine. Music, fireworks and a commercial fair.

- Last Sunday in March—Domingo de Ramos. Varying celebrations throughout Bolivia: a cattle fair in El Alto, a procession of child angels in Sucre.

April
- Semana Santa—Easter Week. The pilgrimage to the shrine at Copacabana blends Catholic ritual with offerings to the gods by Aymara Yatiris (shaman). Tarija's Semana Santa is more Spanish. Similar religious festivals are held around the Jesuit mission communities near Santa Cruz.
- 15 April—Tarija's Departmental Anniversary. Serenaders and dancers in the streets. Competitive events including a rodeo the following day.

May
- 3 May—Fiesta of the Cross. Throughout Bolivia, this event is more pre-Columbian than Christian. Remote indigenous villages hold T'inkus (ritual combat that may erupt into fierce violence when participants are governed by the effects of hard drinking; occasionally leads to death).

  Bolivian director Mela Márquez's gutsy film, *Sayariy*, is the most insightful portrayal of this indigenous festival ritual. "I was the only member of the film crew," Márquez says, "who didn't have a violent experience."

  The filming took place in a village five hours from the nearest phone, during four weeks of extremely primitive living conditions. The T'inku's nearest equivalent in Western culture is ritual professional wrestling. The moment when a legal rough check in ice hockey erupts into a fracas may also bear something of a visceral resemblance.

  But if a T'inku participant were to witness a professional wrestling match, he might be overcome with bewilderment. Why does the audience sit there without getting involved? Why does this imitation brawl not erupt into the real thing?

  Most Bolivians and visitors alike would agree with me that of all the events in Bolivian culture, the T'inku is most likely to provoke a culture shock. But let us turn the tables.

Give a T'inku crowd the opportunity to observe British hooligans at a football match, or East Los Angeles street gangs in warfare. The T'inku is a once-a-year event, a chance for releasing profound historical and economic frustrations which date back to the Spanish colonisation of the Andean indigenous peoples.

During The Festival of the Cross, the faint hearted should opt for other villages, where old men (Awki-Awkis) perform a comical dance that satirises aristocratic gentlemen.

- 26 May—Espíritu Santo or Pentecost. Combines the Holy Spirit with the Pachamama (Mother Earth God). In mining communities and agricultural villages, magical plants adorn houses and llamas are sacrificed. Not recommended for animal rights activists.
- 27 May—Heroínas de la Coronilla, also Mother's Day. In remembrance of the women who fought to protect Cochabamba from the Spanish.

June

- 2 June—Santísima Trinidad. The most important festival of the Beni, with dancing dogs, pigs, tigers, bullfights and games.
- 2 June—Gran Poder (Great Power). La Paz's greatest party, with more than 60 dance groups, including dances such as La Diablada and La Morenada. Resembles the Carnaval entrada.
- 24 June—Día de San Juan. The Pachamama receives yet more offerings in rural Altiplano, this time in hopes that she will provide fertile soils. In Tarija, bonfires and water games. In Santa Cruz, a mass, and lots of drinking. In the Beni, a walk over hot coals. Everywhere, fireworks.
- 29 June—San Pedro and San Pablo. Cleverly scheduled to unload the fireworks left over from Día de San Juan.

July

- 16 July—Fiesta de Nuestra Señora del Carmen. In La Paz, the religious celebration is combined with a culture and tourism fair. In Los Yungas, there is a macabre medieval dance, while Sucre and Oruro host processions, fairs and masses. Los Yungas is the place to be. Also known as Dia de La Paz.

August
- 15 August—Virgen of Urkupiña. Held in Quillacollo, Cochabamba, includes symbolic rock smashing, as well as the usual dancing, eating and drinking.

September
- 14 September—Fiesta de Sorata. This cliffside town wakes up from its sleepy rapture once a year. Not the most well known fiesta, but the setting may be the most beautiful in all Bolivia. (*Sorata is featured in a later section of this book.*)
- 14 September—Cochabamba's Departmental Anniversary. Culture and tourism fair, with handicrafts and typical food.
- 21 September—Spring Equinox, Tiahuanaco. Observe the first ray of sun cross the line that marks spring, in the ambience of the most elaborate pre-Inca ruins in Bolivia. Don't miss!

October
- 13 October—Virgen del Rosario, Tarija. Onlookers toss flowers on a street procession, creating a colourful carpet.
- 24 September—San Rafael. A four day festival in Santa Fe, a mining town in Oruro, with folk dancing and more drinking.

November
- 1 November—Day of the Dead. Visits to cemeteries include eating, drinking and music to be shared with the spirits. Most interesting rituals in Potosí. The dead are celebrated rather than mourned. Closest equivalent in the US is the New Orleans jazz funeral, where the song *Didn't He Ramble!* honours the dead.
- 10 November—Santo Domingo. Three days of revelry and excesses in where else but Oruro, Bolivia's festival capital!

- 18 November—Beni's Departmental Anniversary. Bolivia's most carnivorous region celebrates with a cattle fair, bull fights and folk dancing.

December
- 8 December—Day of the Immaculate Conception. Typical dances, food and drink in the towns around Santa Cruz, with a more solemn version in Cochabamba.
- 24 December—La Navidad. Christmas is not a major holiday in many indigenous communities. Best place to enjoy the choral concerts and Christmas displays is in La Paz. Don't miss the performance of the Nova Chorus. Most extensive celebrations in Tarija, lasting until the end of January. Vallegrande, Che Guevara's Waterloo, hosts unusual Christmas festivities.

Fitting In To The Fiesta
If a passion for fairs and revelry moves you to travel to Bolivia, consider the Department of Oruro, which exemplifies the Octavio Paz thesis; perhaps the most sombre region of Bolivia is also the site of the longest and wildest festivals. With the decline of mining, the fiesta has become Oruro's greatest industry.

Once you've attended a few fiestas it takes no analytical skill to conclude that dancing is a favourite Bolivian pastime, an activity that bridges the culture and age gap. What then are the 10 most 'friendly persuasions' that will ease the foreigner's adjustment to Bolivia?

The Suitability Test
Should you have an affinity for at least seven of the 10 pastimes in the following checklist, your adaptation to Bolivia will be effortless. From four to six affinities will mean a moderate degree of effort in dealing with culture shock. Fewer than four affinities suggest a more trying adjustment period, although I've met a few trekkers who find total fulfilment in Bolivia when limited to affinities (3), (6) and (7).
- Football (Soccer): a universal language.
- Dancing: another universal language.

- Trekking or climbing: the Inca trails are literally built into the Bolivian culture and hundreds of magnificent but attainable peaks of over 5,000 m (16,404 ft) await the amateur climber, with higher ones available if you have something to prove.
- Art fusion: artists have created a colourful fusion between the indigenous and European heritage.
- Street life: most Bolivian cities are pedestrian friendly, with mixed-use zoning and a hyperactive informal economy.
- Pluricultures: this country is not a 'melting pot' and some degree of autonomy for Bolivia's more than 30 ethno-cultural groups is foreseeable, if not already established in some cases.
- Wild geography: a feast of microclimates, topographies, cloud forests, glaciers, rainforests, high-plain melancholy, tropical exuberance, raging rivers, old growth forests and people who gather to defend this diverse environment.
- Political agitation: democracy in Bolivia is considered a participatory happening, and activist groups don't wait around for an election. Since the last revision of this book, two presidents were toppled and one of the most powerful multi-national corporations expelled by non-violent grass roots movements.
- Creative, non-mainstream business: lots of untapped voids and niches in the economy.
- Unpredictability: if your motto is 'The best surprise is no surprise,' Bolivia is not for you.

GETTING INVOLVED:
Non-Governmental Organisations

Bolivia's struggle for survival breeds an extensive community of non-governmental organisations (NGOs), most of which have their main offices in urban areas.

NGOs serve the poor and the handicapped, operate medical outreach programmes, provide assistance for business, support the arts, do important research in ethnology, social sciences and human rights and defend the environment.

Some of these organisations fill a void that would be occupied by the government in wealthier countries. Sceptics like James Petras, in *Imperialism and NGOs in Latin America*, argue that NGOs were supported by neoliberal privatisers as part of the trend to disenfranchise the state and, at the same time, depoliticise or co-opt potential leaders of grass roots movements.

In theory, Petras may be right, and certainly many NGOs have been opportunistic and have pushed more paper than progress. On the other hand, the people served by some of these organisations could not have waited around for a distant utopia, and I have witnessed more than a few NGO participants who were also involved in social movements. Foreigners in particular may not fit in the front lines of union or peasant marches but can fulfill a role in creating opportunity or resolving problems.

The existence of NGOs offers a rare opportunity for visitors to participate in the daily struggle of the country and not just admire its marvels. NGOs are not the only vehicle for a participatory stay in Bolivia, but they improve one's odds for finding purposeful activities.

Working With NGOs

With a maturing awareness of the root causes of social problems, numerous NGOs have transcended the immediate and limited goals of charity and opted for programmes of sustainable projects in self-help and development.

Others, unfortunately, become bureaucratic and fundraising takes priority over dedicated service. A little research will link travellers planning to stay in Bolivia to an NGO within their speciality, with far too many to list here. Some actually offer a salary, but the majority, as exemplified by FOBOMADE, an activist environmental organisation, write that 'we are looking for volunteers to join projects in different parts of Bolivia.'

Bolivia is a magnet for a large community of expatriates who work together with idealistic local citizens in ambitious economic, cultural and ecological programmes. These programmes allow visitors to get to know Bolivia from the ground up, literally. In the next section, we will get to know Bolivia's odd cities from the top down. Then we'll wander away from the asphalt road and into more remote corners of this land of authentic adventure. These narrative descriptions will be complemented by a Resource Guide at the end of this book, with practical place-related information (distinctive restaurants, hotels of special value or character, adventure tours and other primary or aesthetic tips).

LA PAZ: THE GREAT HOLE

Many non-governmental organisations are strategically headquartered in La Paz, where they have direct access to key government agencies and foreign embassies.

Long ago, La Paz lured the Executive and Congress away from Bolivia's official capital and more beautiful city, Sucre. Lovers of idyllic settings like Sucre, hillside villages like Sorata or the jungle lavishness of Rurrenabaque and the Mamoré will be inevitably seduced by the stunning, appalling, exquisite, repulsive, magnificent city of La Paz.

Chuquiago, the original Aymara name for this ex-indigenous mining settlement, is the antithesis of its flatland namesake Chicago. La Paz is an inside-out version of hilly

San Francisco, California. One looks up into San Francisco and down into La Paz.

Tearing through the gut of La Paz is the river-turned-sewer, the Río Choqueyapu. Fed by countless tributary-sewers, the Choqueyapu carries sludge, chemical waste, animal carcasses and other glorious products of civilisation from north to south-west. The Choqueyapu runs roughly parallel to La Paz's straightest and longest avenue, whose central point is El Prado.

On El Prado, one may sit on a boulevard bench without smelling the Choqueyapu, which has been encased in the downtown area. A thorough cleanup would require a ten-year commitment, involving a zealous education campaign and massive investments in sewage systems and the recycling of industrial wastes. Repercussions from the Choqueyapu are felt all the way down where it flattens out in the Zona Sur (South Zone). Eventually, past a town called Mallasa, marshlands attempt to absorb and neutralise the tainted waters.

I'd never think of using water from the Seine for my morning coffee in Paris, nor catching my fish dinner from a New York City dock on the Hudson River. But the Seine and Hudson are still rivers. The Choqueyapu is an ex-river. (In fairness to the Choqueyapu, La Paz is not the first city to have encased and partly buried a river-turned-sewer. Consider, for example, the forgotten Bièvre River that once ran through Paris and now flows under it, emptying out into the Seine.)

Choqueyapus

Wherever you go there are Choqueyapus. The answer to the Choqueyapu is not to escape but to stay and fight. Conservative estimates say that the river can be cleaned and revived for a little more than US$ 50 million in five years.

La Paz is not a beautiful city—'imposing' is a better adjective. It does have its nooks and crannies of superb grace and splendour, for sure, especially in the old, preserved streets of its north-west quadrant.

El Prado, downtown La Paz.

Most travellers arriving in La Paz, by plane, bus or automobile, will be entering by way of El Alto, perhaps the only city in the world where the airport is the neatest place in town.

The city of La Paz is found beyond the ledge, deep down in the gashing hole. At the far end and bottom of the gash (which has been carved out of chalky badlands by the Choqueapu) is the more affluent Zona Sur (South Zone), which tries hard to emulate a North American suburb, as exemplified by a Mexican restaurant that advertises it's 'MEXICAN BAR' ... in English!

But La Paz's south zone still looks like Bolivia, as the more onerous aspects of North American suburbia, single-use zoning, windowless department stores, motorway degradation and the absence of public transportation have not yet been adopted.

The view of La Paz, as you pass over the lip of El Alto into 'The Hole' will 'knock your socks off,' according to Peter Hutcheson, former editor of *Bolivian Times*. The redbrick slums at the edge of the lip give way to more developed neighbourhoods and then the downtown skyscrapers in varying pastels, with the blazing white peak of Mount Illimani monopolising the background. With few exceptions, the higher the neighbourhood, the poorer the people and the more feeble the infrastructure. Killer landslides in the rainy season are not unknown to these precarious hillside settlements called collectively *las laderas* (the sides). When the chalky, claylike limestone gives way under the incessant rains, the mess arrives downtown.

By night under a full moon, Illimani shines and the city becomes an inverted heaven; the poorest neighbourhoods are granted the consolation of having the best view.

In colonial times, the author of *Don Quixote*, Miguel de Cervantes, applied for the position of Mayor of La Paz. Today, the city is in need of a real Don Quixote, and may have found one in its mayor Juan del Granado, nicknamed Juan Sin Miedo (Fearless Juan).

In the 1700s, a throng of the original Aymara inhabitants laid siege to the city, under the leadership of Tupac Katari, inflicting considerable damage against the colonial regime.

In modern times, Plaza Murillo has been the scene of a series of violent conflicts, including the controversial lynching of President Villarroel in 1946. Not surprisingly, the presidential palace in that plaza is named El Palacio Quemado (The Burned Palace).

Today, the most intrepid of all La Paz residents are the roller bladers, who must navigate the city's sharp inclines and jarring cobblestones.

All rolling stones from the north, east and west will land in El Prado. Using the southern tip of El Prado, a traffic circle called Plaza del Estudiante, we can divide the central city into its four quadrants, nicknaming each one according to its most defining trait.

Purist geographers may object to our labelling the quadrants North-west, North-east, South-west and South-east, since the main avenue cuts through La Paz at an angle. But some sort of pattern recognition is vital to get around a city of such anarchistic design.

Map of La Paz
For a detailed map, visit http://bolivia.gotolatin.com/eng/Info/Hbook/LaPazMap.asp.

The Big Agora

The north-west quadrant bustles with outdoor speciality markets. Behind the San Francisco Basílica on Calle Sagárnaga, the artisans' neighbourhood unfolds like peacock feathers, into the textures and colours of silver work, alpaca sweaters, typical musical instruments, paintings of brilliant colours, wood carvings and a seemingly infinite variety of traditionally-made textiles with unpredictably dazzling patterns.

The artisans' turf overlaps into the Mercado de Hechicería (Witch Market): llama foetuses for religious ceremonies and wandering shaman who shun tourists. Stall owners consider cameras as enemy armaments.

North of the San Francisco Cathedral is Mercado Lanza, with meat, fish, produce, eating stalls, alcohol, flower stands, toys and trinkets such as key chains with a coca leaf embedded in transparent plastic.

The Huyustus

Life gets even raunchier further up from San Francisco, with the Mercado Negro (black market), the Huyustus (with everything from furniture to contraband electronic products) and one crowded street dedicated to the sale of stolen goods. People say the street is called Sebastian Segurola. Someone stole the nameplates.

Bargains in this neighbourhood are allegedly tied to money laundering. Enter at your own risk.

My wife goes shopping in the hair-raising Huyustus. La Paz is one of the safest cities in the world, but in this section, preventive measures against pickpockets are recommended.

La Paz pickpockets are less sophisticated and less violent than their colleagues in most major cities in the world, though some can steal your socks without taking off your shoes. The best safety rule: do not broadcast your valuables or you will be a walking invitation for the redistribution of wealth.

Since passports are a valuable commodity, I carry a photocopy of the personal data and visa pages of my passport when going to this neighbourhood or anywhere else.

Pickpocketing Bolivian Style

A pickpocket once ripped a gold necklace from my wife's neck. (She had forgotten to remove it before leaving home.) She chased the adolescent, caught him and forced him to return the necklace.

If this same incident had occurred in Bogota, Río de Janeiro, Los Angeles or Washington, DC, the kid may well have whipped out a shiny knife and slit her neck from ear to ear.

The Huyustus specialises in clothing, bedspreads, pyjamas, shoes, toys and musical instruments. Surrounding speciality areas are nicknamed by their primary street: Calle Eloy Salmón (furniture, bikes and electronic products); Calle Graneros (black market specialising in shoes and clothing); Miamicito or Little Miami (linen and women's clothing); Pasaje Ortega (kitchenware, plastics and shoes); Max Paredes and Rodríguez (lowest priced groceries in La Paz).

After purchasing more than can be carried in a minibus or *micro*, your vendor will help you flag down a taxi, or if necessary, a truck.

I enjoy a trip to this neighbourhood mostly when I am not buying anything. Otherwise, the visit can be harassing. Times Square on New Years' Eve is roomy and underpopulated compared to the Huyustus. The term agoraphobia is reputed to achieve its maximum definition in this north-east quadrant of La Paz.

Market Shopping

In outdoor markets, expect to eventually get a 5–10 per cent reduction in quoted prices. If you look like a gringo, there is a 50 per cent probability that you will be overcharged on the initial price.

My wife tells me to 'go take a walk' when she is negotiating an important purchase but I have not found the overcharging of gringos to be as prevalent as she insists.

Near the Huyustus is the cemetery. Like the Père-Lachaise Cemetery in Paris, the La Paz cemetery is a campus for lessons in the country's military and social history.

San Pedro Prison—these prisoners couldn't afford more luxurious cells.

Across the traffic circle from the cemetery may be the most exciting attraction of the north-west quadrant. In an empty parcel of terrain, a man with recently slaughtered snakes gives a sales pitch to a crowd of people. The proverbial 'snake medicine' salesman is not just a folk tale!

When you've become bewildered by the crowds in their humming labyrinth, the way out is down. Streets with the steepest incline will get you to the main avenue the quickest. An alternative way out is south, parallel to the downtown drag, at a mild incline, to the Plaza San Pedro, a community meeting place for medicinal herbologists and old fashioned portrait photographers.

The high painted adobe wall occupying a whole quadrangle is the San Pedro Prison. Visiting hours at the San Pedro Prison are Thursday and Sunday afternoons. Foreigners are allowed in to visit their countrymen.

Many inmates are stuck here because they cannot afford a lawyer, or worse, because they could not afford to pay an escort on the date of their hearing. They may linger in jail for months or years before their day in court. René Blattmann's presumption of innocence law has been difficult to put into practice.

Within the prison, money talks, and prisoners pay for their cells and other amenities. I visited with Guillermo Gutiérrez, an entrepreneur charged with violating banking rules in a controversial case. He had been locked in for five months without a trial. He resided in the 'five-star' La Posta section, in a cramped, two-floor apartment, including kitchenette and bath.

Through the other entrance is the proletarian section of the San Pedro jail. Here, the ultimate redundancy is possible: to be homeless in prison. Those prisoners who can't afford to pay for a cell must sleep in the cold corridors.

A prison population of over 1,600 fits into a space originally designed for 300. In the worst section, there are 111 prisoners for each shower. However, proximity to visitors is a priority and thus San Pedro inmates oppose being transferred to the frigid and more spacious Chonchocorro on the Altiplano.

The Outdoor Museum

If the north-west quadrant of La Paz looks like a rugged capital of Third World survival artists, the mellow north-east quadrant contains La Paz's finest examples of preserved colonial architecture, centred around the narrow Calle Jaen.

The best of these streets is just north of Plaza Murillo, and includes boutique size speciality museums. The mixture of commerce, tourism and residents adds flavour to the neighbourhood. The Museo Costumbrista Juan de Vargas, the Museo Litoral (in remembrance of Bolivia's lost coastline), la Casa de Don Pedro Domingo Murillo (liberator of the city) and the Museo de Metales Preciosos Pre-Colombinos are all within short walking distance and worth a visit.

Don't miss the carved-stone colonial-style Museo Nacional de Arte, on the north-west corner of Plaza Murillo. This three-story 1775 building with pillared balconies, surrounding a courtyard of stone mosaic with a central fountain, is an ideal setting for soothing meditation. On the various floors, all periods of Bolivian art are represented.

In the same neighbourhood, within one of the great old colonial buildings, is the Peña Marka Tambo (Calle Jaen), with an exuberant cast of Bolivian folk music and dance groups. Not far from there is the Peña La Casa del Corregidor (Calle Murillo).

A Plaza Murillo focal point is Hotel Paris, a restored anachronism of the old aristocracy. Everything within its expensive suites will take you back a century; wood carved furniture, lacy bedspreads and curtains, original rugs, traditional bathroom tiles—only the fax machine breaks the illusion.

> Also at Plaza Murillo is the Congress building, where a heated debate may be more thrilling than the blurry double feature at the cinema next to Hotel Paris.

International Village

The affluence of the south-west quadrant of La Paz is deceiving as owners of stylish mansions may have their total financial wealth invested in the one piece of property.

The personality of this neighbourhood comes from the large contingent of expatriate residents and the institutions that serve them, including embassies, foreign restaurants, the Alliance Française and Goethe Institute, and a host of avant garde cafés and night clubs.

The downtown of Sopocachi is Plaza Abaroa. Abaroa was the hero who died in a fruitless defense of Bolivia's seacoast. Once a year, the Plaza is the scene of a celebration of the Day of the Sea.

Plaza Abaroa is also the practising ground for festival dancers. On any given weekend, the chance is you'll encounter free entertainment. The neighbours living in the high rise condominiums around the Plaza have memorised the festival songs that perpetually fill the air and would rather hear a telephone busy signal or a dripping faucet.

In the blocks to the north and east of Plaza Abaroa is La Paz's night club and café district. Café Montmartre, by the Alliance Française, Thelonious Jazz Bar, Matheus Bar, Andrómeda and Café Equinoccio are a few upscale places with good, down-to-earth jazz, rock 'n' roll, traditional Bolivian folk music, Latin music and an occasional classical string quartet. Políticos hang out in Matheus, while the younger crowd at Café Montmartre is treated to a perpetual blue haze of smoke doubtlessly imported from a Paris café.

Not Always What it Seems
The skirts of upper Sopocachi are beaded with outdoor staircases. A friend who took a room with a view in that area complained that, when he needed a tube of toothpaste from the grocers, he had to go down 68 steps, and then back up. You think you're living on the second floor, but in reality, you're living on the seventh floor of an eight-storey walkup.

At the foot of upper Sopocachi, along Avenida Ecuador, are a number of fine art galleries, including Simón I. Patiño and the Solón Foundation (Ecuador at Rosendo Gutiérrez) and Museo Marina Nuñez del Prado, several blocks north.

A short, steep hike above Plaza Abaroa will take you to El Montículo, a tree shaded hill, with a popular wedding chapel. El Montículo is a hangout for proletarian picnickers with spectacular views of Mount Illimani and the rugged foothills around the south suburbs.

Sunday Refuge
The south-east quadrant, primarily occupied by the Miraflores neighbourhood, is an old middle class haunt with bustling streets and rows of inexpensive

restaurants and snack hangouts. The medical school of Bolivia's national university gives the neighbourhood a student atmosphere.

The focal point of Miraflores is the Hernán Siles football stadium, where Wednesday nights and Sunday afternoons are prime time for professional football. The nickname 'Sunday Refuge' refers to the football games and comes from a popular tango.

Some South American football federations have lobbied (unsuccessfully) for banning World Cup qualifying matches at above 3,000 m (9,842 ft), which would have disqualified the Miraflores stadium.

In 1997, this stadium hosted the international Copa America tournament. Among the participating countries were the US, Argentina and Brazil. Bolivia made it to the final, only to be defeated by Brazil. For once, the eyes of the world were on Bolivia.

In a surreal administrative decision, then mayor Gaby Candia chose this precise moment for a massive tear-down-and-put-up-again refurbishing of the El Prado downtown hotel area, thereby disfiguring the city of La Paz for visiting journalists.

> **The Fast Pace of Chess**
> When they're not playing football in the stadium, La Paz's Chess Association, whose members pay a US$ 3 a year membership fee, meets Mondays through Fridays from 5:00 pm to 11:30 pm on the fourth floor of the stadium. Those folk not used to the aesthetics of football may perceive the chess matches to be more quick paced than the world's most popular sport.

Visitors may join La Paz fitness advocates in jogging early morning laps over the stadium's tartan running track, before 50,000 empty seats.

An unheralded and idyllic spot in the midst of hyperactive Miraflores is the Jardín Botánico, with its labyrinthian paths of exotic trees and flowers, and its views of various La Paz proletarian neighbourhoods.

La Paz's human and vehicle congestion and malignant webs of tentacular electric and phone lines often provoke in city boys like me, a thirst for peace, quietude and refuge. The little known Jardín Botánico is the best refuge in La Paz, Sundays or any other day.

All four quadrants have their serious ups and downs, but the south-east quadrant wins the contest for the roughest terrain.

Down in a deep gorge near the Choqueyapu is the Teatro al Aire Libre (Open Air Theatre), where famous visiting performers are expected to offer one show at moderate cost for those who can't afford to shell out 50 bucks at the Hotel Radisson.

Jutting straight above the Teatro al Aire Libre is a towering hill within a gorge, called Laikakota, an outdoor park for children with a dramatic 360 degree view of La Paz. It is at this bizarre outcrop where the Quipus Foundation's cultural centre and childrens' museum is located.

'Sunset Boulevard' La Paz

Like Sunset Boulevard in Los Angeles, La Paz's main avenue cuts through the whole city changing its personality along the way.

Walking from north-west to south-east where the main avenue is called Montes, you'll find the main bus terminal a block to the left. Down a few blocks is the San Francisco Church, whose construction began in 1549. After a heavy snowfall caused the collapse of the original structure, San Francisco's reconstruction was completed in 1753. The art work on this Basilica's stone-sculpted façade represents the intervention of indigenous customs on Spanish baroque models. The Spaniards, not desirous of getting their hands dirtied, sent the Indians up the scaffolds. Once alone above, the native craftsmen were free to add their own motifs.

On Calle Sagárnaga, across from the south façade of the San Francisco Church, the Peña El Parnaso puts on an animated show of folk music and dance.

Across the avenue from the Basílica is La Casa de La Cultura, a sometimes forgotten corner where ongoing expositions of art and literature grant a welcomed respite from the *micro-* and minibus anarchy of this congested corner.

Back to the main avenue, a few blocks farther down on the San Francisco side, is the modern post office, Bolivia's Tower of Babel, where English, French and German vie for second place behind Spanish in the language standings.

Directly across from the post office on what is now Avenida Mariscal Santa Cruz is yet another *peña*, Los Escudos.

Within three blocks behind Los Escudos are both the Secretariat of Tourism (Calle Mercado, Ballivian Building) and the Immigration building on Avenida Camacho, where you'll find one of the most photographic views of Mount Illimani, with telephone wires crisscrossing in the foreground.

El Prado

Back down the main avenue, which is now called 16 de Julio, the centre island with benches and trees is referred to as El Prado, La Paz's favourite outdoor hangout.

The old El Prado was lined with colonial buildings similar to the ones in the north-east quadrant. A few of these remain, in particular, El Club Libanés, but most of those grand old structures were torn down and replaced by business high rises.

> **The Delights of Street Eateries**
> On various streets across from the university, family eateries attract bargain searchers, with the full course lunch menu at less than US$ 1.50. I invited a Bolivian friend to one of these spots, Nelsy's. His reaction: "This is exactly the way my mother cooks."

At the end of El Prado, is the Plaza del Estudiante, the traffic circle that acts as the axle between the four quadrants. Just beyond is the main campus of the Universidad Mayor de San Andrés (UMSA), Bolivia's underfunded university with high quality professors and significant research projects.

The university also runs a quality television station, Channel 13. Surrounding the university are numerous photocopy shops, where text books are routinely copied. A textbook author will never get rich in Bolivia.

Foreign Embassies

It is at this spot by the university, Nudo Villazón, where the main avenue splits into two parallel thoroughfares, Avenida 6 de Agosto with traffic moving south and Avenida Arce moving north.

Walking down Arce, you'll pass the five-star high rise Radisson Plaza Hotel, an attractive traffic circle called Plaza Isabel La Católica, and the Centro Boliviano Americano (CBA), which features an English language library with an annual membership fee.

> Avenida Arce ends abruptly before the breathtaking dropoff into deep gorges, but the road continues, via hairpin turns, passing the presidential residence and then moving roughly parallel to the Rio Choqueyapu.

You will now pass various embassies. Visitors from Great Britain, Australia and New Zealand will be attended by the UK Embassy on the right side of the avenue.

Just past the UK Embassy is a lifeless stone block fortress that happens to be the United States Embassy. Canadians, Germans and Swedes will also find their embassies on the same Avenida Arce. Across from the United States Embassy is the neo-medieval Brazilian Embassy.

The Womens' Prison

Once down in Obrajes, the road levels out to a slight incline. Middle class Obrajes is the home of the Womens' Prison.

"Children often live in prison with their mothers," explain two former prison employees, Daniela and Nancy, interviewed for this book. "You don't see any loving games among the children," Daniela says, "only violent games. It is ironic that a prison that is supposed to protect society is breeding new criminals."

Daniela and Nancy explain that the women imprisoned for terrorism have become leaders among the inmates. "When the terrorists were seized after a riot that I witnessed," says Daniela, "the rest of the prison population came to their defence."

Daniela often attempted to convince the terrorists that there is no justification for violence against innocent human beings. In the process of these discussions, she made a few friends. "Because of these friendships," she laments, "the government began to be suspicious of me."

Out of prison and past downtown Obrajes, the road runs precariously close to Rio Choqueyapu. If the wind is blowing, do not breathe through your mouth.

Plaza Humboldt

Plaza Humboldt is the final stopping place, the gateway to the south suburbs. This is the scene of Sunday outdoor art exhibits of attractive popular art with typical Bolivian scenes.

For parents with children, most of the best private schools, including the German-Bolivian School, the Colegio Franco-Boliviano, the Montessori School, the Saint Andrews School and the most expensive of them all, the English language Colegio Calvert, are all found in this warmer southern tier of La Paz.

In 1999, a group of students, mainly from Calvert, at least one the son of a United States Embassy official, went on a rampage, damaging parked cars and harassing Chola street vendors. In a city whose abject poverty and lack of recreation facilities should breed street gangs but rarely does, this youth rampage involved the bored and affluent, many of whom belonged to exclusive private recreation clubs. Racism was an ugly factor in the disturbance. The oasis of the Zona Sur became yet another contradiction in the city's superimposed human geography.

La Paz is a rugged piece of earth where the city never ceases to be an intruder, no matter how many streets are paved or bridges built. Every day, one way or another, people in La Paz must do battle with its incongruent, deterministic geography. An upstairs climb into Alto Sopocachi at 1.5 km (2.5 miles) above sea level is never an unconscious act.

So many people are crammed into this hole, like a thousand clowns in an old automobile, while the Altiplano, 400 m (1,312 ft) above, retains its barren melancholy. The lack of more than one straight path through town results in vehicle–pedestrian anarchy.

La Paz: Best Bets

The following rankings are primarily based on interviews with numerous native Paceños and visiting residents. I have used two criteria: (a) Which places will one want to revisit? (b) Which places appeal to both foreigners and Bolivians? Luckily, La Paz does not have too many 'Oh-I've-already-been-there' type of places.

- The view from La Ceja (The Eyebrow) when literally dropping into La Paz from El Alto, with Mount Illimani in the background. Best time is late afternoon through sunset, as La Paz puts on its evening dress of a sea of lights.

    An alternative, lesser known site with an equally spectacular view is found at the top of the other side of 'The Hole', in Pampahasi, a high ridge where La Paz glistens below to the west, and hidden green valleys lie to the east. *Micros* and minibuses marked Pampahasi can be caught moving south on Avenida Camacho.

- The art scene. The Museo Nacional de Arte and smaller galleries, a few of which include Fundación Solón and Fundacion Simón Patiño. Marvel at the potent mix of two great legacies, the European and the Andean indigenous.

    La Paz's remote location prevents her from receiving exhibits of foreign art, but the local product admirably fills the void.

- The Tiahuanaco ruins (also spelled Tiwanaku). This is pre-Inca architecture with a style of massive but precise stonework similar to that of Macchu Picchu in Perú. The civilisation that led to Tiahuanaco originated somewhere around 600 BC and La Puerta del Sol (Gate of the Sun) gives some indication about Tiahuanacan cosmology. Some of the stone slabs fashioned into finely carved façades of Tiahuanaco weigh as much as 175,000 kg (385,808 lbs).

    Nearby, raised agricultural fields surrounded by canals illustrate an ingenious farming methodology that has excited agronomists and anthropologists around the world.

Micros to Tiahuanaco cost about US$ 1. If you want a more comfortable trip, organised guided tours run for about US$ 10.

- Music scene. Andean music has become universal, and is best heard in small clubs called *peñas*. Local jazz groups straddle the avant garde: a fusion of Andean instruments/ harmonies with classical African American jazz.
- International and league football at Hernán Siles Stadium. No programmes are sold, so buy any one of the local newspapers with a colour sports insert for the line-ups.

  Bolivian football is especially exciting/frustrating, because the artistry of ball passing is superior to the power of goal scoring. Bolívar, the best local team, often dominates a game whose outcome remains in doubt until the final seconds.

- Tear gas demonstrations. These should be observed at a distance. Here is history in action, participatory democracy, ritual confrontations that always end up with negotiated settlements.

  Bring a wet handkerchief, and be placed where your escape is downhill, not up, in case the gases spread more quickly than expected.

- The Calle Jaen neighbourhood, north-east quadrant. One of the best strolls in the world. Besides the cornices, balconies and sculpted windows, take a peek inside the open doors.

  Most buildings here have beautiful cobblestone courtyards, with fountains and lush gardens. Museum-haters don't fret; boutique museums on these streets are not at all laborious.

- Outdoor markets in the north-west quadrant, surrounding Plaza Marcelo Quiroga Santa Cruz, including the Huyustus and the Black Market.

  All of La Paz is selling something. How can they find enough buyers? Is this Third World basic survival or the beginning of a thriving system of free market commerce?

- Basílica San Francisco and surrounding artisans. We may be stretching it here, as this barrio hangs on the brink of classical tourism. However, this is your chance to

The Calle Jaen Neighbourhood in La Paz offers one of the best aspects of the city's architectural heritage. A number of small museums are also situated in this area.

purchase a piece of artisanry directly from the person who made it. Shops operated by middlemen are no less attractive.
- Day-Hikes from La Paz (avoid the height of the rainy season between October and March). Amazingly near the congested 'Hole', hikers can enjoy true wilderness.

Day Hikes

Much has been written about various Inca trail treks: including the Cumbre-Coroico Choro trek beginning at La Cumbre and the Taquesi Inca Road from Ventilla (near Palca) to Sud Yungas (maps and tours available at adventure tour agencies in and around La Calle Sagárnaga). Many visitors, however, would like to end the day's adventure in a comfortable bed, and few guidebooks offer information on day hikes.

Many vigorous day hikes begin at La Cumbre: flag down a mini-bus or hitchhike from Villa Fátima to La Cumbre, about 4,600 m (15,091 ft) above sea level. This is the mountain pass just before the descent to Los Yungas.

Hike 1

To the right of La Cumbre, a jeep path takes you up past llama herds and glacial lakes to the top of Mount Valeriani, where an Entel phone station rests at 5,000 m (16,404 ft). At the edge is the straight-down canyonesque descent to Unduavi and Los Yungas. Look across the gap into the face of stark glaciers. Difficult to believe that one can arrive at such a spectacular view with no mountaineering equipment and little physical challenge but for the altitude.

Hike 2

Similar landscapes are found walking up to the left of the Cumbre. Passing several glacial lakes, choose between Abra Chacura at 4,860 m (15,944 ft)—the beginning of the Inca trail to Coroico—or two rugged peaks to the left, at above 5,000 m (16,404 ft), both of which offer 360 degree panoramas that include the incredible glacier of Wila Mankilisani and straight-down views, not meant for the faint-hearted. The only safe period for this day hike is the dry season between May and August. Dark glasses with UV-ray protection are indispensible. The climbing angle gets steep and insecure near the top of these pointy peaks. Watch out for loose shale and precarious footing on narrow snow paths.

(I thought I knew the territory like the proverbial palm of my hand, but I once got lost when coming down from one of those peaks, under an uncharacteristic blanket of mist in late August. I discovered two rare Andean flamingos wading in their private secluded bog. Flamingos were not supposed to hang out in this region! I had no camera but the imprint is alive in my soul. I had to make two more climbs to 5,000 m (16,404 ft) in order to feel my way out. It took seven hours of uncertain trails in near zero visibility, with lots of lifesaving meditation along the way.)

Hike 3

For a more fertile hike from La Cumbre, continue down from La Cumbre in the mini-bus until the police checkpoint at Unduavi. Walk right at the Sud-Yungas sign. The fern-lined road plunges past a ghost town. A few trucks and buses will pass by, kicking dust in your face, but traffic is sparse and you'll have the path to yourself for the most of the hike.

You're moving from cool to hot, so be prepared to strip off layers on the way down as you pass through narrow gorges with brilliant green cover, by transparent rivers and leaping cascades. The goal is to arrive at a narrow but towering waterfall aptly named El Velo de la Novia (the Bride's Veil). Two primitive restaurants will greet you.

> **Important Note**
> This hike takes about five hours, including a riverside picnic. To make it a day trip, you'd have to flag an infrequent bus or truck back to La Paz.

Hike 4

Don't get off the bus at Unduavi. Bypass the Sud Yungas turnoff, and ask to be let off where the new Yungas Highway

This photo of 'The World's Most Dangerous Highway' was taken by Mark McMahon (http://filmtrips.com), author of *Driving to the End of the World*.

turns left. You proceed straight ahead. At first you'll have the view into Sud Yungas gorge to your right and later the Nor Yungas gorge to your left. Known as 'the World's Most Dangerous Road', for its breathtaking hairpin turns, thousand-metre dropoffs into green abysses and crosses marking the dead that serve as warning signs, this road carves down through limestone as the vegetation thickens and humidifies. With a new highway on the other side of the gorge, less vehicle traffic interrupts this stroll, which ends seven hours later at the hotland river town of Yolosa at 1,100 m (3,608 ft). From here you can flag a bus back to La Paz or better yet, hop on a pick-up truck, past the other side of the river, 300 m (984 ft) up to the pretty town of Coroico, where you can find a relatively inexpensive hotel with swimming pool. This same hike can be done by mountain bike with a tour company. For more information on the Yungas region visit http://www.enjoybolivia.com/english/what-new/la-paz-valley-yungas.shtml.

Hike 5

Take a mini-bus marked Ovejuyo-Tranca in the direction of the Zona Sur. Get off at the *tranca* (police checkpoint) above Ovejuyo (past the Zona Sur). Continue up the road until your eyes get a double blast of white from the pointed Illimani and the flat-peaked Mururata. Descend through the agricultural Valle de las Animas, veer right at a junction in the village of Huni, and you'll descend over an ancient Inca trail into the magnificent Palca Canyon, where, in the shade of natural ramparts, you'll weave over a meandering stream. An occasional mini-bus now roughs it through here, but that's an infrequent event. Pay attention for an odd complex of farm buildings up to the left. That's the exit out of the canyon for the uphill stretch to the old mining river town of Palca. From Palca, return to La Paz by mini-bus from the central plaza. (Alternatively, the road outside of Palca winds up to the town of Ventilla, near the beginning of the longer Taquesi trek.)

To measure the safety factor, I've done all these hikes at least twice, in the dry season only! To do them in a day, you must begin early. Although I've done it, you should not hike alone.

From La Paz, you don't have to go far to find the rough and primitive.

Chacaltaya, Bolivia's only ski resort, was excluded from this list because, at 5,100 m (17,000 ft), it will leave you literally breathless. Says writer and ski enthusiast Gary Rosenberger: "Even bunny runs have a way of becoming booby traps the closer they get to outer space."

FROM HIGHLAND TO JUNGLE: ALTERNATIVE CITIES

A comparative description of Bolivia's other major cities will help sort out the pros and cons of life away from the 'Big Agora.' Each city is outlined according to altitude, population, climate, distinguishing features, assets and liabilities.

Potosí

At 4,070 m (13,350 ft) above sea level it looks like a valley and acts like a valley but wins the prize for the highest city in the world. In the year 1545, silver was discovered and by 1650, Potosí was the largest city in the Western Hemisphere. Today, with the decline of the mining industry, and with aluminium having defeated tin, its other resource, in the industrial arena, Potosí's dwindling population has now levelled off at about 110,000.

Potosí exemplifies the functioning of colonial and neo-colonial economies. From its heyday of silver mining to its tin boom during the middle of the 20th century, Potosí had 400 years to change from an exporter of raw material (the bottom of the economic totem pole) to an exporter of value added products. It never made the transition.

Its three tin barons, led by the Frenchified Simón Patiño, were vilified in the Revolution of 1952 for having sent Bolivia's mining wealth abroad. Yet, after the nationalisation of the mines in 1953, this country continued to dig up its riches and send them abroad. The tragically glorious and corroded Cerro Rico that overlooks the city is the imagistic testimony of this plunder. Between the mid-1500s and Bolivia's independence in the third decade of the 19th century, eight million miners of African and Indian descent died working under brutal conditions in the mines.

Of the silver extracted from the Américas by the Spanish colonisers, 80 per cent came from Cerro Rico alone, from this one rugged hill. Grated with hues of deep orange, Cerro Rico still contains operating mine shafts. Fleeing this depressed area, many ex-miners have relocated to the Chapare to farm coca leaves, after the promised post-layoff jobs were never delivered by the government. But most of Potosí's fierce residents are sticking it out, defying the harsh winter cold of highland nights. They have purposely built in bends in streets such as the narrow Calle Quijarro, a block from the market, in order to break the force of wind gusts.

Not So Cold
"The cold in Potosí is overrated," says Jaime, a former zinc miner and now attorney. "Potosí is mild compared to what you are dealt in the winter in the United States."

Today, many Potosínos work their own mining collectives, extracting zinc and gold under precarious conditions. Largely a Quechua city, a significant Creole population has an

Façade of San Lorenzo Church, Potosí—Spanish Baroque and indigenous Andean art converge.

understanding of the Quechua language but is separated by class and cultural barriers.

Potosí's depressing history contradicts the beauty of its colonial architecture, highlighted by the Casa Real de la Moneda (Royal Mint), whose only imperfection is the incongruous French mask of Bacchus hanging over an archway. People who hate museums will be thrilled by Casa Real de la Moneda. The old wooden minting machines and the circular ruts in the stone floor made by burros and humans used as beasts of burden who propelled them are a central attraction in a structure of various stone mosaic patios and colonial balconies.

An array of primitive coins will make coin collectors levitate in ecstasy. The museum's colonial art, highlighting the work of Holguín, contains a treasure of anonymous mestizo paintings. Painted by indigenous artists, these works sneak Andean motifs into the mould of the Spanish baroque style of the times.

Museum Musts

A cast of venerable museums and convents provides an escort for the Casa Real de la Moneda. The Museo Universitario is a must for lovers of modern art, pottery and cultural artefacts.

Churches with elaborate baroque façades, wooden and wrought iron balconies overlooking narrow cobblestone streets and orange colonial tile roofing make Potosí an outdoor museum. The stone carved façade of the San Lorenzo Church is a brilliant example of indigenous motifs adapted into a classic baroque design.

Sensorial contact with Potosí's arduous history is accessible through tours that descend mine shafts. Don't expect Disneyland stylisation; the horrors will be real. A 20-minute bus ride will take you to the Pailabiri tin mining encampment, where, after paying an entrance fee, you'll be given protective gear, boots and lamps. You'll get to feel the humid tunnels and the intense heat, up to 45°C (113°F) which obligates miners to strip down for work. Only the toughest of men could survive the bizarre contrast between the stifling heat of the mine and the furious cold outside the pits, at an inhumane altitude of 4,500 m (nearly 15,000 ft).

A visit to a cooperative silicosis mine is recommended for the most masochistic of tourists. Check ahead of time to make sure someone is not dynamiting in his own little niche of the shaft. Mining is a strong family tradition, and most of the miners you meet are friendly fatalists. Tour companies that sponsor inexpensive visits to the mines also contribute to miners' clinics and health expenses.

In the depth of the Potosí winter, a quick, two-hour ride (three hours by bus) to Sucre's high valley eternal spring climate will be therapeutic. Potosí also serves as base camp for a visit to Bolivia's version of the 'Great Salt Lake,' the spectral Salar de Uyuni.

Potosí was named as a World Heritage Site by UNESCO, in tribute to its exquisite colonial architecture and the living remnants of its tragic history.

The human cost of massive layoffs in the mining industry, Potosí's primary liability, is embedded in the stoic suffering of its people today. I expected to find a sombre city, yet nights on Calle Bolívar have a festival atmosphere, as throngs of cheerful strollers defy all pessimism. Potosí's winter nights with no central heating and its inhumane altitude only serve to make its residents more resilient.

Perhaps no place in the world offers such a contradictory mix of beauty and affliction. The 'city of contrasts' cliche, which is true for most places on the globe, is an understatement when referring to the sad yet cheerful city of Potosí.

El Alto

Can a squatters' settlement be converted into a city? Just above the rim of La Paz, El Alto attempts to answer in the affirmative. Even the name El Alto (the High Place) doesn't sound like a city. At 4,018 m (13,180 ft) you don't get a break in the altitude. At least Potosí has the protection of wind-breaking hills.

El Alto's embattled inhabitants, mostly indigenous Aymaras who have immigrated from the country, receive the extra punishment of an occasional light snow on a frigid winter's night and sometimes even in summer.

El Alto is the Tijuana of Bolivia, a stop-off point for immigrants searching for a better life in the metropolis. There is no border patrol between the ridge that separates this city and La Paz, but many arriving pilgrims end up imprisoned in this settlement that has sprawled out anarchistically over the Altiplano with endless, half finished redbrick monuments to frustrated ambitions. The city spills beyond its haphazard infrastructure into rutty dirt streets with open sewers.

Blending within El Alto's population are invisible people who have no birth certificates and no identification cards, and who, when they die, often prematurely, are buried in clandestine cemeteries. Officially, they never existed.

Sometimes El Alto pioneers buy a cheap piece of land, begin their house brick by brick, then discover that the same plot has been sold several times over. In El Alto hospitals you may have to bring your own medicine and supplies if you expect full service. Clandestine El Alto butchers slaughter pigs without government inspection. A slow and silent catastrophe awaits arriving settlers.

Internal immigration from Bolivia's more desperate rural areas has inflated El Alto's population, which is now approaching a million.

El Alto's more fortunate indigenous and Cholo residents make the long commute to La Paz to work as domestics, bricklayers and day labourers. Llojeta, a panoramic highway that winds down to La Paz's affluent south zone bypassing upper La Paz, opens low wage employment opportunities for El Alto residents in the Zona Sur.

El Alto's main consolation is its dramatic view of the snow covered *cordillera* (mountain range). Magnificent Illimani bulges from this vantage point like a glowing, white robed Buddha on the horizon. In the opposite direction, El Alto is a quick drive to Lake Titicaca and the ruins of Tiahuanaco.

These features are not enough to diminish El Alto's emerging gangs, abandoned children who become addicted to sniffing paint thinner and freelance prostitutes who avoid weekly medical check-ups. The alienation of displacement from agricultural roots has stimulated a proliferation of honkytonk bars catering to alcoholics.

Alteños Suffer Too
The late El Compadre Carlos Palenque would listen to the misfortunes of the suffering masses who visited his populist television programme, *La Tribuna Libre del Pueblo*, and would refer them to medical, legal or social services. But when one confused Alteño exhibited the wounds from a beating from an employer, a frustrated and impotent Palenque exhorted him to return to his farming community.

And yet El Alto has become the epicentre of change in Bolivia. El Alto residents have overcome every obstacle in the Book of Impossibility, very much thanks to a grass roots organisation that sprung forth from traditional Aymara community democracy, under the banner of FEJUVE (La Federación de Juntas Vecinales, roughly, Federation of Neighbourhood Committees). Today, FEJUVE continues the struggle for natural gas control and for water rights (that

ENJOYING BOLIVIA 185

began with the La Coordinadora in Cochabamba in 2000). La Coordinadora had an identifiable spokesman but in El Alto it is difficult to identify any one leader. At any moment, a new face may rise to the surface in community assemblies, through charged debate that outside observers would think were out of control.

Without fixed leaders, FEJUVE gets the job done, to the extent that it served as the catalyst for the social movement that led to the expulsion of president Sánchez de Lozada in 2003.

Roberta, a Chola resident of El Alto.

FEJUVE's Aymara identity has an historical antecedent in the 1781 anti-colonial milicias of Tupac Katari, whose command centre was in what is today known as El Alto, and who conducted a siege of La Paz from this strategic point 4,000 m (13,123 ft) above sea level. But it was not until the 1940s, following the establishment of railroad and airforce installations, that landowners parceled out their holdings and anarchic urbanisation began. As late as 1952, there were only 11,000 inhabitants on this high plain outpost.

The development of urban committees that would eventually coalesce around FEJUVE was based on rural Aymara social structures. Three approximate zones developed and partly merged, one mainly of rural migrants from the Altiplano (north), who practiced artisan and commercial trades, another with larger commercial interests, including public services (centre) and the other based primarily on light industry (south) with significant numbers of migrants from other regions of Bolivia.

The foundation for FEJUVE's activism was set out in 1959 when locals began to demand the installation of basic services, and when unanswered, would take matters into their own hands, with electricity and water and other services connected by neighbourhood volunteers. These ad hoc neighbourhood organisations merged into FEJUVE in 1966.

In later years, FEJUVE began to participate with the COR (Central Obrera Regional or 'Regional Workers Central') and with national mobilisations such as the 1985 March for Life led by miners.

You wouldn't know it by observing meetings during crisis time but FEJUVE does have an executive committee which incorporates local neighbourhood committees. The crucial link between leadership and neighbourhoods are weekly or monthly assemblies, and it appears as if the executive committee primarily carries out the will of the neighbourhoods. In theory, members should not carry the agenda of political parties and women should have an equal role in decision making, but some critics from within allege that both of these rules are not strictly adhered to.

Visually, El Alto would need major renewal to match the conditions of a war torn Bosnian city. A silent war of survival is raging in El Alto, including myriad heroic acts that do not meet the eye, with various NGOs attending to some of the needs of the mentally and physically impaired, the destitute and unemployed youth.

El Alto's altitude, its highland frost and its shaky or nonexistent infrastructure are serious liabilities. Its petty crime rate is juiced up by heavy drinking. But as the epicentre of social change, El Alto is now a source of hope and many down-and-outers have been able to compensate for their grinding poverty by engaging in the good fight. For more information visit

Oruro

If La Paz, Potosí and El Alto have not met with your approval, this cool Altiplano city of 160,000 inhabitants, at 3,702 m (12,140 ft), is your last chance for life at the top before we descend to the eternal spring, high valley cities.

In Latin America, sometimes the most taciturn, melancholic and distressed places engage in the most intense and passionate annual festivals. Oruro is Bolivia's unofficial folk capital, with a yearly Carnaval in late February, featuring La Diablada, an ornate mestizo allegory in which masked dancers act out the victory of good over evil. Carnaval is no ordinary parade; it is a total experience, and the audience is just as entertaining as the impressive dancers.

Like Potosí, Oruro has been hit hard by the decline of the mining industry. Visits to mines, the old Patiño mansion and a mining museum, make this history come alive. The tin mines around Oruro made Patiño the wealthiest man in the world, but no one knew about trickle down economics at the time and most of Patiño's profits were siphoned off to Europe.

Other features of Oruro include an interesting Museum of Anthropology and the old fashioned Palais Concert cinema, with its stone Rodinesque mask hanging over the entrance. Outside the small city, delicious *pejerrey* (kingfish) are waiting to be caught beneath wading flamingos in nearby Lake Uru Uru, a 3 km (1.8 mile) walk from the university.

When I bring up the subject of Oruro to my Bolivian friends, the consensus adjective is 'sombre.' In one couple's Oruro ordeal, the husband, with a well paying, prestigious job, suffered from such a potent case of 'culture shock Oruro' that he'd drive to La Paz every weekend for an escape. Finally, against the material needs of his family, he ditched his Oruro job and took a lesser position in another city.

His friends believe he was never willing to give the closed society of Oruro a chance. Sometimes, a place that seems more insular simply requires more time in order to establish rapport with the locals. Learning to play an indigenous instrument (the *zampoña* is easier than the *charango* or *quena*) or getting involved in Oruro's fervent football tradition, are two possible bridges in communication.

Various foreign visitors to Bolivia interviewed for this book have testified with delight that, from the indigenous highlands to the primeval jungles, seemingly impenetrable cultural barriers break down when they play football with the locals.

Oruro is neither as picturesque as Sucre nor as culturally stimulating as Potosí, but in my short stay, I had nothing but positive experiences. If you get lucky, you'll find *peña* music or several legendary women cooks who've been selling homemade food from stalls at the market (*see Restaurants-Oruro in the* Resource Guide *at the back of the book*).

Oruro is the gateway to the Salar de Uyuni, the world's highest saltlake, twice as large as its counterpart in Utah. Get there by bus or if you've got more time, a picturesque railroad. The Salar has a split personality. In the dry season, it defines the meaning of infinity. If the rains are fierce and the lake reappears, other-worldly reflections will give you a natural high. You're above the treeline. Our friend, the artist Walter Solón Romero, originally from the railroad town of Uyuni, went through most of his childhood without knowing what it was like to touch a tree. His boundless imagination may have been nurtured by so much emptiness.

HIGH VALLEY CITIES

Many millions of years ago, Bolivian dinosaurs made a clever decision to bypass both cold Altiplano and steamy lowlands and instead hang out in the year-round spring climates of the high valleys. Dinosaur fossil footprints have been found precisely in areas near Bolivia's three main high valley cities: Sucre, Cochabamba and Tarija.

Sucre

If aesthetic surroundings are your primary motivation in choosing an ideal place, this 'city of four names' is arguably the prettiest city site in Bolivia. At last, we have descended to the eternal spring altitude, where the breathing is easier, at 2,790 m (9,150 ft).

Sucre is a city of only 150,000 inhabitants, but in name it is the capital of Bolivia, hosting an annual symbolic legislative session and maintaining the seat of the Supreme Court. Sucre's political influence dates back to 1825, when Liberator Antonio José de Sucre drafted a declaration of Bolivian sovereignty, with the belated approval of his boss, Simón Bolívar. At various times in its history, this city has been called Charcas, La Plata and Chuquisaca, with the latter name still used today.

Aesthetically oriented locals are secretly happy that La Paz has become the de facto capital, liberating Sucre from the contradictions of hyper-urbanisation.

Culturally, Sucre exerts more influence than its size; it is the site of the Universidad de San Javier, founded a quarter of a century before Harvard, in 1624.

Sucre's colonial splendour is enhanced by a government edict requiring all structures in the central city to be painted white or annually whitewashed. Contrasting with varying shades of white are the black wrought iron and carved wood balconies and the heartwarming orange tile roofing. Float into a Zen trance by gazing down on the city from La Recoleta Convent's stone mosaic plaza.

A more people oriented spot for observing life is a bench in the wooded Plaza 25 de Mayo, where one can watch university students, Quechua vendors and children playing on the bronze lions surrounding the monument to Mariscal Sucre. Every night, but especially at weekends, the Plaza becomes a true community gathering place, the type of downtown that has been foolishly dislodged in suburbanised cities. Students and families with children flood the park, strolling over its

Folk group, Raza Milenaria, singing in a Sucre *peña*.

mosaic walks, cavorting, chatting and reading on benches under street lamps until past midnight.

As a daytime gathering place, nearby Parque Bolívar rivals the Plaza. A wide variety of trees satisfies nature lovers. Children are amused by boat rides, games and climbing bars in the form of a mini Eiffel Tower.

Some years ago, a 'guerrilla gardener' attacked both the Plaza 25 de Mayo and later Parque Bolívar by secretly planting marijuana. He or she was never caught.

Sucre's horticulture is complemented by its salon culture. There is a German Goethe Institute, an Alliance Française and three university museums covering colonial to modern art and anthropology. Colonial Sucre's old convents and churches are the foundation of its architectural unity.

Popular culture can be appreciated at the Mercado Campesino (Peasants' Market). Any one of the restaurants in and around the Plaza may offer a *peña* on a weekend night. In particular, Arco Iris's interactive *peña* eliminates the boundary between musicians and audience. As in Mississippi's blues juke joints, people from the audience may rise and dance in any available space of floor, to a group like Raza Milenaria, which plays music from all regions of Bolivia. In the uninhibited musical atmosphere of Arco Iris, foreigners and Bolivians find a common ground.

A major feature of Sucre, rarely mentioned in travel guides, is the presence in many government buildings, the university and the normal school, of grand historical murals by Bolivia's great 20th century artist, the late Walter Solón Romero. Solón, who grew up in the barren Uyuni and had never seen a tree until late childhood, arrived in Sucre after being the sole survivor of a plane crash in Chile. During his year-long recovery period, from his hospital bed, he organised the arts collective Grupo Anteo. Solón's and Anteo's murals, in the genre of the Mexican muralists, are Sucre icons.

Sucre's slower pace makes it a better hangout city than La Paz, with unusual and sometimes bookish cafés and taverns at or near the Plaza 25 de Mayo, including the multipurpose Joy Ride Cafe, La Repizza (good food), Tertulias Coffee Bar Restaurant, Bibliocafé and at the nearby Alianza Francesa,

La Taverne, moderately priced considering the fine food and cosy atmosphere. Too bad that the outdoor seating so typical of Cochabamba establishments is not found on Sucre's narrower streets.

Sucre's liability? Commercially eclipsed by La Paz, Sucre may be a bit too placid for folks who demand lots of action. For a side visit 65 km (40 miles) away, enjoy the Mercado Campesino of Tarabuco, especially for the richly colourful textiles. A quicker escape is the hour-and-a-half pilgrimage trail through shady woods to the top of the hill above La Recoleta.

Cochabamba

The bus from La Paz stops at the final summit before its spiralling descent into Cochabamba. The passenger peers down from the rim of a precipice over an immense and jagged cavity into a city grid three hours below—Cochabamba, sweeping out over the only flat space in sight.

The open space of Cochabamba, a wider and deeper hole in the Andes, alleviates cases of La Paz-triggered agoraphobia and other more exotic maladies such as hyper-asymmetry syndrome. With my first stroll through Cochabamba's expansive parks, bicycle-friendly streets and alternate routes that elude congestion, I identify with the mouse that has just been released from a maze.

Once nicknamed 'The Garden City' and still referred to as the breadbasket of Bolivia, Cochabamba has been stricken in recent years by a drought so prolonged that the city's once voluminous river has dried to a trickle.

Yet coming from La Paz, I was impressed by the greenery on Cochabamba's wide boulevards and in its large parks. On 24 September 1995, Cochabamba made a symbolic commitment by declaring Ecology Day and prohibiting the use of private vehicles for the day. Shortly after, as if responding to the declaration, the summer rains arrived, with more zeal than in previous years.

The word 'water' has been the mantra of most local residents in recent years, and triggered massive uprisings in 2000. The 'Water War' (*detailed in Chapter Two, Overview of Land and History)* eventually led to the expulsion of a Bechtel-led group of privatising companies that had hiked water prices beyond the budget of the average Cochabamba resident.

Cochabamba's warm days, and its cool nights so ideal for those who like to sleep under a comforting quilt, are the result of its 2,570 m (8,430 ft) altitude. Lacking a profusion of tourist attractions compared to Sucre or Potosí, this city of nearly half a million inhabitants is just a good place to be.

One of the best ways to 'be' in Cochabamba is on a bicycle. No need for a 10-speeder; Cochabamba's mountains have moved back to allow space for its flat streets.

Cochabamba's most captivating feature is the Centro Cultural Pedagógico, also known as Palacio de Portales, a mansion of the infamous tin mogul Simón Patiño, which houses an exciting museum of modern art, a fine reference library and totally preserved interiors. Designed by French architect Eugene Bilaut to satisfy a whim of the Frenchified Patiño, the mansion also hosts concerts and lectures, in the shadow of the mini-Versailles gardens that embellish the mansion. The Alliance Française and Goethe Institute complement the cultural ambience.

Cochabamba is known for the best open-air markets in Bolivia, called *canchas* from the Quechua. The best view of the central city is from above, looking down on the intricate tile patterns of its roofing. Try the view from the towering statue of Cristo Rey, on a hill just outside of the city. You can't miss it.

Cochabamba's Plaza 14 de Septiembre is a refreshing hangout, surrounded by colonial arcades and a cathedral collage of diverse architectural styles. Various churches and convents, including San Francisco, Santa Teresa and Santo Domingo, help save the city from reckless modernisation, but Cochabamba has long ago abandoned the architectural unity that characterises Sucre.

> Hiking in the nearby Parque Nacional Tunari's forested slopes above the city, one encounters small waterfalls, wildflowers and trout lagoons. This park is more developed and accessible than the usual Bolivian national parks. Surprise: it has a picnic area and a playground!

Breathing is easy, the air warm and fresh, and the blend of modern urban life, colonial ambience and the Quechua heritage is hard to beat, if you don't mind fewer cultural activities in comparison with La Paz.

The park at Plaza Colón is an attractive stop-off, although locals warned us to take extra care of our belongings there at nights. Gangs of children, called *polillas* (moths) reputedly lurch in the trees. The only fringe activity we saw there during several night promenades was a lone street walker trying in vain to flag down a customer.

Cochabamba is about six hours from La Paz via a comfortable bus ride. On our trip we were treated to an old Pedro Infante Mexican film and a Bollywood romance on the in-bus monitor. Bus fares are quite economical. By air, it's only a 35-minute trip. Cochabamba serves as Bolivia's neutral ground; since it is neither lowland nor Altiplano, it remains aloof from regional antagonism between Cambas and Kollas.

Cochabamba's liabilities include occasional cholera outbreaks and a nagging drought, and the region is not exempt from floods when the rains come. Cholera is avoided by boiling drinking water, cooking vegetables and maintaining normal sanitary habits.

Exciting sidetrips are numerous and include scaling the 5,035 m (16,519 ft) Cerro Tunari (with a base camp about 25 km/15.5 miles from the city), the Fiesta of the Virgin of Urkupiña in nearby Quillacollo (15–18 August), the Macchu Picchu-like ruins of Incallajta (132 km/82 miles east of the city) and the Toro Toro National Park with its fossils, caves, waterfalls, ruins and dinasaur tracks (198 km/123 miles south-east of the city). With the exception of Quillacollo, access to these exciting places is difficult and a formalised tour is recommended.

Tarija

This lowest and warmest of Bolivia's high valley cities dozes at 1,924 m (6,310 ft) in southern Bolivia near the Argentine border. Dr Gustavo Zubieta Castillo laments that this Andalucia-like paradise of 60,000 inhabitants has passed from the acoustic to the electronic age, sacrificing its romantic heritage. But those of us from New York, Sydney or London will still find a rural Mediterranean soul, including long afternoon rest periods, in this clean and friendly city of festivals. The Iglesia de San Roque is the Eiffel Tower of Tarija, watching the city from a hill—the best balcony in town. Other impressive views are found in the gardens of Iglesia de San Juan and at Mirador (lookout) de San Juan, a student hangout.

Other features of Tarija include its festivals, whose musical harmonies are brighter and more joyous to Western ears than their Altiplano counterpart, palaeontological sites and wineries. The Museo de Arqueología y Paleontología features an overview of the region's ancient animal heritage, a prelude to treks in the Tarija ravines and badlands, with their profusion of prehistoric animal fossils.

Should you make a discovery of consequence, the Archeology and Palaeontology Museum should be advised. Access to prehistoric fossils is much less complicated here in Tarija than it is in Cochabamba and Sucre. The dinosaur tracks at Torotoro are 120 km (74 miles) from Cochabamba while the Fancesa Cement Factory's dinosaur quarry is not far from Sucre. Meanwhile, a taxi ride to Tarija's fossil areas costs only US$ 1.

Tarija's wineries may be worth a visit for connoisseurs. Most Bolivians swallow their national pride and drink wines from loathed Chile, but a few of Tarija's delicate wines deserve more credit.

Tarija's main liability is its remoteness. Cowboys are still found amongst the Chapacos, and Tarija's tidy streets will not evolve into cosmopolitan pandemonium for years to come, in spite of the laments of Dr Zubieta.

In recent years, moneyed interests in the gas-rich Department of Tarija have formed a united front with those of Santa Cruz, with Prefect Mario Cossio expecting to negotiate energy integration agreements with neighbouring Argentina, Paraguay and Chile. Both Departments were informed by the central at the end of January 2006 that natural gas is a federal resource and only the government can negotiate its exploitation.

Once in Tarija, you're not far from Tupiza, a small but cultivated railroad town at nearly 3,000 m (9842 ft) above sea level surrounded by rough and colourful badlands.

LOWLAND CITIES
Santa Cruz

Santa Cruz is Bolivia's gateway to the sparsely inhabited tropical lowlands, various protected national parks and the Chaco plains. With 1,140,000 inhabitants this cosmopolitan city on the edge of the wild has about a sixth of Bolivia's population. The combination of its low altitude and proximity to the equator should make for sultry weather year round. But in Bolivia's May-through-October dry season, chilly *surazo* winds may slash away the Santa Cruz heat. The region is not exempt from an occasional winter torrent, but humidity during this relatively dry period remains tolerable.

A thriving agricultural region, Santa Cruz has also grown as an industrial centre. Cruceños have a reputation for being more entrepreneurial than Paceños. With more than a fifth of Bolivia's largest companies based here, Santa Cruz may be surpassing La Paz as a business hub.

Santa Cruz is a three-ring city, with its inner *anillo* (ring) containing most of the city's highlights. Its second and third rings are mainly residential or industrial. Bolivia's premier hotel resort, Los Tajibos, is cast way out in the third ring.

Santa Cruz has Bolivia's best zoo, a fine art museum (Casa de la Cultura Museo de Arte), an insect exhibit (what better place than in the tropics) at the Natural History Museum and a profusion of parks and gardens.

The Santa Cruz region is a montage of totally diverse and sometimes contradictory cultures and subcultures, including Mennonite farmers who wear Pennsylvania outfits in tropical heat, Sikhs from India, Okinawans and a fertile movement of environmental activists acting as an alternative to a conformist culture of 400 beauty pageants.

Defenders of the environment are invited to visit the office of the Asociación Ecológica del Oriente (ASEO), 681 Cristóbal de Mendoza Avenue. Over a cup of coffee with

ASEO's executive director, young and dynamic María Teresa Vargas, I learned of the frightful use of illegal pesticides, whose importation to Bolivia involves international accomplices from countries where the same pesticides are also banned.

Vargas tells of a Santa Cruz man who used the banned DDT to murder his three children and then committed suicide. "Many peasants employ no protective measures when using these illegal poisons," she says. "Some actually mix the stuff with their hands."

Tourist books often refer to the exotic sloths who live in the trees in Santa Cruz's Plaza 24 de Septiembre. Vargas explains that the sloths' inadequate diet leaves them too weak to sustain themselves on the branches of trees. Some have fallen to their deaths. Others are run over by automobiles.

> **The Plight of Sloths**
> Plaza 24 de Septiembre is frequently the scene of protest marches and strikes. When the authorities repress these demonstrations with toxic tear gas, the sloths have no way to flee.

Ecologists are lured to Santa Cruz because of its proximity to the virgin Amboró National Park, which has been relatively successful in repelling those who would wish to rape her hidden natural treasures. The Amboró National Park covers an area of over 630,000 hectares, within three distinct ecosystems: the Amazon Basin, the Chaco scrubland and the cloudforest foothills of the Andes. Both highland and lowland species of flora and fauna prosper in the park. At least 700 species of birds have been identified as native residents of Amboró. Monkeys, peccaries, capybaras, jaguars, ocelots and the rare spectacled bear make this their home. It's a place to become goggle-eyed over virgin rainforest, natural swimming holes and numerous waterfalls coming from tributaries of the Yapacani and Surutu Rivers.

Once you get to the park, don't expect Yosemite-like amenities. But at least it is accessible, only three hours from

Santa Cruz, just off the main highway to Cochabamba. Santa Cruz travel agencies sponsor tours of the park.

Santa Cruz also functions as a convenient base camp to the European Jesuit missions and the ruins of Samaipata. Jesuits from Bavaria, Bohemia and Switzerland organised indigenous communities between 1720 and 1760, and the missions have been declared Patrimony of Humanity by UNESCO. Seven different towns continue to use the mission temples, preserving their unique wood-carved architecture.

The ruins of Samaipata have been radiocarbon dated at around 1500 BC. They are located at the comfortable altitude of 1,650 m (5,413 ft), 120 km (74 miles) from Santa Cruz.

Amboró, the Jesuit missions and Samaipata are not about to become Club-Med centres. An enlightened breed of tourists seek out these places and visitor facilities are improving.

Back in the city, several *peña-pubs* (folk music pubs) can be found not far from the Plaza. Foreigners feel at home here, enjoying the best Bolivian music in town.

Reports of isolated cases of cholera require the usual preventive health measures. Nasty microbes that would not survive on the Altiplano take kindly to the tropical heat of Santa Cruz. Some Bolivians arrive here and go straight to the Los Tajibos resort and stay in the refreshing pools, never venturing downtown or into the wild.

The winter dry season is the best time to avoid the steamy hazards of this exciting city.

The current issue around Santa Cruz is regional autonomy. The Pro Santa Cruz Civic Committee presided over by businessman Ruben Costas is the hotbed of autonomy sentiment. Creole Santa Cruz is seen by regionalists as subsidising 'Indian' Bolivia. In fact, the city of Santa Cruz generates 38 per cent of state tax revenue while the much-maligned indigenous La Paz produces 45 per cent.

Racism is perceived by highland Kollas as an undercurrent of the Santa Cruz autonomy movement, an allegation denied by Camba leaders. However, the rightwing groups Nacion Camba and Juventud Cruceñista have been accused of beating up indigenous demonstrators from the Landless

Peasants Movement, as if they were shock troops for large landowners.

Autonomy advocates boast the presence of natural gas reserves in their department, but in fact, most of these reserves are in the Chaco, whose Guarani inhabitants have supported Kolla demands for nationalisation of gas. In all there are 11 different original ethnic groups dispersed throughout the Department of Santa Cruz.

The Kolla Evo Morales won more than 30 per cent of the presidential vote in Santa Cruz, and anti-racists claim this as proof that the autonomy movement is simply an exclusive capitalist movement. Nacion Camba, whose motto is Camba Fatherland or Death, discounts the argument, claiming that all three major candidates were from the highlands and votes were not so much for Morales as against the traditional parties.

At the centre of Santa Cruz autonomy is the soy agribusiness which boomed in the mid-1980s thanks to subsidies from La Paz. According to agrarian expert Miguel Urioste, most soy producers are Mennonites from Canada, Japanese from Okinawa, Brazilians and assimilated Kolla colonisers.

Meanwhile, environmentalists have been warning the public that genetically modified soy is in the works.

Trinidad and Cobija

Two other tropical lowland cities also serve as gateways to the jungle. As previously detailed, Trinidad, population over 40,000, capital of the Beni Department, is the base for Fremen's jungle tours.

A mere 14 km (9 miles) from Trinidad, one can visit Chuchini, a little known ecological centre run by the dedicated Hinojosa family, built in the vicinity of a pre-columbian mound that was part of a vast man-made agricultural drainage system. Chuchini's ma-and-pa caretakers can orient you to piranha fishing, ancient artefacts, observation of jungle animals (crocodiles, wading birds, monkeys), tropical lagoons and cleared hiking trails. The dry season is preferred but in the rainy season there's access by motorised canoe. This centre is part of a protected area. For years, Efrem Hinojosa had been promised financial help in caring for wildlife that was sent to him from the local zoo, but the help never came. An overworked Hinojosa was bitten by a zoo animal, provoking a heart attack. He recovered, and perhaps the shock of the event triggered the local university to provide the help he well deserved.

Cobija, capital of the forlorn Department of Pando, may hold the record as a capital city with the lowest population—9,000. Cobija's greatest distinction is its role as port of entry to Brazil. The Department of Pando, to the extreme north of Bolivia, would be an ideal site for a frontier film portraying the dramatic and violent rubber boom in the early years of the 20th century. Rubber from Malaysia would replace the Brazilian and Bolivian variety, and then synthetic varieties further diminished the business, which has been replaced by another gathering enterprise, Brazil nuts: hardly the right trademark for this native Bolivian product.

BOLIVIA PLAYS HARD TO GET
Travel in Bolivia

In his *Holidays in Hell*, P J O'Rourke writes: 'Like most people who don't own Bermuda shorts, I'm bored by ordinary travel.' There is nothing ordinary about travel in Bolivia. At least 13 distinct life zones, from the highest cities and lakes in the world, to green valleys and gorges of eternal spring, to the steamiest jungles, are separated by the roughest and most inaccessible terrain imaginable.

To the geographic barriers, add human barriers: three major nations within a nation, Hispanic, Aymara, Quechua and a host of other smaller nations/languages, including the Guaraní and the Afrobolivians.

Bolivia is only beginning to create an infrastructure of highways, hotels and restaurants that will facilitate access to many of her remote villages and stunning backlands. The obscene altitude of Potosí, La Paz and Lake Titicaca also discourages classical tourism. There are three broad categories for adventure travel.

First, there are the virtually inaccessible parts of Bolivia which contain Inca ruins waiting to be unearthed, prehistoric fossils, yet-to-be-discovered bird, animal and plant species and indigenous communities where savvy inhabitants have deciphered many of nature's mysteries. These are places that proclaim 'I dare you!' to the most intrepid adventurers.

A second category includes similar natural and cultural treasures that used to be unaccessible but are now within reach through organised eco- and ethno-tourism.

Mount Illimani presides over El Alto like a robed Buddha.

Finally, there are larger cities, rural paradises and impressive ruins of ancient civilisations, easily accessible via highway or air, but still offering fulfilling discoveries and culturally rewarding human contact.

This leg of our Bolivian adventure shares all three types of experience. Beginning with the most inaccessible, we shall see how untrained, non-professional adventurers have crossed over prohibited thresholds into places reserved for the gods.

Can a Non-Professional Reach the Peak of Mount Illimani?

Peter Hutchison came to Bolivia by accident. Back in England, he had earned a degree in Latin American studies, yet in all of his courses, there was no mention of Bolivia.

"It's amazing to me," he explains, "just how absent Bolivia is from international awareness. It's a brilliant secret."

Peter was staying in Lima, Peru when friends of his decided to travel to La Paz. Peter has never baulked at exploring a new place, and the possibility of employment at an English-language weekly called *Bolivian Times* made the trip up into the Andes even more appealing.

Life at the edge.

ENJOYING BOLIVIA 203

"The first view of La Paz from El Alto is enough to blow your socks off," Peter exclaims with joy. Capping off the extraordinary panorama is the snow-covered Mount Illimani. "For me," Peter continues, "La Paz is the most impressive city, location-wise, in the world, even more so than Hong Kong. It's the mountain that does it for me."

Peter eventually got the newspaper gig, and a room with a view in the Alto Sopocachi neighbourhood, part ways up the side of the gorge leading to El Alto.

"From my porch you can see the richest and poorest people in Latin America," he pointed out. "But the *barriadas* of Lima are more depressing; poor people in the hills of La Paz can go down to the centre of town, grab a piece of sidewalk and sell something. They have an outlet.

"Everywhere I went, I had a different view of Illimani," he continued. "It was right there, and it kind of had to be done. For it to take so much of my attention, I had to meet it in person." Peter had always wanted to climb a real mountain. He'd made it to the top of a smaller mountain in Ecuador, but Illimani was the ultimate challenge.

Yossi, a fellow Englishman working as a climbing guide in Bolivia, explained to Peter that a good guide won't climb a mountain for you. He can only help you avoid problems.

Those problems were formidable. Deep crevasses crossed only by a daring leap. A 45 degree ice wall. And an invisible enemy: the altitude.

Climbing Mount Illimani

La Paz itself is already 3,600 m (11,811 ft) above sea level, higher than many of the world's mountains. "In the beginning," Peter advises, "you have to get plenty of rest as you get accustomed to the altitude."

Base camp is at 4,400 m (14,435 ft), and "the second the sun goes down, you'd freeze if it were not for the five-season sleeping bag."

The real climbing begins on the walk up to Nest of the Condors, at 5,500 m (18,044 ft). "There," Peter warns, "you really start feeling the lack of oxygen. Climbing up slate outcrops, it gets steep in parts."

The second night of camp, climbers melt snow for a water supply. "You sleep cradling your jar of water to stop it from freezing. If you left it exposed, it would freeze and the hour or two it took to melt the snow would be wasted.

"The second morning we woke up at 2:00 am to avoid slush and fragile ice. I had muesli for breakfast. Unless there's a full moon, you have to use a head torch. You don't sleep very well because of the altitude. The lack of oxygen causes eerie dreams."

Peter's guide was able to take deep breaths that would switch his body off for five to seven seconds at a time. "I thought he was about to die, but it's a way for the body to conserve energy by breathing less."

On the night prior to the third and final day of ascent, one can see La Paz, 57 km (35 miles) away as "a little hole in the ground, bursting with light." There is awe in Peter's voice; he is right there on the mountain, reliving the experience.

The third day is called Summit Day. It's snow on the ground from then on, but the dry season, from June through August, pretty much assures that there will be no blizzards. No one should climb Illimani in the wet season.

"Both of us were struggling with our mental state, especially after we reached what we thought was the summit, only to discover it was a false summit: at 6,462 m (21,200 ft). One hundred more metres (328 ft) to climb doesn't seem like much in the abstract, but they were the longest 100 m of my life.

"The brain is still thinking on the basis of what the body is capable of doing, but physically your body is no longer capable. The brain is groping to come to terms with a body that can't respond."

There must be a great degree of masochism among mountain climbers, I suggest.

"Mountaineers in general may have some degree of masochism, but primarily its the pure and simple challenge. We had both nearly given up, so it was a good test.

"We stayed on the top for between 10 and 15 minutes. Everest is taller but here you feel on top of the world. Depending on the time of year, you can see all the way down to the Amazon basin. This was perhaps the best thing I'd done in my life."

Mountaineering can be expensive. According to Peter, an expedition to the Himalayas costs around US$ 20,000 just to enter the mountain range, but in Bolivia there are neither restrictions nor climbing fees.

These financial advantages mean a lack of controls that can lead to accidents. In 1995, there were three deaths in climbing accidents in Bolivia.

What Peter calls expensive is based on Bolivian standards. He was able to rent his gear for US$ 20 per day with the guide costing US$ 50 a day. There is also the cost of plastic boots. "Normal boots would freeze," Peter explained.

Peter spent over a year and a half in Bolivia, eventually becoming an editor of *Bolivian Times*. We interviewed him as he was preparing to leave for England. His climbing of Illimani was the highlight of his stay. Had his visiting English girlfriend decided to live in Bolivia, Peter would have gladly remained. For Peter, Illimani will always be the other woman in his life that he had to leave behind.

Before trying Illimani, visitors might wish to climb the equally impressive Huayna Potosí, at 6,088 m (19,973 ft). Nearly 400 m (1,312 ft) lower than Illimani doesn't sound like much, but it makes a great difference; Peter's guide,

Andrew Valder, second from left—the Apolo Terranaut.

Yossi Brain, a hero to those of us who have hiked in Bolivia's highlands, died in an avalanche in the remote Cordillera de Apolobamba.

The Apolo Terranaut

The Apollo astronauts knew what was awaiting them on the moon, but modern day terranaut, Australian, Andrew Valder, had no idea what was in store for him beyond the bizarre town of Apolo, deep within the misty shroud of Bolivia's Madidi National Park.

The Bolivian government claims success in protecting vast areas of its country by designating national parks. Thus far, protection of these treasures of nature has not been a demanding feat. Sunday drivers find most Bolivian national parks inaccessible. Even your normal breed of adventurous backpackers do not arrive in droves to these remote and inviolable places.

When Andrew Valder first came to South America from his native Australia, like Peter Hutchison, he had never even heard of Bolivia. In his twenties, he had become disenchanted with the artist-and-repertory company where he commanded a high salary. "Sick of the lifestyle of the music industry," he growls, "its afterhour social requirements," he quit and travelled to South America.

He made contact with an NGO called TREX (Tropical Research and Exploration), through a Norwegian agricultural research acquaintance. TREX managed to secure enough funding for travel expenses alone, but no salaries, from the British Embassy and a US organisation called Conservation, Food and Health.

The area that he was to explore with three companions, the Madidi National Park, was reputedly a haven for the greatest variety of bird species of any region in the world, as well as remote ruins of ancient Inca villages camouflaged in the profuse foliage. This northern Bolivia region includes highlands, valleys and lowlands, from snowy mountain passes to wild rainforests.

Apolo and Beyond

The port of entry to the region is the obscure town of Apolo. To reach Apolo from the tip of the highlands, the explorers were fortunate to find a spot in the metallic cargo compartment of a merchant driver's utility truck. The metal surface collected both cold Altiplano air and direct highland sun rays. It was simultaneously hot and cold.

The route passes Lake Titicaca, where the pavement ends, then bounces over a pass on the skirt of Mount Illampu, winding down to Apolo, a semitropical mile above sea level.

Until 1994, there was no vehicle access to the town. Andrew calls Apolo a bizarre place; its isolation has fostered inbreeding, creating an underclass of near midgets who cannot talk. Like the imported Oompa-Loompas in controversial Roald Dahl's *Charlie and the Chocolate Factory*, Apolo's peculiar muscular outcasts do heavy labour, mainly toiling as carriers.

The town's large plaza is surrounded by adobe structures with corrugated roofing. The people are friendly. There are three restaurants. But you'd better tell them in advance if you plan to eat; there's not enough volume for steady service. The façade of one of the restaurants is covered with pornographic photographs. The town's primary mode of subsistence involves 15-day round-trip forest treks, to collect incense.

Andrew was to make several trips from Apolo, through

> Coca consumption was once restricted to the Inca nobility, but was later introduced to farm labourers and miners, as a means of increasing stamina and killing hunger. For Andrew, chewing coca was an obligatory example of cultural adaptation.

the cloud forests that rise up again to 2,800 m (9,186 ft), then down to the tropics, with a final destination in the town of San José.

In the 1940s, this route was a cattle trail. In the 1980s, it became a cocaine trail. Today, coca is still grown, but only for domestic use. Hard boiled, independent gold prospectors are the newest breed to penetrate a territory that is wilder than the old Wild West.

During the long hours of tough hiking, Andrew and his colleagues chewed the native coca leaf, learning first hand that the leaf's celebrated attribute of generating unprecedented endurance was not a mere legend.

During the trek out of Apolo, the travellers were able to listen over their guide's radio to the international Copa America football matches, including the game in which Bolivia defeated the United States 1–0.

At a place called Machariapo, the explorers found a hacienda style house where a Bolivian ex-forestry official, consumed by the semitropics, had abandoned civilisation forever, living a hippie existence. He fed the travellers glasses of orange juice, again and again, until he acquired the nickname Don Naranja (orange).

Don Naranja, in the tradition of his ancestor Don Quixote, had a wild scheme. This paradise he had chosen, with the world's greatest biodiversity, would become an exciting tourist lodge. I fear Godot will arrive there before any tourists do.

Undiscovered Birds and Ruins

The trekkers pushed on, still in search of ancient Inca ruins. They were able to plot the altitude, longitude and latitude of key sites along the way with a GPS (Geographical Positioning Unit).

Red-helmeted Jacinto, nicknamed Mr Good Vibes for his positive spirit, was the guide. Jacinto worked the trails along with his son. Their mules carried tarps, field books, medical gear, snakebite remedies and navigational equipment. Jacinto promised the imminent arrival to a town called Turnia. Turnia was found to be one solitary house.

There, they negotiated for more guides, finally reaching an agreement with a reluctant woodsman who wondered what gringos were doing in these remote forests. Andrew was baffled by a cultural communication gap; the new guide saw no purpose in projects of ecotourism and searches for ruins.

It was then, in the heart of the Madidi National Forest, that the explorers came across remnants of an old village, with Inca-style stonework. They found broken walls and what appeared to have been pens for animals. After a proper time for reverence, the exact location was recorded and the trekkers moved on.

The next stop was a hamlet called Mamacona, where Jacinto could go no further because the path had disappeared. He would not risk leaving his mules behind. The guides from San José, who should have met up with the trekkers in Mamacona, never arrived. One reluctant porter, picked up in the metropolis of Turnia, remained with the group.

With no path ahead, the trekkers explored the area surrounding Mamacona, slashing their way through liana vines and bamboos, with 30 kgs (66 lbs) on their backs. When they discovered a new set of ruins, it became apparent why the porter was so reluctant; he had feared that visitors would be coming to the region to pillage.

US born astrologer and hypnotherapist, Melissa Johnston, who has also been through the region (with gold prospectors), explained that, "with these people, if you establish good rapport, they will help you all along, but if you don't have the right attitude, you will be shunned and receive no help at all."

The trip beyond Mamacona was still in doubt. Andrew explained to the guide, as best as he could, that the group's purpose was to set up an ecotourism route that would be managed exclusively by the local residents.

Mamacona was an improvement over Turnia: two houses instead of one, with a stunning view of the green, velvet hills and deep precipices of the semitropics. "Such an exotic view," Andrew marvels, "from huts of such squalor."

Here it became necessary to negotiate for guides. The Mamaconians awaited their local fiesta a week later, and offers of cash were not enough to divert them from that momentous occasion. Finally, the offer of a machete to go along with the money convinced two men to act as guides: 20 per cent of the Mamacona population. This deal was good for a limited time only, since the guides would be needed to hunt down their fiesta feast.

"Past Mamacona, we reached one of the most beautiful places on earth," Andrew marvelled. "Rolling fields of what looked like broccoli, with protruding plate-like mountains and rivers crashing through deep gorges. We walked along the edge of a gorge in order to avoid the thick vegetation, chewing coca along the way."

The cultural gap between Quechua-speaking guides and the English/Spanish-speaking trekkers was bridged by a young boy who translated. The locals wondered why anyone would want to take their photos. They hadn't made the national football squad, nor were they soap opera stars.

The guides were treated to tapes of Bob Marley and the ornithologist's bird recordings.

In the thickest jungle, Andrew and his companions were left without guides, forced to carry burdens of 30 kgs (66 lbs) each. They knew they were more than a day's trek from their destination of San José, a town of 400 people, on the Tuichi River, reachable only by foot or by boat, eight hours to the nearest road.

At a moment when it seemed they could advance no longer, when even the coca leaves were losing their effect, the promised guides from San José showed up. 'There is a god,' Andrew thought, as his backpack thudded to the forest floor.

To most folk who travel around the world, San José would seem like a disappointing backwater village. But after the jungle of pitiless beauty, San José was a welcome refuge, "where a piece of fresh bread comes over like a great delicacy," Andrew explains.

Andrew and his three companions, with the indispensable help of several shifts of guides, had made it through inhospitable uncharted territory, discovering ruins of ancient Inca villages.

A True Discovery
On Andrew's next trip through the region, the ornithologist, Bret Whitney, was going to discover a new species of bird! Whitney had been there before, and in one of his bird recordings, picked out a new 'tune.' He returned to discover what is now named Sevialapus Schienbergi.

A few years later, San José received a grant and a world-class ecotourism lodge was built.

Bolivian Paradise
Adventurers Peter and Andrew find weird joy in exploring places where their lives are in danger. Their wilderness machismo requires 30 kgs (66 lbs) on your back and a trail only navigable with a machete. Anything less is for wimps.

Maybe I'm a wimp, but I prefer to venture where I have at least 97 per cent chance of survival. Sorata is one of these places. It is less awesome than La Paz's Palca Canyon, less sensational than Potosí, less prominent than Lake Titicaca's melancholic beauty. But Sorata is mellow and sensorial, as it hides within virtually inaccessible mountains.

Sorata in Style

Once you get to this tidy town of pastel façades that resembles an Italian hillside village, Sorata continues to play hard to get, with snow covered Mount Illampu offering only an occasional glimpse.

Peter and Andrew crave frontiers where no human being has set foot before, I like to see people. There are plenty of people in the crevices and on the inclines of this Sorata Yungas, a few expatriates from places like Italy, Quebec and Germany, but mainly indigenous farmers with subsistence plots of land.

> In Sorata, stone stairways connect streets that are lined with wrought-iron balconies. The lush town plaza is nurtured by recurrent silky drizzles.

These tilled fields are suspended at angles up to 45 degrees, producing a quilt of colourful ripples, looking much like the Quetzaltenango area of Guatemala, but without the death squads.

The town of Sorata is poised on a foothill, beneath the seducing Mount Illampu and above the San Gabriel River, which has won the battle against the unwilling bedrock, carving a gash as it hurtles towards the tropics.

Sorata benefits from the fact that the more famous Yungas are on a different road. Instead of Yungas resorts, you get Residencial Sorata, a gem of hotel artisanry, right on the plaza. Thanks to the altitude at 2,650 m (8,694 ft), none of the famous Yungas mosquitos are here to dispute the beauty.

Finding Sorata

But first you have to get here, and that is not easy. Transportes Larecaja sends buses from behind the La Paz cemetery every morning. You can reserve a seat, but the wooden stools in the aisles tell you that the bus is going to be packed with farmers from Altiplano communities, some of whom have hopped on the bus directly from the stable after their last shovelful of manure. The dominant language will be Aymara, but Spanish will do just fine.

The trip is only 152 km (94 miles) but you are told that it will take four and a half hours, so you know the road will be tough. There are no rest stops along the way, so if a morning toilet break is a habit of yours, avoid breakfast beverages. After the first 40 minutes, you conclude that the trip will be a breeze, as you capture a mellow profile of Lake Titicaca. But at the adobe town of Huarina, the asphalt ends and the road winds toward the *cordillera*. At Achacachi, a focal point of indigenous activism, foreigners are asked to get off the bus and register with their passports.

The road makes a winding ascent of the Cordillera Pass. When you've reached the top, you can see the road ahead as an erratic ribbon winding into an immense cavity. (For more information on the Andean Cordillera visit http://www.ecuaworld.com/discover/sierra.htm.

The precariously perched villages below seem on the verge of plummeting into the deep green gorges. Halfway down, you spot Sorata, and you think you are there, but you are not, unless you descend by parachute. Even after you arrive, you are still not all there, for you cannot catch a glimpse of the bashful Illampu above.

To the Bat Cave

My wife Martha, our then 11-year-old son Marcus and I, set a goal for this, our first but not last, trip to Sorata: to hike to the bat cave, 12 km (7 miles) north-down, just past the town of San Pedro.

By the high road, it's a two and a half hour hike. By the low road, along the San Gabriel River, add another hour. Even if there were no bat cave, this trek would still be spectacular. But with an 11-year-old, an enticing destiny is motivational.

I promise him that the path is downhill and that we can hitch a ride with a truck on the way back. Soon the first promise is broken. Marcus protests. "We must take one step up in order to go two steps down," I say, distorting a phrase by Mao.

The directions are easy; out of Sorata turn left at the first fork in the road. At the second fork, make a right for the high road or a left for the river path. If you have any doubts, just say the word *gruta* (cave) at any of the settlements along the way, and they will point you to the right road.

When you have reached a peak in the road and Sorata has disappeared, you are at the halfway point. Scattered hamlets across the gorge are reachable only by footpaths. A fine drizzle refreshes without drenching. The river roars from below to express its supreme authority.

Here, the road winds downhill. When you finally spot San Pedro below, you are about three-quarters there. San Pedro is a square of pastel painted buildings surrounding a green football field.

Once at San Pedro, the cave is still 10 minutes ahead. Since only three or four people visit the cave on weekdays, and not more than a dozen or so at weekends, there is no permanent attendant, nor are there signs that locate the home of the bats. In San Pedro, a girl sells fizzy drinks from a tiny shop by the roadside. Let her know you are going to the cave. Let anyone else know, too. By word of mouth, the lady who caretakes the cave will find you before you find her.

When you reach a white hut with a wooden bench, you are there. The caretaker will arrive behind you by bicycle. You climb a hill to the cave. You pass a whitewashed adobe structure with urinals, then a roofless adobe hut with a one-cylinder motor for turning on the electricity in the cave.

The guide, if you can find her, will handcrank an electric generator for about US$ 1 each, and you will enter the dimly lit cave.

Aside from a lake about 150 m (492 ft) inside the cave, the attraction is the chance to share the same space with bats. There are no stalagmites or stalactites. Beyond the lake, you'll need *spelunking* (caving) equipment. Vampire bats allegedly nest in the deepest recesses of the cave.

As you near the lake, the bat squeaks get shriller. Shadows sweep by your eyes. If you don't blink, you will see the profile of a bat. As your eyes adjust to the relative darkness, you will perceive other bats as they slumber from a hanging position on the roof of the cave. At this lower altitude, the farmers of San Pedro would have to contend with mosquito infestation if they were to lose their bats.

After watching the bats, Marcus had forgotten about my first broken promise. We emerged from the hot cave with a nagging thirst. We walked back uphill to the pathside stand, bought a papaya drink and waited for a truck. To this very day, any time I sip a papaya drink, I remember that soothing moment in a silent paradise.

The girl at the shop said there would 'probably' be a truck or two coming by. "Maybe later in the afternoon," she added. We had a two and a half hour trek back, with only two hours of sunlight remaining. We started back uphill, this time with the sun emerging from the clouds behind us. Promise number two might still be fulfilled if just one truck appeared.

> The three of us sat down on boulders and admired the perfect panorama. The view of Illimani from La Paz is ruggedly awesome but Illampu shyly peering down over Sorata is sensual beauty. Marcus had relished the challenge. He let us know he was tired, but without complaint. He was distracted by the frog croaks.

At the halfway point, Marcus had gained a second wind and no longer asked about the awaited truck. After 18 km (11 miles) of hiking, we turned a bend and there she was: Illampu, undraped, her smooth white form tempting us to move ever closer. After the next two bends in the path, with the sun behind us still peeking through clouds, we had our first view of Illampu and Sorata below her within the same frame. The San Gabriel River roared its approval from far below.

The bats were down below, cleaning the gorge of mosquitos. And we were ready for a long sleep, knowing that Illampu would continue to play hard to get and would probably not expose herself again while we were in Sorata.

Accommodation in Sorata

Hotels around the plaza are priced at backpacker rates. Residencial Sorata is a funky work of hotel artisanry, a maze of balconies, interior gardens, rooms with antique furniture, a dank atmosphere and bulging mattresses. Right next to it is the colonial Paraíso Hotel. Full course lunches in plaza restaurants range from just under US$ 1 to US$ 2.50, and the eating is remarkably good considering that this town is so remote.

These prices will remain relatively low as long as Sorata remains elusive and is eclipsed by the other more resort oriented part of Los Yungas.

A Wealth of Exploration

The bat cave is only the beginning of Sorata hiking experiences. The soft-spoken Quebecois, Louis, at Residencial Sorata will point you to guides, beginning at about US$ 12 per day for groups. Hiking and trekking are just as challenging as they are rewarding, from simple lagoons to the complex circuit around Illampu. Old gold miner trails offer a Wild-West experience.

The most ambitious can take the roughest of Inca roads, the Mapiri trail, which drops more than 2,000 m (6,561 ft) into the rainforest. Guides and porters are absolutely necessary.

TOURS FOR PEOPLE WHO DON'T LIKE TOURS

Once hard-to-reach sites are now made accessible through innovative travel companies that sponsor authentic tours that are ethnically and environmentally hip. Blending modest but appreciated comforts with a tolerable dose of roughing it, these tours allow for the thrills of do-it-yourself escapades, minus (some of) the hazards. (*A selected list of contact numbers of reputable tour companies is found in the* Resource Guide *at the end of the book.*)

Island of the Sun: The Dawn of South American Culture

Bolivia has long been maligned by statistics on per capita income, which qualify it as the second poorest nation in the Américas. But such statistics do not consider self-sufficient communities with virtually no income, where money is not the primary tool of the economy.

One such place, with three interconnected communities, is Island of the Sun, a half hour boat ride from the popular pilgrim shrine village of Copacabana (where fervent believers celebrate marriage ceremonies and spend their honeymoons).

Island of the Sun and Copacabana are focal points of the Bolivian side of Lake Titicaca, the highest navigable body of water in the world at around 3,800 m (12,800 ft) above sea level.

Tourism and Exploitation: Finding the Balance

Before exploring the Island of the Sun, the inevitable question must be confronted. Will contact with modern lifestyles decimate a way of life that dates back hundreds of years?

The romantic extreme says leave these places alone. The realist opposite says that abandoning such communities is tantamount to delusive paternalism, which will exclude

Island of the Sun, Lake Titicaca, during the dry season. High altitude and ancient cultures make the island one of Bolivia's most satisfying travel destinations.

citizens of the world from partaking in advances in medicine, education and other arenas of modern life.

Lake Titicaca may be both too high and too remote for the overdevelopment that comes with excesses of tourism. The more enlightened tour companies (we had a very positive experience with Transturín; Crillón is also a Titicaca specialist of high repute) have attempted to interact with locals by alternating visits to local homes so that everyone would equally benefit from the contact, complying with the island's self sufficient, egalitarian way of life in which there is no misery or wealth and where resources are pooled in times of need.

Contact with the island's children illustrates the dilemma. On the more visited side, children now ask for *caramelos*. The healthy diet of the islanders is virtually sugar free. A dentist who ventured here to live would remain unemployed. If you aren't accustomed to eating sweets, you don't miss it. But once children taste it, they are hooked.

At the home of José, a resident of Challapampa on the opposite side of the island, the local foodstuffs were decked out on the patio in a dazzling collage: numerous varieties of corn (the buzzword 'biodiversity' has never been needed here), fava beans, *quinoa* and various types of potatoes, including the *oca*, a cross between a yam and a potato.

Cheese did not become part of the diet until the Spanish Conquest. The lake's various species of fish comprise the primary non-vegetarian staple.

"The islanders love the pigs, sheep and cattle that loiter on the beach," José explained. Every family has its own animals. They are used for food only in emergencies or for special festivals.

What is lacking on the island is fruit. Nutrients from fruit are recouped through various types of vegetables. The claimed presence on the island of a fair share of centenarians speaks well for the diet.

As one approaches the island of steep cliffs, crevasses and coves, it hardly seems the place where a community can be self sufficient agriculturally. But this pre-Inca culture had long ago created an elaborate system of terraces, embellishing the lake's hilly shore with a ribbed texture.

Each terrace is engineered with five layers, including topsoil above and stones on the bottom level. The wall of the terrace is also made of stone. The five levels filter and nourish the water as it sifts down from one terrace to another. The island has been the site of sacred pilgrimages with visitors bringing samples of their own soil from other parts of the Aymara nation, and for a brief 60 years, from the Inca empire. These soil samples thus enriched the variety of microorganisms and the agriculture of today thrives on this fertility.

Each family has its own plot of land, from six to 12 hectares, but in the tradition of the communal *ayllu*, there is considerable collective work and families help each other during harvest time.

Challapampa

The town of Challapampa is on an isthmus between two splendid bays. The frigid lake has lost much of its ancient salinity, but when the wind is right, one senses a seacoast aroma.

Pre Inca ruins, Chinkana, Island of the Sun.

Housing is primarily adobe with straw roofing. Each family has three rooms, the largest one for the whole family, providing human warmth to resist the frosty nights, plus a storage room and a stable. The kitchen, not considered a room, is housed in a separate structure.

At lake level is a cosy museum, financed by Bolivia's National Institute of Archaeology. Many of the museum's pieces of ceramic, gold and silver artwork were protected from scavengers in the homes of the villagers until the museum was built. The museum is truly a community project.

Hiking above the lake level part of town, you'll pass through a sacred stone portal into an upper section, where an attractive school house is one of the structures surrounding an informal, grassy pedestrian plaza.

Chinkana Temple
Beyond this level, a stone marked path winds up to breathtaking views of coves and beaches, past a sacred stone outcrop, to a peak where pilgrims and travellers alike receive the Kallawaya mystic ceremony, the burning of coca leaves by an island shaman. After this purification of the soul, one is ready to visit the Chinkana Temple, a large stone edifice built in the form of a maze, with numerous interior doors and passageways.

The stone Chinkana Temple, a 3–4 km (2–2.5 mile) walk from the village, is perched on a high cliff overlooking a magnificent deserted beach. The whole hike, from Challapampa to Chinkana and back, is a little more than 8 km (5 miles). Each point in the hike offers a distinct panorama of the lake, beaches, crevasses and coves.

The Great Lake

Impressionist spirits will delight as the rich blue of the lake changes to a soothing emerald in some of the coves. At certain angles, the lake is so wide that one cannot see the opposite shore.

If you see the world the way Monet did, then there are at least seven distinct times for viewing the lake. The brown terraces at rest in winter are replaced by a quiltwork of varying patterns of green in summer (December through March).

With only limited electric lighting on the island, a full moon allows for such a spectral view of the shore of Challapampa, with hushed adobe dwellings between shining volcanic bedrock polished smooth by centuries of winds. When the moon is absent, the village and waves are eclipsed by a sky whose brilliance is unknown at lower altitudes and would have inspired 'Starry Night II' from Van Gogh.

With the arrival of rudimentary hostels and small snack stands, campers may no longer need to be housed in private homes, and homestay adventures may shift to smaller islands in the lake.

Before the more adventurous sorts reject a formalised tour of the island, it must be noted that some La Paz tour companies offer options with both adventuring and respect for the visited culture in mind, whether one sleeps and eats in a simple yacht or is introduced to local facilities in a mellow way that does not upset that balance of life on the island.

Tours allow for acceptable access to local homes, shamans and native musicians. Guides fluent in Aymara can help bridge the wide culture gap, providing lessons in ethnic studies along the way.

ENJOYING BOLIVIA 223

Tours to Island of the Sun can be combined with visits to smaller islands, villages on the Peruvian side of the lake or to Copacabana.

If you're on your own, you can negotiate the price of a motorboat ride from Copacabana to Island of the Sun.

Daytime temperatures on the lake range from the 60s to the 70s (Fahrenheit) year round while night temperatures are cool to cold, sometimes dipping below freezing.

The Bolivian Amazon: How Rough Can it Get?

As development penetrates Bolivia's Amazonia, natural predators such as the jaguar become endangered species. The delicate balance between sustainable development and tourism practised by some Island of the Sun tour companies departing from La Paz parallels what Fremen Tours has accomplished in Bolivia's Amazonian region.

As part of its adventure incursions into the jungles of Bolivia, Fremen has brought rodent control experts and funded school construction. Education laws attempt to

Flotel Reina de Enin tours the Mamore River exploring Bolivian Amazonia. A combination of cruising and trekking is an ideal way to explore the more rugged parts of Bolivia.

integrate the vast country but also encourage the preservation of distinct ways of life through bilingual education. Fremen publicises Amazonian medicinal plants, provides a market for local artisans, and celebrates the diet and customs of the indigenous communities that host its tours.

Profits from the sale of local artisanry to visiting adventure tourists are divided 50 per cent to the artisan and 50 per cent to community projects. Fremen's ideology of authentic tourism includes acting as an advocate for the original community. On one occasion, the Mojeña village of Villa del Carmen lacked four children to reach the minimum 20 students that would qualify it for services from Bolivia's Secretariat of Education. Fremen initiated and followed through on paperwork that eventually allowed the settlement to receive the teacher and supplies it required. Fremen set aside a portion of its tour profits to build the school.

At a point on the Mamoré River which separates one Yuracaré community of six families from another community of three

> Before ethno-ecotourism was conceived, forays into tropical jungle areas were a hit-and-miss proposition as far as observing exotic animals or, more importantly, achieving any type of meaningful cultural exchange with local inhabitants.

families, Fremen boats the children from the smaller community to their school.

As with Island of the Sun tour specialists, Fremen's financial self-interest coincides with the preservation of habitat and customs.

'In contrast to most of the Brazilian or Peruvian Amazon,' writes Aimée Sullivan, 'it is easy to see animals such as alligators, turtles, *capybaras* (the largest rodent on earth) and innumerable species of birds in the Bolivian Amazon.'

Fremen admits that sighting of reticent jaguars is not likely, but it guarantees that tour clients will get within 20 m (65 ft) of caimans from 2–7 m (6.5–23 ft) long, sweet-water dolphins, river turtles and various types of monkeys, including the monkey-squirrel.

The Llanos de Moxos Tour

Fremen's Llanos de Moxos tour combines trekking and nature with cultural exchange. The main thoroughfare of the tour is the Mamoré River, upriver from the site of the infamous construction of the Madeira–Mamoré Railroad at the turn of the century, built by indentured servants, including North Americans and Europeans. The construction of the railroad through malaria swamps resulted in 'one death per crosstie' according to a needless exaggeration by the television programme *Ripley's Believe It Or Not*.

The date of completion of the railroad, which is now within Brazilian territory on the border of Bolivia, coincided with the smuggling of rubber seeds to Malaysia, where they grew in a more conducive environment. Result: the Madeira–Mamoré Railroad, at the moment of completion, was obsolete.

Exploitation by the rubber barons extended throughout the Amazon region, including natives of the Llanos de Moxos region explored by Fremen. Most of the saga took place many kilometres downriver in the area of Guayaramerín. The primary victims were the indigenous communities of the Amazonia.

Today, both the Yuracuré and the Mojeños are poor but self sufficient. They speak Spanish to visitors, but the bilingual school projects partly financed by Fremen Tours may help to preserve their original languages.

The tour of this area may be anywhere from three to five days, including round trip air fare between La Paz and Trinidad, the point of departure. Visitors sleep on the river in a 'flotel', called the Reina de Enin, a simple but comfortable sleeping quarter with private baths. The tour includes visits to three indigenous communities. Thanks to the organisers, a fine rapport between visitors and locals adds delight to the tour.

Included is a visit to a cattle ranch, an hour-and-a-half horseback ride into the jungle and across the savanna, observations of river fauna on the Mamoré, a visit to a protected rainforest sanctuary and a free afternoon for swimming or trekking. The river cruise itself allows for observation of local flora and fauna, with the aid of a trained guide. If the fishing is good, visitors will dine on piranha soup. My brother-in-law was able to catch a big one, which looked like a surubí. The combined catch of the group resulted in a fine fish dinner.

The city of Trinidad, capital of the Department of Beni, is only 16 km (10 miles) from nearby Mamoré ports. Trinidad is the most important city in the Department of Beni. But Benianos and foreign travellers interviewed for this book speak with more enthusiasm for the towns of Guayaramerín and Rurrenabaque.

Guayaramerín's great advantage is that it lies across the Mamoré river from Brazil. Railroad enthusiasts are best situated here to appreciate the remains of the Madeira–Mamoré Railroad.

Guayaramerín's Brazilian counterpart is Guajará–Mirim. A road from there to Porto Velho, the terminal for the ill-fated train line, uses the original railroad bridges that were supposed to connect with Guajará–Mirim.

Rurrenabaque: the Fine Line Between Tourism and Penance

"Unlike other lowland places in Bolivia," says expat astrologer, Melissa Johnston, "Rurre is not flat. If you come in the dry season, between May and October, there won't be much of a mosquito problem and the weather can actually become quite cool!"

ENJOYING BOLIVIA 227

Let's go to Rurre, stay in a comfortable hotel with a private bath, walk the streets of the prettiest town in the Bolivian lowlands, watch the luxuriant Beni River from the banks of the town, climb a steep hill for a magnificent view of the Beni lowlands, and then bathe in El Chorro, an exotic pool and luxuriant waterfall only 1 km (0.6 miles) from the town.

For most people, this would make a fine vacation. But for some, the easy way is not enough. To discover 'the hidden secrets' of the mysterious Amazon basin there are customised adventure tours up the River Beni to the Tuichi River.

Instead of sleeping Fremen style in a comfortable river boat with bathrooms and a dining room, the adventurer must spend the night in a sleeping bag in order to keep the local wildlife from joining.

For some seasoned travellers, the Bolivian Amazon is more interesting than its Brazilian counterpart because the rivers are narrower and the population less dense, thus one can better observe the exotic wildlife.

Typical trips begin with motorised canoes, with your guide's machete clearing the way. On the river bank one sleeps beneath an individual mosquito net. Net or no, mosquito repellent is indispensable.

Dinner consists of fish that the guides and tourists manage to catch. Dessert is crocodile watching under torch light.

This tour may involve a trek through the jungle, drinking fresh water from the vine-like medicinal Uña de Gato. Clients learn the art of medicinal plants by chewing on pain-killing leaves. The day's diet is limited to local vegetation, which may include almonds, bananas and the sap from a tree nicknamed the 'garlic tree.' Hours later, the travellers emerge from the thickets covered with insect bites and bathe it off in the cool river.

That would be enough for most of us, but the more intrepid endure a third day of penance, building their own rafts and then travelling over the violent Tuichi River. The penance topped off with a steep mountain climb to visit a colony of macaws.

An optional fourth day includes the 'ethno' segment of such tours: a visit with the Chimane villagers, all of whom are impervious to the mosquitos. The visitors have a choice. Insult their Chimane hosts or eat the superpungent tortoise stew. It would have been sufficient to partake of the Chimane gardens of papaya, yuca, guava and lime. If you don't agonise, though, then you haven't really taken this tour.

More medicinal herbs, and then it's back to the motorised canoes, where the travellers may get cleansed by a drenching rain all the way back to Rurre. After removing ticks from various parts of their bodies, they will sleep until noon the next day.

> **Useful Tip**
> Hotels are friendly, basic and cheap. With Rurre tour companies expanding faster than they can be clocked, it is necessary to consult Bolivia's Secretariat of Tourism for recommended companies.

I originally wrote that Rurrenabaque emplifies how so many potentially prime tourist spots in Bolivia will remain undisturbed for years to come; it is difficult to reach, and once you're there, the infrastructure is not tourist-friendly. But between 2000 and 2005, the number of annual visitors to Rurre jumped from 5,000 to 37,000, and local tour companies sprouted up accordingly. Not bad for a town of 11,000 inhabitants, or maybe not good for preserving the reason why one would want to visit Rurrenabaque in the first place. Tours have expanded in dimension to reach the Madidi and Pilon Lajas national parks.

Bussing from La Paz during the dry season (when roads are most passable) takes 18 hours; it's only 45 minutes by plane.

No one says that we must travel with a tour, but when culture shock or inaccessible geography are constraints, macho travel may not be the answer. Many Bolivian tour companies are well aware that the type of customers who arrive in such remote territories are adventurers who do not want to degrade the environment and would like to interact with local inhabitants without disrupting their way of life. In such cases, a tour is not contradictory with adventure and enrichment.

LEARNING THE LANGUAGE

CHAPTER 8

'The native Bolivian word *La yapa* is remarkably similar to the Cajun word *Lagniape*, with the same meaning: the extra amount that the vendor throws in with the purchase in appreciation of a good customer. Other Aymara or Quechua word comparisons are more mysterious. When *Chuquiago* (the native word for the city La Paz) is pronounced, it sounds nearly the same as the Native American word *Chicago*'
—Author's journal

SPANISH LANGUAGE

Your trip begins with a continuing education course in Spanish. Spanish is phonetic, and its grammar, although distinct from English, is quite sensible, consistent and easily reduced to basics. It is the type of language that can be picked up abroad once one has learnt the basics.

My experience, having taught Spanish at both the university and continuing education level, is that mastery of the minimum basic concepts will provide a sufficient foundation for one's arrival in Bolivia.

The Basics
Pronunciation
Spanish is a phonetic language, with only five vowel sounds that never vary. Learn these simple sounds:
- **a**   'ah'
- **e**   'eh'
- **i**   'ee'
- **o**   a shortened 'oh'
- **u**   a shortened 'oo'

Discover that most consonants differ only slightly in pronunciation between English and Spanish, with Spanish consonants softer or less explosive. Although some sounds in Spanish may be represented by letters that don't correspond to English, there are only two sounds in the whole language, both consonants, that 'feel foreign' to the

English-speaking tongue: the rolled 'rr' sounds like a trill, and the *j* (or *g* when it comes before *e* or *i*) sounds like a heavily aspirated 'h'.

For English speakers, Spanish is one of the most pronounceable languages in the world.

Vocabulary

Once you've settled into the sounds, take advantage of the numerous cognates—words that are identical or nearly the same in both English and Spanish (for example, all words from English with a 'tion', and their derivatives, are the same in Spanish, with a 'ción' ending).

- *Invitación*—invitation
- *Invitar*—to invite
- *Invitado*—guest

These two simple and basic principles, simple vowel phonetics and cognates, will allow most sceptics who think they can't learn a foreign language to acquire a rudimentary knowledge of Spanish in a short time.

Cuánto cuesta...?	How much does it cost...?
Cuánto es...?	How much is it?
Dónde está...?	Where is...?
Dónde están...?	Where are...?
Gracias	Thank you
Hable más despacio por favor	Speak more slowly, please
No hablo español	I don't speak Spanish
Tiene Usted...?	Do you have...?
Perdón	Excuse me, pardon me
Por favor	Please
Quisiera or *Me gustaría*	I'd like (followed by either a noun or an infinitive)

... and places you may need to find quickly in order of urgency ...

Banco	Bank
Baño	Bathroom
Boleto	Ticket
Casa de cambio	Currency exchange
Correo	Post office
Farmacia	Pharmacy or chemist
Oficina de turismo	Tourist office

Grammar

Between Spanish and English, grammar does not vary a whole lot. In Spanish, verbs change their endings (conjugations) according to the subject pronoun, so that the ending of the verb will usually indicate the subject. Even though *yo hablo* means 'I speak,' the *yo* is not necessary except for emphasis, since the *o* ending tells the listener you are in first person. An excessive use of the pronoun *yo* could make you seem egotistical. The following rules demonstrate some basic differences concerning adjectives:

- Descriptive adjectives **follow** nouns instead of preceding them (*lección difícil* instead of 'difficult lesson')
- Adjectives agree in gender (male/female) and number (singular/plural) with nouns. Example: *casa blanca* (white house) is female, *edificio blanco* (white building) is male, and *casas blancas* (white houses) is feminine plural. An *a* final letter usually indicates the word is feminine; an *o* ending is masculine.

There are two significant differences in perception between Spanish and English. First, Spanish has two verbs for 'to be': *ser* and *estar*. *Ser* comes from essence and relates to characteristics or identity; *estar* refers to state or condition. 'To be or not to be,' from Hamlet, would be *Ser o no ser*, since it concerns the character's identity.

Spanish also has two past tenses: the preterit, which looks at an event as completed or factual, and the imperfect, which describes or re-experiences an ongoing past. The most frequent form of expressing the future is virtually identical to the English 'going' plus infinitive.

Spanish has other grammatical differences, but none are crucial to basic communication. These basics, plus a working vocabulary of a few hundred words, can be mastered in a short but intense continuing education course, which you should take before doing business in Bolivia.

Aymara and Quechua

Quechua is the fourth most spoken language in the Américas while Aymara is the sixth. Bolivian Spanish is heavily spiced with words and phrases from both Aymara and Quechua, both fascinating languages in their imagery, conceptual nuances, built-in world views and sense of humour. Aymara prevails in La Paz and the Lake Titicaca region while Quechua is more common in Cochabamba, Sucre and Potosí. Spanish-speaking Bolivians fancy seasoning their speech with words and expressions from both Quechua and Aymara.

Code switching is nurtured when the indigenous culture has food, clothing, concepts and customs nonexistent in the conquering culture. The conqueror thus adopts the indigenous vocabulary. Indigenous words also replace Spanish

LEARNING THE LANGUAGE

words when they are perceived to be more expressive, and especially when their tone conveys a sense of humour not found in the original of Spanish. A number of Spanish words, such as *alpaca*, *choclo* (corn on the cob), *llama* and *mate* (herb tea) come from Quechua.

Communication between Spanish speaking Bolivians and Quechua or Aymara speakers is sometimes hampered by the distinct world views of their languages. For example, you can't 'look forward' to something in Aymara because this culture sees the past as in front and the future as behind. It's natural when you consider this logic because we can see the past but we cannot see the future. Thus, the Aymara word *qaruru* is a combination of *qaru* (right behind) and *uru* (today).

The Aymara concept of *ayni* is vital to understand for education and business. Roughly, *ayni* is a system of community, collaboration, support and relationships: a collective consciousness.

The following is a list of some key words from Quechua (Que) and Aymara (Aym) that spice up Bolivian Spanish. Bold print indicates those words that are an integral part of everyday language. Both Aymara and Quechua only have three vowels, the **a**, **e** and **i**. Vocabulary may be more limited than some other languages but a richness of metaphors more than compensates.

Achachi (Aym)	Old
Api (Que)	Hot corn cereal
Asna (Que)	Stinking
Camisaqui (Aym)	How are you?
Ccuchu (Aym, Que)	Corner
Cha'lla (Aym)	Housewarming in which *pisco* alcohol is sprinkled on the floor to feed the Pachamama
Chaqui (Que)	Hangover
Charque (Aym, Que)	Dried meat
Chenco (Que)	A mix-up

Chiji (Aym, Que)	Grass
Cunasa sutimaja (Aym)	What's your name?
Huaironco (Que)	Originally 'bumble bee,' more frequently used as a metaphor meaning indecisive or beating around the bush
Ima sutiqui (Que)	What's your name?
Imilla (Aym)	Girl
Inti (Aym, Que)	Sun (used in names of businesses and organisations)
Jaccha (Aym)	Big
Janihua (Aym)	Literally 'no,' metaphor is 'stubborn'
Juntucha (Aym)	The leftovers
Khencha (Que)	Jinx
Llokalla (Aym, Que)	Boy, Indian
Puchu (Aym, Que)	Leftover
Sullu (Aym, Que)	Literally 'abortion,' metaphor is 'malnourished'
Tata (Que)	Father, old man
Tatai (Que)	My father
Taya (Aym)	Cold
Ttanta (Aym, Que)	Bread
Tucsa (Aym)	Stinking
Yapa (Que, Aym)	This is equivalent to the 13th piece of bread in a bakers dozen, the bonus that a steady customer receives. *La yapa* is remarkably similar to the Cajun word *Lagniape*, which means the same thing.

LANGUAGE AND TITLES

Next comes a more sensitive issue which I hope I shall handle fairly. When you meet someone of obvious indigenous background, specifically if that person is wearing typical Indian dress or work clothes, you may be addressed as *caballero* (roughly 'gentleman') for men, and *señora* for women. The old caste system is built into the language. (This casting of the language may suddenly diminish now that Bolivia has elected a president of Aymara heritage.)

When called *caballero*, egalitarian principles may move you to respond with the same terminology. If you do so, rather than being seen as fair-minded and socially conscious, the person who addressed you will feel he is being ridiculed. So much for good intentions—you are not going to change the social structure of a country with one out-of-context egalitarian response. If addressed as *caballero*, the proper response is to address the person by first name.

Bolivian film director, Mela Márquez, has given her own analysis of this 'almost unbridgeable gap' between the classes. "I don't think I fully realised the level of racism here before I went to Europe. Of course it exists there as well, but here there are explicit rules as to the level at which you must live. The rich here are more likely to know Miami or Buenos Aires than a small village just down the road from their homes."

I have expressed my discomfort about these linguistic manifestations of caste to a Bolivian friend who had lived in the United States.

"In the US," he responded, "there is a social prohibition against all expressions of race and class difference when the company is mixed. But I have been in rooms with no blacks present, when the racist garbage I heard was nauseating. I'm not sure which is better," he added, "our brutal honesty or the hypocrisy back in the US."

Before Bolivia became a nation, the Spanish language was already burdened with both a formal and a familiar 'you.' If you are addressed with the formal *Usted* in Spanish, you should respond with *Usted* as well. Only after a social relationship develops over a period of time because of intellectual affinities, do both parties use the *tú*. However, many Bolivians of indigenous background use the *tú* exclusively, even if they are speaking to the president of the republic.

In socially conservative Andean countries such as Bolivia, cross-class relationships are less likely to develop than in Mexico, Chile or Argentina, although Bolivia's class structure has loosened up considerably in recent years, a process that will be escalating as these words are written.

In Bolivia, you may also find a middle road. You may be speaking with a distinguished middle-aged or elderly person in a setting that has become informalised following prior conversations. You want to speak with respect but you do not wish to overdo it with '*señor Portales*' or '*señora Medina*.' The middle path is the title *don* for males and *doña* for females. If I were to bump into Senator Leopoldo López on the street, for example, after having previously had a friendly interview with him, I could say, "*Buenas tardes, señor López,*" or, "*Buenas tardes, don Leopoldo.*"

THE BUSINESS OF LANGUAGE

The Spanish language is an important factor, even if business is conducted in English. A few phrases of Spanish on the part of the visitor can establish rapport. Take special care to learn pronunciation of the names of hosts or companions. In certain businesses, a few phrases in Aymara or Quechua could also go a long way in establishing rapport.

Spanish, as we have seen, has two words for 'you': *Usted* and *tú*. The first is formal, and should be used until you are invited to use the familiar *tú*. This invitation may be phrased as: '*Podemos tutearnos*' ('We can speak to each other with the *tú*'). Or your associates may simply begin addressing you with the *tú*. You should respond in kind and begin addressing them with the informal *tú*. If you continue using the *Usted* after having been addressed with *tú*, it may be perceived as an insult.

The visitor is not expected to have a command of Spanish, however, and Bolivians and all Latin Americans show remarkable empathy for your language weaknesses. On the other hand, your ability to communicate in 'bad' Spanish is greatly appreciated. The English language is not considered a necessity as it would be in Mexico, for example. Many well educated Bolivians do not speak English.

Slips of the Tongue
Spanish is not without important subtleties, and if you are preparing a product or advertising campaign, it is best to seek consultation, in order to make sure that you are not stumbling upon a double meaning.

The most famous error of this type concerns General Motors' attempt to market its popular Nova automobile in Mexico. The disastrous coincidence was that *no va* in Spanish means 'It doesn't go.'

A beer company once translated its advertising slogan 'Turn it loose,' in a way which, in Spanish, sounded like a powerful laxative.

WORKING IN BOLIVIA

CHAPTER 9

'Incorporating a new business in Bolivia... takes fifty-nine days, entails fifteen separate procedures, and costs twice as much as the average person earns in a year. So, according to a ... World Bank study, most of Bolivia's businesses remain 'informal,' which means that they have no legal protection, and limited access to credit markets.'
James Surowiecki, 'The Financial Page: Morales's Mistake,' *The New Yorker*, 23 & 30 January 2006.

Working in Bolivia requires an awareness of both the social and economic dynamics of business. This chapter opens with experiences on social business customs and then follows up with some insights on economics, including a response to the oft-repeated question, "why are countries that are so rich in natural resources so poor in development?"

BUSINESS AS NOT USUAL

Festival Entradas may begin long after their scheduled starting time, but once they get going, there is no end in sight. Patience is rewarded in Bolivia, whether you're anticipating a party or a business event.

In business, practice the art of waiting, especially between 12:30 pm and 2:30 pm, when everything except restaurants and some government-run bodies shut down for an extended lunch break. It seems inevitable, though, that commerce will be gradually switching to the North American model, whereby shops remain open during the lunch period.

The telephone rarely accelerates a business process, and it may be an impediment. A phone conversation is not a worthy substitute for a face to face meeting. Expect office phones to ring busy anyway, with few extra connections or message machines. The technology is available, but anything that interferes with human contact is suspect. E-mail is a useful tool, for sure, but it will never replace direct contact.

THE ART OF WAITING

In any serious business process, much time will be spent reading two-year-old magazines in offices. On average, 80 per cent of life is maintenance time. A universal talent is to convert maintenance time into aesthetic fulfilment. In Bolivian offices, you will not be the only one in limbo. What better time to initiate a conversation with companions in waiting? Office personnel may gladly join in. Subjects range from predictions on various elections or football matches to suggestions for weekend getaways.

After an hour of reading last year's stock quotations, the person you need to see urgently may come out of a meeting and ask, apologetically, if you can return in the afternoon, or better yet, tomorrow. In Bolivia, simple procedures for getting things done do not always exist, and if this person is in a position of responsibility, he has probably been hit with an unanticipated crisis.

In such cases, I have been pleasantly rewarded by postponing my business and returning at a more favourable time. Some of my most enduring contacts are with people

Whether waiting for the fiesta to begin or for a business contact, patience will be rewarded in Bolivia.

for whom I had to wait the longest. On the other hand, impatience rarely reaps rewards.

WHO DO YOU KNOW?

Should you encounter a bureaucrat whose intransigence threatens to paralyse a promising process in its tracks, do not give up. Some bureaucrats have a need to show their importance by making your concerns take a back seat. These human anchors can be set loose with the influence of other important people with whom you have maintained positive contact. A letter or phone call from an influential contact will shake the intransigent bureaucrat into action. Personal referrals are more effective than the most brilliant credentials.

CULTIVATING CONTACTS

Contacts are typically cultivated over lunch. During initial lunches, discussions cleverly elude the theme of business. Your knowledge of local football standings and popular culture is a helpful bridge of communication, as is a willingness to respond to questions about your country.

Family Values

Bolivians are genuinely interested in your family. When you are known as part of a family, your alien shell is discarded. The fact that your brother was a city planner or your daughter is studying to be a dentist may seem irrelevant to you, but if your lunch companions allow this subject to come up, it reflects the importance of family for Bolivian identity.

Manners, including graciousness and attire, are valuable assets in forming business relationships. Generally, the higher the altitude, the more formal the attire. I have attended sessions of Congress in which then Senator Guillermo Richter, who represented the lowland Beni Department, was the only person in the room not wearing a tie. However, now that Bolivia has elected a tieless, shirtsleeve president, La Paz seems to be loosening up.

PRACTICAL BUSINESS/SOCIAL TIPS

- Folks from the United States, and even Europeans, often use the word 'America' when referring to the USA. Don't commit this error; Bolivians are also from America.
- Don't schedule back-to-back meetings. Business meetings often extend beyond the expected time period.
- Don't be conditioned to expect the need for a bribe. (In Bolivian Spanish, the word bribe is *coima*.) While bribery still exists in Bolivia, it is not as prevalent as one is led to expect. That's my visceral reaction, based on on-site comparisons with other Latin American countries. My view is contradicted by the 'Corruption Perceptiveness Index' of the business organisation, Transparency International, which ranks Bolivia in 118th place among 158 countries. The lower the number, the more corruption has been perceived. The best score was 9.7. Bolivia stood at 2.5, equal to Guatemala and Ecuador, and ahead of only two Spanish speaking countries in the Américas. Visiting business people are often caught at a point where an important step in the process is simply not happening. Routinely, the requirement is either patience, or one more reference letter of significance. A willingness to pay an extra 'service charge' is a last resort. (I once did an undercover investigation which discovered what every Bolivian already knew: that military and police procurement involves 'courtesy payments' to high ranking officials who sign for purchase of goods and supplies.)
- Bolivia is a country of more than nine million inhabitants. Subtract millions of subsistence farmers, street vendors and labourers, and you have a business community no larger than a town in Iowa. Most important occurrences are detected through the grapevine. An aggressive community of journalists within an atmosphere of freedom of expression makes it less and less possible to do business in an underhanded way. Campaigns against corruption are commonplace. Corruption lingers on, but the level of scrutiny from journalists and government policing agencies has risen significantly.

- There is a keen awareness of social responsibility as it relates to profitable business. Anyone who can combine transparency and social responsibility will win great respect in the public domain. A business that exports a value-added product rather than a raw material will be appreciated for generating jobs and helping to turn the tide against the colonial heritage of Third World countries as exporters of raw materials.
- Bolivia's 'capitalisation' programme (a euphemism for 'privatisation' of strategic state enterprises) was controversial when it was being implemented in the 1990s and for the most part, the naysayers have been proven correct. This programme made no dent in unemployment and underemployment statistics, but weakened the state's ability to pay for public services. A foreign businessman who can create a new company rather than buying off an old one will be embraced by Bolivia's unemployed.

TITLES

In business situations, unless you know a person of the opposite sex on an ongoing basis, a simple handshake will suffice, as it will with same sex introductions. More crucial is to address the person by their title. If they are lawyers or college grads, the term to use before the last name is *Licenciado*. An engineer or technical professional is called *Ingeniero*. A teacher is called *Professor* since the word *maestro*, used for teachers in other Latin countries, in Bolivia refers to drivers and independent contractors.

BUSINESS CLIMATE: EXPORTS

Knowing the basics of business communication can get you far as long as you know what business sectors are ripe for investment. We conclude the business chapter with a snapshot of Bolivia's business terrain, ending with a summary of possible new directions in economic policy.

THE CURSE OF OIL

Any treatment of natural resources and exports needs to face the reality that resource-rich countries among former colonies develop more slowly or less profoundly than other countries within the same category. It is precisely because Bolivia is so rich in hydrocarbons and minerals that it is so undeveloped.

One explanation is the 'Dutch Disease'. When Holland found natural gas in the North Sea, the sudden inflow of dollar revenues led to a sharp rise in domestic currency. Non-oil sectors like manufacturing or agriculture are rendered less competitive in world markets.

Oil and gas industries employ few unskilled labourers so the wealth reaches a tiny segment of the population. Some governments have tried to set up special funds that would save some of the inflowing revenue for future generations or distribute it directly to the people. President Chavez in Venezuela has used oil revenue to subsidise social programmes and even as aid for neighbouring republics. Governments that do not follow the Chavez example may remain tempted to borrow from hydrocarbons or mineral revenues to patch up the budget or worse, for the personal gain of a few.

Whole treatises are written on the subject, but one thing is clear: natural resources do not correlate with wealth for the general populace.

Colonial structures engrained a system whereby a raw material might be extracted at little cost thanks to near slave labour, exported immediately abroad to a wealthy company where the product was refined and elaborated into something new, with 'surplus value', and this new product was then sold back to the country where its raw material originated. The price was rarely affordable to the masses of people who would have benefitted if this raw material had been elaborated at the point where it had been extracted.

I once asked a Bolivian zinc miner about the potential for uncovering new lodes. He told me, directly, that if I wanted to benefit from zinc, forget mining; I'd do much better as an intermediary trader.

THE RAW REALITY OF RAW MATERIALS

Rubber was once the primary product in the deep rainforests of north-east Bolivia. Working in virtual slave conditions, rubber workers extracted the once valuable sap from wild growing trees in what could be termed 'jungle mining'. There were no bars or walls but escape was nearly impossible. River routes crossed rapids and encountered caimans. Land routes requiring machete mastery were boobytrapped with malaria and dysentary.

Quality of life for lowland rubber workers was as grim as it was for highland miners. With better growing conditions for rubber discovered in Malaysia and synthetic materials on the rise, the whole industry collapsed. Taking its place was the harvesting and processing of the humble Brazil nut. This industry centres around the steamy towns of Cobija and Riberalta.

By 2003, the total market value of Brazil nuts reached US$ 48 million, a tidy sum for a vast but sparsely inhabited region. The industry supports nearly 30,000 families, creating as many as 100,000 collateral jobs in packaging, transport and export. Bolivia controls 80 per cent of the Brazil nut market, with bordering Brazil and Peru accounting for the rest. Like rubber, the nuts grow in the wild, and therefore, no intensive farming will disrupt the rainforest in their harvest. With the help of the Swiss government, quality control (reducing toxins, improving packaging) within the industry has greatly improved.

> The presence of the Brazil nut industry acts to discourage residents from environmentally catastrophic slash-and-burn agriculture.

The relative success of the Brazil nut has spread to other exports, usually non-traditional products for niche markets. These include cotton textiles originating in the lowlands and *cameloid* textiles such as the warm *alpaca* from the highlands; gold and silver jewellery; leather products, wood manufactures (with some mahogany coming from illegal loggers), and certain exotic food products such as fava beans and especially *quinoa*, the supergrain that grows anywhere in the Andes above 2,000 m (6,561 ft) in altitude.

At the moment, *quinoa* is targeted to health food shops in developed countries. For a *quinoa* cereal to make it in the mass market, production would have to expand beyond current capacity.

So that the country does not lapse into the direct export neo-colonial economy, local economists and international non-government organisations are encouraging value added products and goods. The number of derivatives from Brazil nuts or *quinoa* have no boundary. The knowhow of foreigners is also employed in order to help Bolivian producers become adjusted to the requirements of international markets.

With illegal timber operations in remote forests, the hardwood industry needed a more sustainable model. The Cochabamba company Industria Madera Sali has been able to diversify wood products while using a strict environmental management system. By spinning off wood products into a more complex product array, this company is reducing pressure on old growth forests. Madera Sali currently supplies the immense US company, Home Depot Stores.

Quinoa is another example of diversification and production of added value. A company like Andean Valley, also in Cochabamba, has created processed foods from *quinoa*, obtaining organic certification for some of its products. Since *quinoa* is grown by smaller farmers in some of the poorest areas of Bolivia, expansion of this industry and the added value that comes with it can bolster these poorer regions.

A few success stories cannot blind us to the nagging obstacles against the Bolivian economy. Being a landlocked country makes exporting more expensive. Low internal consumption places too much pressure on export, at a time in the globalised economy when many exports gain their original strength from a strong local customer base. Transportation remains a literal obstacle, with a contorted topography of immense mountains, tight valleys, narrow gorges and vast flood plains limiting the potential for ground-based transport. Less than 3 per cent of Bolivian land is technically arable, though small farmers plant on impossible inclines in areas we'd consider unarable, and rainforest industry such as Brazil nuts do not need to be farmed before harvesting.

These obstacles, in combination with the vestiges of dependence on a non-value-added export model, continue to restrict Bolivia's economic enfranchisement. The economic awareness of social protesters should be seen as positive in progressive business sectors, for even the poorest of Bolivians are aware of the difference between the moribund neo-colonial model and more dynamic forms of economy.

> Ultimately, as experience from rising countries such as South Korea illustrates, the nurturing of internal markets creates a vital safety pad for launching the export sector.

Areas of business where foreign visitors of goodwill can be of help are: managerial skills in the logistics of international cargo, trade information systems, marketing tools, quality control, international packaging requirements, product design and support in all these areas from institutions of higher education and non-governmental organisations that specialise in trade and commerce.

BUSINESS CLIMATE: INTERNAL ECONOMY

The government elected in December of 2005 might be described as 'socialist realist'. The middle word of Movement Towards Socialism points to what is referred to as 'Andean capitalism'. Vice-president Alvaro García Linera points out that you can't move toward socialism without an 'organised proletariat and established capitalism, neither of which exist in Bolivia.

In the theoretical terms of the administration that took power in 2006, 'Andean capitalism' is a necessity in a country where 70 per cent of workers belong to a 'family economy'. Andean capitalism may end up as a simple electoral slogan or may develop into a viable alternative model. In theory, it is 'a capitalist regime where family, indigenous and peasant potentials are balanced and articulated around a national development project and productive modernization.'

The prerequisite is a strong state, contrary to the previous Goni and Bánzer regimes, in which the state, drained and sapped from massive privatisation of the most strategic sectors, was capable of no function beyond serving as an intermediary for foreign exploitation.

In the early days of the Morales–García Linera administration, foreign investment was not an evil phrase, but it was expected to be guided by a strong state, with roots formed through local investments, family and small businesses and a communitarian economy.

The definition remains at an abstract level in the evolving and uncertain economy whose context must be understood by those people from abroad who wish to do business with or in Bolivia.

This government was brought to power by five years of social movements led by the majority indigenous population. Whether Andean capitalism can be defined with more precision and then converted into a viable reality depends on whether the demands of this majority population can be met. Another primary variable is the position of the United States. When a similar type of government was elected in Chile in the early 1970s, the USA chose to destabilise the Chilean economy, with grave consequences. Though some mentalities in the US foreign policy community may not have evolved, times have changed. Bolivian activists and intellectuals know that orthodox 'free' market policies have failed and they will be well aware of any signs of destabilisation triggered by a foreign power that wants to reimpose them.

> ### Alternative Trade
> Bolivia remains a wild frontier for business. Much has been hyped about the Butch Cassidy cowboy legend in Bolivia, but considerably more interesting is the survival of Wild-West style gold mining around the rivers north of La Paz and the 'ant' contraband around the borders with Chile, Peru and Argentina, where rivers of humanity flow back and forth across borders, with individuals each carrying their own stash.

Reading between the lines of Bolivian economic advisors, one can project that there will be an attempt to forge an alliance with the most socially responsive sectors of the international business community in order to cushion the financial blows that may sweep in from the north. There's always a chance that pragmatists from the north may realise that no truly free trade instrument can be institutionalised between Bolivia and the United States until both sides are equally enfranchised. The model of countries like Portugal and Greece being subsidised by Europe until they were able to stand equally with their northern partners is more likely to be accepted in Bolivia than the slumming models that have been offered, in which foreign investors reap and run.

Until now, no one has been able to create a model that could harness the vast informal economy into a law-abiding job-creating mechanism. Orthodox free market policy (neoliberalism) was given two decades to dynamise the country, with shameful results. One could say that the neoliberals have 20 years of business experience, but in fact they only have one failed year repeated 20 times. They'd love to continue on the same worn tracks, but it appears as if the majority of Bolivian people would like to give a fair chance to new models.

As of February 2006, half of the ministers in the new government were comprised of new model supporters but the other half seemed to be from the old school. Clearly, the president was attempting to consolidate his government by satisfying everyone, but he also has risked satisfying no one. The Bolivian social movements that led to the election of a revolutionary president will not sit tight for long if old economic models prevail.

FAST FACTS ABOUT BOLIVIA

CHAPTER 10

> 80% OF ALL BRAZIL NUTS ARE GROWN IN BOLIVIA AND THEY'RE STILL CALLED "BRAZIL" NUTS

'Bolivia is... a place of natural highs. It boasts the world's highest city, the highest commercial airport (so high that incoming flights have to ascend to land), the highest navigable lake, the highest ski-run, the highest golf course and, during its turbulent post-independence history, the highest number of military coups. It has close to a thousand peaks over 5,000 meters.'
—Alan Murphy, *Bolivia Handbook*

Official Name
Republic of Bolivia

Capital
The seat of government is in La Paz but the legal capital is in Sucre

Flag
Three equal-width horizontal bands of red, yellow and green from top to bottom. A coat of arms sits in the centre of the flag, within the yellow band.

National Anthem
Canción Patriótica (Patriotic Song), uselessly militaristic since Bolivia has never won a war and has repudiated its past of military dictatorships.

Time
Greenwich Mean Time minus 4 hours (GMT −0400)

Telephone Country Code
591

Land
Located in South America, this land-locked country is surrounded by Brazil, Paraguay, Argentina, Chile and Peru,

with all five of these countries having sliced off parts of Bolivia at one time or another.

Area
total: 1,098,580 sq km (424,164.1 sq miles), nearly the size of France, Germany and England combined, and yet with less than 1/20 the population of those three countries!
land: 1,084,390 sq km (418,685.3 sq miles)
water: 14,190 sq km (5,478.8 sq miles)

Highest Point
Nevado Sajama (6,542 m / 21,463.3 ft), with the central Cordillera Real alone having more than 600 peaks at more than 5,000 m (16,400 ft)

Climate
Varies depending on the altitude and ranges from cold and semi-arid to tropical humid, with radically different climates often so contiguous that one can walk (up or down) from one climate to another.

Natural Resources
Natural gas, petroleum, tin, zinc, tungsten, antimony, silver, iron, lead, gold, timber, hydropower

Population
8,857,870 (July 2005 est), approximately the population of Switzerland but nearly 25 times the size of Switzerland.

Ethnic Groups
Quechua (30 per cent), Mestizo, which is a mixture of Amerindian and white (30 per cent), Aymara (25 per cent), white (15 per cent), with more than 30 minority ethnic groups, most of them with their own distinct languages, collectively representing less than 1 per cent.

Administrative Divisions
9 departments: Chuquisaca, Cochabamba, Beni, La Paz, Oruro, Pando, Potosí, Santa Cruz, Tarija

Official Languages
Spanish, Quechua and Aymara

Government Structure
Republic

Religion
Predominantly Roman Catholic but with indigenous religious traditions and cosmology blended in with Catholicism; about 5 per cent Protestant

Currency
Boliviano (BOB)

Gross Domestic Product (GDP) Per Capita
US$ 2,700 (2005 est.) compared to France's US$ 29,900. The 'average' Bolivian earns less than 10 per cent of what the average French person earns, and it's worse, since GDP averages do not consider inequality of distribution of wealth. On the other hand, the cost of living for basic food staples, housing and public transportation in Bolivia is considerably lower than in France. Thus, GDP is a very rough measurement.

Agricultural Products
Soybeans, coffee, coca, cotton, corn, sugarcane, rice, potatoes, *quinoa*, fruit and nuts

Industries
Mining, smelting, petroleum, food and beverages, tobacco, handicrafts and clothing

Exports
Crude petroleum, natural gas, soybeans and soy products, Brazil nuts, *quinoa*, tin and zinc ore

Imports
Aircraft and parts, automobiles, insecticides (sometimes illegal), paper, petroleum products, plastics and processed

foods. A significant portion of imports are contraband and find their way into the informal economy.

Environmental Issues
Bolivia is part of the richest and most biodiverse region on Earth, the Tropical Andes. The main threats to this rich environment are:
- Deforestation (from slash-and-burn agriculture and both legal and illegal timber operations), though Bolivia remains one of the most forested countries in the world, with 54.2 per cent of its land covered by forest, half of which is intact 'primary forest';
- Soil erosion (from slash-and-burn agriculture and overgrazing); desertification;
- Loss of biodiversity;
- Receding glaciers (due to global warming);
- Polution of water supplies (from mining, agrochemical and industrial runoff).

FAMOUS PEOPLE
Ana María Romero de Campero
Ana María Romero de Campero (1943) has been an award-winning journalist and one-time editor of the prestigious but now-defunct *Presencia*. Romero was once asked to leave her newspaper job to become Minister of Communication at a time of national convulsion. She later authored a book about her experiences. She's written two books since, including a novel about journalism.

More recently, she was the Head of the Human Rights Ombudsman Office. During the government repression of 2003, she initiated a hunger strike calling for the president Sánchez de Lozada to step down. The strike was joined by a number of high-profile Bolivian personalities.

Marco Etcheverry
Marco Etcheverry (1970) led Bolivia's national football team to an unprecedented qualification for the 1994 World Cup, thanks to a dramatic victory against Brazil. He starred for

the US Major League Soccer team DC United between 1996 and 2003.

Evo Morales

Evo Morales Ayma (1959), of Aymara heritage and the son of poor peasants, became a labour organiser and leader of the coca growers' union. Scorned by Bolivia's political elites, Morales was elected to congress in 1997 thanks to his oratory skills and philosophy of creative civil disobedience. He helped develop the Movement Toward Socialism into a political party and was elected president in December of 2005 with a record 54 per cent of the vote.

Felipe Quispe Huanca (El Mallku)

Felipe Quispe Huanca (El Mallku) (1944) has risen in the new century as a militant peasant leader and champion of indigenous enfranchisement, with a component of cultural nationalism that resembles the Black Power movement of the United States. Quispe is perceived by some as more 'radical' than Evo Morales.

Jorge Sanjinés

Jorge Sanjinés (1936) has been one of Bolivia's great film makers. His award winning *Blood of the Condor* (Yawar Mallku, 1969) began a fruitful career in which Sanjinés blended pioneering aesthetics with anti-racist and sociopolitical statements.

Alberto Villalpando

Alberto Villalpando (1942) is one of the main driving forces in Bolivian contempory music. He is an eclectic composer who uses classical instruments, voice and electronic devices to create truly unique compositions.

ACRONYMS

ALCA   The Free Trade Area of the Américas (Area de Libre Comercio de las Américas) is a United States-initiated attempt to establish open

	trade borders throughout the Américas, which has been opposed by a large majority of Bolivians as unbalanced and constricting against Bolivia's agriculture and industry.
APDHB	Permanent Assembly of Human Rights (Asamblea Permanente de Derechos Humanos de Bolivia) which is closely associated with the historical leadership of Waldo Albarracín.
ASOFAMD	Association of the Families of Martyrs and the Disappeared, this organisation struggles against impunity of human rights abusers from former dictatorships and investigates the truth about disappeared political prisoners whose bodies were never found.
CIDOB	The Confederation of Indigenous Peoples of Eastern Bolivia (Confederación de Pueblos Indígenas del Oriente Boliviano) is a grass roots advocacy organisation.
COB	The Bolivian Labor Confederation (Confederación Obrera Boliviana) that, under the leadership of Juan Lechín, participated as co-government following the 1952 revolution. Since then, the COB, mainly supported by miners, teachers and peasant unions, has been involved in most Bolivian social movements.
CSUTCB	Confederation of Bolivian Agricultural Workers (Confederación Unica de Trabajadores Campesinos de Bolivia) has a long and rich history of defending Bolivian peasant rights.
COMIBOL	The National Mining Corporation (Corporacíon Minera Boliviana)
ENFE	Empresa Nacional de Ferrocarriles, former national railways now privatised by a Chilean company.

FAST FACTS ABOUT BOLIVIA

ENTEL	Empresa Nacional de Teléfonos, former national phone company now privatised long-distance company whose temporary monopoly has ended.
FEDECOR	Combining the Coordinating Committee for the Defense of Water and Gas with the Departmental Federation of Water Users of Cochabamba (Coordinadora del Agua y el Gas y Federación Departamental de Regantes de Cochabamba), this grass roots group has been responsible for defending Cochabamba's water resources against transnational corporations and later managing these resources.
FEJUVE	The Federation of Neighborhood Assemblies of El Alto (La Federación de Juntas Vecinales de El Alto) has been a primary player in social movements to defend Bolivian resources such as natural gas and water from privatisation and foreign control.
FOBOMADE	A non-governmental environmental organisation, Bolivian Forum for Environment and Development (Foro Boliviano—Medioambiente y Desarrollo)
INRA	Agrarian Reform Institute (Instituto de Reforma Agrara)
LAB	Lloyd Aéreo Boliviano, flagship airline now privatised by a Brazilian company.
PIL	Former Bolivian milk company now privatised by a Peruvian firm.
UMSA	The largest branch of Bolivia's national university, in La Paz (Universidad Mayor de San Andrés)
YPFB	Yacimientos Petrolíferos Fiscales Bolivianos, former national oil company, now privatised*

COUNTRY STATISTICS: SUPERLATIVE FACT SHEET

- Highest capital in the world: La Paz—3,600 m (12,000 ft)
- Highest navigable lake in the world: Titicaca; 3,800 m (12,500 ft)
- Lowest violent crime rate in the Américas.
- Most sparsely populated country in Latin Américas with population density at 7.4 inhabitants per sq km.
- Largest proportion of indigenous people in the Américas, between 50 per cent to 70 per cent, depending on how statistics are derived.
- Most unknown currency in the world: the Boliviano, more than 8 per US dollar.
- Most abrupt changes in altitude.
- World's least developed rainforest, but watch out for illegal lumber operations and poachers!
- Greatest democratic transformation: until 1983, Bolivia held the world record for most dictators and coup d'états; now it's got the longest running democracy in Latin America, after Costa Rica.
- Most well-organised non-violent protest culture in the world.

261

CULTURE QUIZ

To test your newly acquired knowledge, try this quiz of situations typical of Bolivian daily life. How you respond in the situations you are faced with from day to day will depend on your ability to work through those aspects of the culture that you find very different from your own.

As you begin to pick up language and cultural nuances and recognise and appreciate the attitudes you encounter, your culture shock will pass and then it's really time to start enjoying the rewards of life in Bolivia.

SITUATION 1

It is Carnaval time, the Bolivian Mardi Gras, and you've just been struck in the side of the head by a water balloon, coming from the back of a pick-up truck in slow traffic. Do you:

❹ Take down the license plate number and report it to the police?

- **B** Forget the incident and look around as you walk to avoid potential foam spray and water balloon attacks?
- **C** Write a letter to the editor, criticising such infantile behaviour?
- **D** Quickly purchase water balloons from a street vendor and counter attack?

Comments

If the balloon did not contain urine or ice, the police will laugh off your complaint, so will readers of any newspaper that would bother to print your letter.

B is one correct answer. Events like this one only happen during Carnaval. It beats getting in the way of a drive-by shooting in a gun-toting culture.

D is not a bad alternative. You may discover there is something therapeutic in getting involved in this Carnaval ritual.

SITUATION 2

You are invited to a social engagement in the home of a friend. Many guests are already seated in the living room and dining room when you arrive. How do you greet the host and the other guests?

- **A** If male, make the rounds, shaking hands with each male (embracing them if they are friends or relatives), and shaking the hand of each female while kissing her on the cheek if she is a friend or relative. If female, shake hands and offer your cheek to males if they are friends or relatives while doing the same with females but adding an embrace if you are friends or family.
- **B** Say 'good evening' to the whole crowd at once.
- **C** Take a seat and only begin greeting people as they happen to come in contact with you.
- **D** Make sure that you are the first to arrive so you won't face this dilemma.

Comments

A is the absolute answer. You will be considered unsociable if you apply answers **B** or **C**. If you choose **D** and are the first to arrive, you will also have to be the last to leave if you want to evade the ritual, since the same process used in the initial greeting is repeated by the person who is saying goodbye.

SITUATION 3

You have been injured as the result of falling into a hole left by construction workers. Do you:

A Sue the company?
B Forget the incident as best you can?
C Report the incident to the proper authorities so that no one else falls into the same trap that you did?
D Fill in the hole with sludge as revenge against the workers who left it open?

Comments

B is the only possible answer. A personal injury lawyer would go broke in Bolivia, a non-litigious society. People are expected to be careful; government and private enterprise do not take legal responsibility for injuries, except in the case of employees. For example, if you have a maid who is injured on the job, then it is your responsibility to see that she receives the care she requires. If the development of countries were linked to the litigation industry, Bolivia could be labelled 'underdeveloped'.

SITUATION 4

You are going into business as an exporter but the initiation of your enterprise is being held up by a permit delay in a government office. The last time you asked, you were told that your documents would be ready any day, but any day has long since passed. Do you:

A Ask if there is a 'special fee' (bribe?) that will expedite the signing of your documents?

🅑 Telephone or e-mail the responsible party?
🅒 Make an appointment and visit the responsible party, preferably with a letter of support from an influential person?
🅓 Call a lawyer?

Comments

The more cynical Bolivians would answer 🅐, and in some cases they would be right. However, 🅒, a personal visit with a further support document, usually gets the job done. Telephoning or e-mailing (🅑) has little impact as personal contact remains vital in business relations.

Should the case drag on even more, you may need 🅓, a lawyer. But don't get a lawyer from the phone directory. He might be a friend of the guy who has been sitting on your documents. Your embassy will have a list of lawyers to choose from.

SITUATION 5

You have been invited to a social engagement and are quite concerned about your patchy listening comprehension and your thick accent in the Spanish language. On a one-to-one basis you can function relatively well, but in large groups with noise and confusion, you become anxious. Do you:

🅐 Decline the invitation and wait until you have improved your Spanish in other more comfortable settings?
🅑 Ask the host if you can bring an interpreter?
🅒 Go to the event and hope that you will find one or two people who speak English?
🅓 Go to the event and speak with as many people as you can in Spanish?

Comments

In some cultures, a heavy accent or a difficulty in expression or comprehension of the native language will cause people to avoid you, but not in Bolivia. In general, Bolivians delight in the chance to speak with foreign visitors and will go out of their way to facilitate communication. (Bolivia twice elected a president with an English accent, a man of Bolivian descent who had grown up in the United States.) The answer is **D**. The more you practice, the more you learn.

SITUATION 6

You are at a dinner with eight people at your table. During the dinner, one of the people makes an overtly racist remark against indigenous Bolivians. You should:

A Hope that someone else will respond, but if not, let the incident pass so as to not be unsociable, thus avoiding dinner table polemics.

B Discreetly respond to that person when you can get him/her alone after the dinner.

C Respond immediately, but diplomatically with: 'How strange you make that remark because I have come to Bolivia precisely out of admiration for the great achievements of her indigenous cultures.'

D Let the person in question know that racist remarks cannot be tolerated.

Comments

When the Spaniards conquered South America, they used racism as an excuse for the right to plunder and exact cheap labour. Racism was therefore imposed in colonial education. Until 1952, Bolivia was one of the most caste-conscious countries in the world. Since then, the prevailing ideology has been to oppose racism, though gains were mainly in words rather than actions. Gradually, with the 'incentive' of militant protest, Bolivia has converted many on-paper declarations into real-life practice, to the extent of electing an indigenous president. However, attitudes do not change completely in one or two generations, and nuances of racism remain.

To not respond (**A**) or to respond privately to a public remark (**B**) would imply to the other people at the table that you, as an individual and as a representative of your country, are not concerned with the issue. On the other hand, a combative response (**D**) will only serve to put the other person on the defensive. A diplomatic but firm response (**❸**) will be greatly appreciated by the other people at your table. In fact, they will probably back you up, once you've broken the ice. At the same time, the person who made the remark is more likely to question his/her premise when learning that Bolivian indigenous cultures are admired outside of Bolivia.

SITUATION 7

You are planning to do business in Bolivia and have set up a lunch appointment with a Bolivian businessman who has expressed enthusiasm about your ideas in a written letter and is interested in participating in some way. Do you go to the lunch prepared to:

❶ Present a business plan and to offer specific financial advantages to your lunch companion should he decide to participate?

❷ Talk about your family, the latest international football matches, how you've adapted to the altitude: anything and everything except business? Since this is a first in-person meeting, your companion will want to find out in his own way whether he/she is going to feel comfortable working with you, and you should want to know the same.

❸ Begin the luncheon with conversation about non-business matters, leaving the business talk for dessert and coffee?

❹ Reject the participation of this person if he does not seem anxious to begin as soon as possible, since you want to see someone who is totally motivated?

Comments

In general, the only purpose of a first in-person meeting is for the two parties to get to know each other and develop a sense of whether or not they will feel comfortable working together long term. The most probable answer here is **❷**.

❸ would seem like a nice compromise, but in Bolivia this is not often the case. However, **❸** may become readily applicable depending on the verbal hints you receive from the potential client/customer/partner.

❶ is just what you do not want to see. You are interested in a real commitment; the need for quick action may point to an impatient person who will dump the project at the first sign that there will be no immediate gratification. An excess of enthusiasm from your acquaintance could be just as dubious as an apparent lack it. Today's swelling of excitement may represent an honest but capricious show of support stemming mainly from a momentary sentiment of solidarity, and your counterpart may wake up the next day to feel that his enthusiasm was based more on his liking for you than the feasibility of your project.

DO'S AND DON'TS

DO'S

- Say *buenos días* (good morning), *buenas tardes* (good afternoon) or *buenas noches* (good evening) when entering a taxi, restaurant or house.
- Participate in indigenous ceremonies when invited and respect La Pachamama (Mother Earth).
- Arrive on time for business meetings and classes.
- Behave according to your natural social background while applying principles of justice and fairness.
- Say *provecho* (*bon appétit*) to others when leaving a restaurant or dinner table.
- Speak up critically, using humour or irony to add a civil edge to your comment, when a racist remark has been made.
- Avoid the truth if it can be insulting and if it is not productive.
- Keep certain alternative lifestyles discreet.
- Get somone at home to wire you money should you need it.
- Employ paid help for the handicapped; it is not costly.
- Stay clear of illicit drugs and the people who use them. Consult your embassy should you have a legal problem.
- Practise physical fitness in your everyday life. If you want something more organised, join a private gym or club.
- Make photocopies of your important documents and keep them in a separate place from the originals. If you have other valuables, purchase travel insurance, and read the contract carefully.

DON'TS

- Don't tell the taxi driver your destination before saying *buenos días*.
- Don't participate in indigenous ceremonies without being invited. Never take photos of anything private or ceremonial without permission from all.
- Don't arrive at the stated time for social occasions (you'll be too early.)
- Don't imitate a different social class or you will be perceived as mocking the people involved.
- Don't ignore the people you pass when leaving a dinner or restaurant.
- Don't belittle traditional religious practices based on La Pachamama (Mother Earth).
- Don't be blunt, as social and business relations in Bolivia are cushioned by a thick layer of civility.
- Don't adopt alternative lifestyles unless you know it fits in with the Bolivian culture; Bolivia is an alternative country, alternatives to this alternative are not promising, as traditional customs prevail.
- Don't borrow money from Bolivian moneylenders. Normal lending interest rates here are much higher than what illegal lenders get on the mean streets of New York.
- Don't count on facilities for the handicapped in Bolivia. It's hard for Bolivian authorities to consider handicapped facilities when they can't afford sewage systems in outlying communities.
- Don't hire a lawyer, for the ending of such stories are usually not happy.
- Don't be lazy and refuse to exert yourself physically.
- Don't think you can find a lost item; they're often kept by someone else who needs them more than you do.

GLOSSARY

A comprehensive Bolivian glossary would occupy a whole volume. The most frequent and strategic words typical of Bolivia have been chosen for this selected glossary.

Abra	Mountain pass (important mainly for hikers/climbers)
Api	A nutritious hot cereal drink
Ayllu	Native community structure, within which functions the system of *ayni* (community solidarity/sharing)
Aymara	Language and people of much of highland Bolivia, pre-dating the Incas
Camba	Bolivian from lowlands of the east
Cambista	Money changer working on the street
Carnaval	Bolivian Mardi Gras, celebrated all over the country but especially famous in Oruro
Chagas	Also known as *mal de chagas*: a slowly developing incurable disease coming from vinchuca bug that lives between poorly sealed adobe bricks, mostly in temperate valleys
Cha'lla	Ritual baptism, as homage to the Pachamama (Mother Earth) of a new home, vehicle or piece of land, in which alcohol or an alcoholic beverage is used, occasionally accompanied with confetti and the burial of a llama foetus. Although this is an indigenous custom, Bolivians of all ethnicities and social classes may practice the Cha'lla.

GLOSSARY

Chaqueo	Annual burning of rainforest lands or overgrown fields for agriculture or grazing with disastrous environmental consequences (short-term air pollution/long-term soil degradation)
Choclo	Corn on the cob
Cholo/Chola	Aymara or Quechua man or woman with urbanised culture
Chullo	Andean woven woollen hat with earflaps
Chuños	Freeze-dried potatoes
Cordillera	Mountain range
Cueca	Of all Bolivian dances, this may be the most exquisite. Folk dances like the *diablada* and *tinku* are more for group spectacles. You're more likely to try a *cueca* on the dance floor. The classic *cueca* song is Viva Mi Patria Bolivia, a type of ad hoc non-militaristic national anthem.
Ekeko	Dwarf-god of abundance /annual miniatures festival
Flota	Long-distance bus company
Kallawaya	Wandering medicine men and natural healers from the Apolobamba region near Pelechuco
Kolla	Aymara or highlander
Kollasuyo	The Inca name for Bolivia
La Diablada	Dance of the Devils, typical group dance in festivals and Carnaval
Llajhua	Hot sauce with hot pepper, tomato, onion and herbs
Llapa	Equivalent to the 'baker's dozen'; a little extra given to a regular buyer

Micro	Small bus used in urban public transportation
Pachamama	Mother Earth, god of nature, whose influence trancends indigenous communities and reaches both religious and secular Bolivians of diverse backgrounds
Peña	Folk music scene
Pollera	Thick bulky embroided skirt used by *chola*. The trend is away from using the word *chola* and instead saying *mujer de pollera* (woman with *pollera*).
Quechua	Language of the Incas, still spoken in the Bolivian, Peruvian and Ecuatorian highlands
Quena	Andean flute
Quinoa	Andean supergrain, now a popular product in health food shops around the world
Salteña	Chicken or beef pie, with semi-sweet dough and mildly piquant sauce, usually a mid-morning snack
Saya	Afro-Bolivian dance recalling black slavery in Potosí mines, today a primary dance of Carnaval and other festivals
Soroche	Altitude sickness
Surazo	Cold wind coming from the south into normally hot Bolivian lowlands
Tinku	A traditional dance that often breaks into a ritual fight between communities
Tranca	Police checkpoint at designated points on highways

GLOSSARY

Tupac Katari	*Aymara* anti-colonial resistance leader
Whipala	Flag of the Andean nation from pre-Inca times, composed of 49 squares with the 7 different colours of the rainbow, symbolising diversity and unity, and used as a banner in movements to defend natural resources
Yatiri	Medicine man, priest or sage who presides over religious ceremonies
Zampoña	Pan flute made from reeds, highlighted in indigenous music

RESOURCE GUIDE

This Resource Guide was compiled from the most current and up-to-date information at the latest possible moment prior to handing in the completed manuscript of *CultureShock! Bolivia*. Given the fragile nature of contemporary business and the evolving reality of Bolivian telecommunications, it cannot be assured that each site or establishment will still be around or have the same phone number when you get there.

This guide is selective rather than encyclopaedic. In the realm of tours, restaurants and hotels, we attempt to avoid what would be easily found or obvious, preferring to explore for special surprises, unusual bargains or local legends. That said, we also highlight practical solutions.

PRIMARY WEBSITES

- http://www.bolpress.com
  Best source of news, current events, and culture commentary.

- http://www.boliviaweb.com
  The all-purpose guide with a comprehensive network of cross-references.

- http://www.funsolon.org
  The site of the Solón Foundation, some of Bolivia's foremost thinkers and doers keep us apprised of current social movements, human rights; features the work of the later Walter Solón Romero, one of South America's great international artists.

PHONES

If you plan to call/fax to or be called in Bolivia:
- Country Code: 591
- City Codes: La Paz   2
                 Santa Cruz   3
                 Cochabamba   4

Sucre	4
Tarija	4
Oruro	2
Potosí	2

WEATHER REPORT
- http://www.boliviaweb.com/weather.htm

INTERNET FACILITIES AND CAFÉS
In any major city, you won't have to look for the ubiquitous Internet café. It will find you. Competition is serious and the price is right. Try several in order to choose your best nest. Off-peak hours like lunch time offer the best chance for immediate accommodation.

PRE-ENTRY VACCINATIONS
Yellow fever vaccination is not required but is recommended for rural travel in the humid lowlands. Any other vaccination depends on your own threshold of concern. Consult your physician about the Tetanus booster. Rainforest explorers should consider Typhoid vaccine or capsules. Also consult your physician about the feasibility of a Hepatitis A vaccination.

BUSINESS ORGANISATIONS
- http://www.boliviaweb.com/business.htm
  Has practical links to business information by sector and company

TRAINS AND BUS
Bus service is relatively comfortable to and from large cities, and less so the farther off the main trail you go. Terminals are easy to find but larger cities like La Paz have different subterminals for various specialised routes.

Not necessarily more practical if time is of the essence, train travel is the little-known alternative (only a few routes) with a possibly more pleasing or at least more aesthetic experience taking the Expreso del Sur, on the Red Occidental (Western Network).

The Red Oriental focuses on a main line between Santa Cruz and Quijarro on the Brazilian border. Heat and humidity and possible overcrowding may remove the pleasure from this trip unless you travel first class.

The main line on the Red Occidental is between Oruro and Argentine border at Villazón, with the main stop at Tupiza, a small, underrated and cultivated city where one can stretch out and tour by renting a bicycle or stay overnight in any of several economical hotels. At nearly 3,000 m (9,842 ft) above sea level, Tupiza is comfortably mild, with rough and colourful badlands surrounding the town.

The higher-class Expreso del Sur travels on Saturdays and Tuesdays while you can ride the Wara Wara on Sundays and Thursdays. Within these two broad classifications are three subclasses in order of quality: executive, business and *salon*.

Service is evolving since the privatisation by a Chilean company, and the future remains in limbo, since privatisation of railroads does not have a good record for passenger travel in other countries.

Tickets are purchased the same day at the railroad station, and first-class tickets may be purchased on the train with a surcharge, but this system may change from one moment to the next. Timetables are estimates. The *jefe de estación* (stationmaster) may be the best source of information.

Travellers in La Paz will have to bus it to Oruro to catch the train, as the passenger service from La Paz was terminated.

SELECTED TOUR COMPANIES

The following tour companies have been recommended by multiple sources, and in several cases, used by the author or his family. Many of the companies listed here sponsor tours to places of difficult access, and Bolivia is one of those countries where many organised tours seek adventure and interact with local inhabitants, contrary to the 'tacky', encyclopaedic tours in the mainstream industry. For other companies not on this list, check out http://www.boliviaweb.com. One can discover small and inexpensive tour companies on one's own, near main plazas of most cities and in the Calle Sagárnaga area of La Paz. For the most part, these companies offer a good product, but you can always double-check by making sure they are approved by the Bolivian Secretariat of Tourism. Our having mentioned specialities with each entry should not imply that these companies are limited to one niche. Most addresses are in La Paz, for pragmatic reasons, but some of these companies have branches in smaller cities, while others go far and wide.

- **America Tours SRL**
  Edificio 16 de Julio (El Prado)
  Tel: (2) 237-4204
  Website: http://www.america-ecotours.com
  Specialising in the incredible Madidi National Park with 1,000 bird species and 44 per cent of all new world mammals, as well as being a hot spot for endemic species.

- **Andean Summits**
  Calle Sagárnaga 189, first floor
  Tel: (2) 231-7497
  Website: http://www.andeansummits.com
  Including mountaineering and any related adventures in which people commune with geography.

- **Crillón Tours**
  Av Camacho 1223
  Tel: (2) 236-1990 / (2) 236-7533
  Specialising in Lake Titicaca, including hydrofoil excursions.

- **Fremen Tours**
  Calle Pedro Salazar 537 (near Plaza Abaroa)
  Tel: (2) 236-7329 / (2) 241-7062
  Website: http://www.andes-amazonia.com
  Covers all of Bolivia, including tailored trips and is known for river trips on the Mamoré.

- **Gravity Assisted Mountain Biking**
  Website: http://www.gravitybolivia.com (associated with America Tours, listed above)
  Featuring exciting downhill mountain biking on the 'World's Most Dangerous Road', dropping from 4,600 m (15,092 ft) to 1,100 m (3,609 ft) in about 61 km (38 miles). (A safe adventure thanks to excellent equipment and trained guides). If you become addicted, they'll take you on other spectacular roads.

- **Hidalgo Tours**
  Bolivar, corner of Junín, in centre of Potosí.
  Tel: (2) 622-5186 / (2) 622-9512
  Specialities include visits to Potosí mines and excursions to Salar de Uyuni (the Uyuni salt lake).

- **Paititi**
  Av 6 de Agosto, Edificio Santa Teresa
  Tel: (2) 244-0586
  Seeks out unusual adventure locations.

- **Sky Bolivia**
  Calle Sagárnaga 367
  Tel: (2) 231-3254
  For climbing and hiking, with equipment furnished.

- **Terra Andina**
  Calle Chaco 738, fifth floor
  Tel: (2) 242-2241
  Website: http://www.terra-andina.com
  Satisfies the intellectual demands of various disciplines of 'ologists', mixing on-site adventure with entirely comfortable lodging.

- **Transturín**
  Alfredo Azcarrumz 2518, Sopocachi
  Tel: (2) 242-2222
  Especially catamaran overnight cruises on Lake Titicaca and other lake-related activities.

RESTAURANTS

CultureShock! Bolivia opts for the minimalist rather than encyclopaedic approach, picking out a few of the best bets in restaurants, considering the quality-price ratio.

In most cities, a multitude of small, family-operated restaurants offer Bolivian dishes at very reasonable prices. In general, if you see a lot of people inside, the food is good. For generic international food, simply find the nearest five or four-star hotel. When no reservations are ever necessary, no phone numbers have been included. Remember that the daily full course fixed-price lunch menu is the best bargain.

La Paz

A restaurant guide for La Paz alone would occupy an entire volume. Here are a few unique eating places with loyal regulars. Apologies to many superb La Paz eateries not included here.

- **Café Torino**
  Torino Hotel, Calle Socabaya 457
  Situated in a superb colonial patio of Hotel Torino. Fixed-price lunches are like *abuela* used to cook, basic but authentic. Good drinking atmosphere and cultural happenings as poets and professors show up in groups from time to time.

- **Chicharrónería Irpavi**
  Irpavi, south zone
  Best fried pork in La Paz. This proletarian, weekend-only patio restaurant began as a small riverside stand, later winning an international award in Madrid. You can see meat hanging behind a glass window before you eat it. Served with indigenous brew, *chicha* and white corn. This insider's place is now a living myth.

- **Gringo Limón (01)**
  Plaza Abaroa 2497 at 20 de Octubre
  Tel: (2) 243-4429

Offers a chance to eat Tarija's food without travelling to Tarija. Speciality is grilled meats. Recommended is lamb, *lechón al horno* (roast baby pig) and the *parrillada* (mixed grilled meats).

- **Gringo Limón (02)**
  Plaza Humboldt
  Tel: (2) 279-0991
  The copious salad bar is the alternative, with both easily recognised from afar thanks to the lemon-yellow façade.

- **Hotel Plaza**
  El Prado
  Almuerzo Buffet. This may be the best five-star bargain in town, all you can eat for a reasonable price at an altitude where you're not supposed to have big meals. Plenty of variety for all courses, including superb desserts.

- **Iglu**
  One branch in Miraflores, near the stadium, another at Plaza del Estudiante. Thirty years of hamburgers. For US$ 0.60 you get a crisp, tasty hamburger and fries. Only place in La Paz serving juice of the tumbo fruit. A worthy rival of McDonalds and Burger King. Iglu will survive the competition.

- **Nelsy's**
  Right across from the university. Cheap, ma-and-pa food. Try *pejerry* (kingfish), usually Fridays. Excellent *salteñas* in the mornings, or *cuñapes* and *humintas*, afternoons. This place is another living myth for insiders on a tight budget in search of authenticity.

- **Restaurant Naira**
  Calle Sagárnaga 161
  Tel: (2) 235-0530
  Specialises in a house recipe for fish and fondue bourguignone.

Santa Cruz

Many restaurants here have both indoor and outdoor seating. If you're tired of potatoes and corn in the highlands, you'll enjoy tropical side dishes here: fried *yuca* (replaces potato), cooked or fried banana and rice with cheese (replaces corn).

- **Casa del Camba**
  Second ring, Cristobal de Mendoza 539
  Tel: (3) 342-7864.
  Economical creole food. Try the *locro*, a unique chicken soup. Also, *picante de gallina*. Good way to taste the Camba culture with generous portions and maybe music thrown in as well.

- **La Bella Nápoli**
  Independencia 635
  Tel: (3) 332-5402
  Rustic, woodsy, upscale Italian food, a spirited walk from the main plaza.

- **Yorimichi**
  Avenida Busch 548
  Tel: (3) 334-7717
  With Santa Cruz known for Japanese immigrants, why not try this truly fine restaurant. Reservation advised.

Cochabamba

- **Mercado 25 de Mayo**
  25 de Mayo and Jordan
  Clean market stalls, it's safe to have a typical Cochabamba breakfast of *api* (hot corn cereal drink) and *buñuelos* (a greasy pastry).

- **El Palacio del Silpancho**
  On Calle Baptista near the corner of Mayor Rocha
  This establishment is often recommended. We have eaten there just to say we've experienced the typical Cochabamba dish called *silpancho*, which is a flattened,

fried steak with a fried egg on top, along with an onion-tomato salad, rice and and friend potatoes. Like it or not, at least you're not in a tourist place.

- **Plaza Colón** (north side)
  Just north of Plaza Colón on the Avenida Ballivián boulevard is a row of several European style restaurants with pavement seating. Economically priced lunches, mainly of traditional Bolivian cuisine but some international as well.

Sucre

Aside from the listed entries, the traveller will find several interesting restaurants and cafés in the vicinity of Plaza 25 de Mayo. Many Sucre eateries and drinking holes have book shelves, book exchanges or other signs that this is a university town.

- **Airport**
  Amazingly, one of the best restaurants in town is at the airport. Sucre is famous for its spicy sausage. If you love sausage but are afraid to take a chance, this is the best bet; virtually greaseless but doesn't sacrifice on taste.

- **Chinese food**
  At and near Plaza 25 de Mayo are several Chinese restaurants with affordable food and good service.

- **La Repizza**
  Not far from Plaza on Calle Ortiz 79
  This low-cost place has a friendly, artsy atmosphere; perhaps the best fixed-menu lunch in town or try the vegetarian lasagna.

- **Joy Ride Café**
  Calle Nicolás Ortiz 14 at Plaza 25 de Mayo
  A multi-purpose gathering place with Euro style bar, a patio,

a book exchange, artwork and sometimes entertainment and dancing, plus food.

- **La Taverne**
  Avenida Aniceto Arce 35, a half block from Plaza.
  Moderate prices considering the quality of this French, Bolivian and international food. Video cassette French films, French magazines on table at entrance. Housed in Alliance Française.

Potosí

- Doña Eugenia does not pop up at the main plaza, but it's worth looking for, by walking north to Calle Santa Cruz and then staying on Santa Cruz until you reach the intersection with Hermanos Ortega. Very authentic food, including *fricasé*, a typical pungent stew, *chicharrón* (pork cooked in its own fat), with a unique regional hot sauce to add.

- **La Manzana Mágica**
  Oruro 239, one block from the main plaza.
  This is a favourite of vegetarian backpackers. Small place, good food, get there early if you want a table.

- **El Mesón**
  Plaza 10 de Noviembre, corner of Tarija and Linares
  Tel: (2) 622-3087
  Good food in an elegant ambiance, with prices that are reasonable, given the quality.

- **Sumac Orcko**
  Calle Quijarro 46, near Plaza
  This is second consensus choice of locals, extensive menu, fills up at night; you can tell by looking through the window that folks are enjoying their food. Fixed-price menu. *Picante de pollo* is recommended if you can handle piquant.

Tarija

- **Pizzerias** are ubiquitous in Tarija

- **Restaurant Bufalo** (on the main plaza)
  Receives good reviews and also serves American style breakfast. Miss Bolivia dined here, so it's no hole in the wall.

- **Taverna Gattopardo**
  La Madrid 318
  Tel: (2) 663-0656
  This is the most popular restaurant for the locals, and is used as a landmark for finding other places. Recommended by many travellers is the *fondue bourguignone*, but you can also get good salads, fish dinners, desserts and unusually good coffee for Bolivia. Outdoor seating on the Plaza adds atmosphere.

Oruro

- **La Cabaña**
  A block and a half from the plaza, Junín 6095
  Tel: (2) 525-8023
  Crowds line up for its fixed-price lunch menu; get there early for authentic Bolivian dishes.

- **Nayjama**
  Aldana 1880 at Calle Pagador
  Tel: (2) 527-7699
  Dishes up more authentic cuisine, including meat from parts of the cow that Americans throw out, as well as tasty *pejerrey*. This place gets great reviews.

- Ask around for two legendary cooks who've had their stands for decades. Doña Cristina Mena may still be serving fried llama with all the trappings at **El Puente**, a few steps from Plaza Sebastian Pagador and hopefully Doña Rosa Calizaya is still there ladelling out her *thimpu* (a mutton and potato stew with lots of endemic Bolivian goodies thrown in with a natural tomato sauce) at **Mercado Fermín López.**

HOTELS

- Practical website: http://www.boliviaweb.com/hotels/htm
The Bolivia website is an all-purpose reference. You can search for a hotel by city/region, by number of stars or with other cross-references. With the above website available, we've opted here for the minimalist approach, listing a few hotels considered by *CultureShock! Bolivia* to have an excellent quality-price ratio, based on a combination of some or all of the following criteria: authentic colonial décor, facilities, location and comfort.
L = luxury, M = moderate, I = inexpensive

La Paz

If you just want to bed down at the low end or bathe in luxury at the high end, there are numerous generic places available. We've tried to pick out some of the most unique lodging choices for all budgets.

- **(L) Gran Hotel Paris**
Right on Plaza Murillo, which provided a view of revolutionary confrontations in the first five years of the century
Tel: (2) 220-3030
Our tour of this hotel seemed like a museum visit. Built in the early 1900s in a post-baroque style, it was remodelled near the end of the century. This is the most respectful of European heritage of all La Paz upscale hotels. Includes substantial breakfast. Attached to a stylish café-restaurant.

- **(M) Hotel Sagárnaga**
Sagárnaga 326, in the heart of the hilly tourist/artisan/bargaining district
Tel: (2) 235-0252
You might be able to bargain for a discount in the low season. Bolivian breakfast. Occasional *peña* music.

- **(I–M) Hostal República**
Calle Comercio 1455

Tel: (2) 235-6617
Situated in a venerable historical building, with courtyards, gardens, reading materials and jovial service.

- **(M) Hotel Rosario**
  Av Illampu 704
  Tel: (2) 245-1658
  Colonial decor, Aymara motifs, artisan neighbourhood and pleasant courtyard. This hotel is meticulously ecological.

- **(I) Hotel Torino**
  Calle Socabaya 457
  Tel: (2) 234-1487
  Among the best of low budget hotels, with a colonial courtyard and central location.

Cochabamba

There's no competition in Cochabamba for 'most imaginative hotel name'.

- **(I)Hostal Colonial**
  Junín N-0134
  Tel: (4) 442-1791
  Cheap but friendly; not terribly comfortable but clean and with an attractive courtyard garden.

- **(M) Mary Hotel**
  Calle Nataniel Aguirre S-601
  Tel: (4) 445-2487
  For seekers of the practical and comfortable: modern and not far from the bus station.

- **(M–I) Americano Hotel** (corner of Aroma and Arce)
  Tel: (4) 445-0552
  Bright and colourful enough to earn three stars.

Sucre

In some hard-to-reach places, we recommend a luxury hotel as a reward for a tough journey but in this beautiful city, the bottom- and medium-end hostals are all colonial clean and picturesque pretty. It's difficult to figure how Sucre can be so easy for a room seeker while Potosí can be so 'challenging'.

Website http//www.boliviahostals.com is the all-purpose contact number for dozens of fine hostels and hotels for all budgets, most within walking distance of the central plaza.

- **(M) Hostal Cruz de Popayán**
  Calle Loa 881, at the corner of Calle Colón
  Tel: (4) 644-0889
  Housed in a historic 17th century mansion acclaimed by UNESCO. It's relatively cheap, given its credentials.

- **(I) Hostal Alojamiento Backpacker**
  Run by the same people at the same address, this is a decent place for rock-bottom budgets.

- **(M–I) Grand Hotel**
  Aniceto Arce 61
  Tel: (4) 645-1704
  Half a block from Plaza, best value, pretty courtyard garden, funky rooms (all of them different) and friendly service.

Oruro

- **(M) Hotel Monarca**
  Av 6 de Agosto, corner of Ejército
  Tel: (2) 525-4300
  Comfort and facilities.

- **(I) Hotel Bernal**
  Calle Brazil 701
  E-mail: bernal@boliviahostels.com
  Tel: (2) 527-9468
  Near bus terminal (for a few dollars more than the dirt cheapest, you get much more value and comfort).

Potosí

- **(I) Hotel El Turista**
  Calle Lanza 19, corner of Nogales

E-mail: turista@boliviahostels.com
Inexpensive, basic but quite friendly service. Ask for a third floor south room with a view. Beds in some rooms may be on the hard side. In a city with few lodging alternatives, this hotel does best in surveys.

- **(I) Hotel María Victoria**
  Calle Chuquisaca 148
  Tel: (2) 622-2132
  Email: mariavictoria@boliviahostels.com
  With colonial style and courtyard, prettier than Hotel El Turista but doesn't match the friendliness of El Turista.

- **(L–M) Hostal Colonial**
  Calle Hoyos 8
  Tel: (2) 622-4809
  Email: colonial@boliviahostels.com
  Central location. Visually more stunning and comfortable than the above two (4 stars), but you will pay for the difference.

Santa Cruz

- **(I) Residencial Bolivar**
  Calle Sucre 131
  Email: bolivar@boliviahostels.com
  Hammocks in the courtyard, hearty breakfasts, fair comfort for low-end lodging.

- **(M) Hotel Bibosi**
  Calle Junín 218 (in a sprawling city, this is centrally located)
  Tel: (3) 336-9173
  This place is not elegant but the spaciousness, jovial service and great rooftop view give it good value.

- **(L–M) Hotel Lido**
  21 de Mayo 527
  Tel: (3) 336-3555
  Most high-end hotels are luxury resorts far from the centre of town (ubiquitous advertising), but this place is centrally located and has all the amenities without being luxurious.

Tarija

- **(L) Hotel Los Ceibos**
  Five blocks from central plaza, Av Victor Paz Estenssoro, at La Madrid
  Tel: (4) 663-4430
  For swimmers; rooms with balcony.

- **(M–L) Hotel El Salvador**
  Alexandro del Carpio 840
  Check travel agency for new phone number

- **(L–I) Pensión Facundo**
  Batalla de Salado 47 (near bus station)
  Best feature is bicycle rental.

Amboró National Park

This area, in ancient times the exclusive domain of the Chiriguano and Yucaré cultures, is at once the scene of incredible biodiversity and environmental threats from civilisation.

- **(L) Amboró Eco Resort**
  Buena Vista, 103 km (64 miles) from Santa Cruz
  Tel: (3) 932-2048

Concepción-Jesuit Missions

- **Gran Hotel Concepción**
  Tel: (3) 964-3031
  Considering the rough voyage to get here, why not stay in luxury, right across from the Jesuit mission church in a complex partly built in the elaborate carved wood styles of the Jesuit churches. This hotel has a pool and luxurient gardens.

Coroico

Dry season is best: May through October.

- ***(L) El Viejo Molino**
  Camino a Santa Barbara km 1, Coroico

Tel: (2) 220-1519
One of the most advertised hotels in Bolivia.

- **(M–I) Hotel Esmeralda**
  A few blocks up the hill from the central plaza
  Tel: (2) 213-6017
  Luxuriant, spectacular views, location, pool and woods. This gets our vote for best value and location.

- **(M) Hotel Don Quixote**
  Camino a Coripata
  Tel: (2) 213-6007
  Colonial, good looking escape, good bargain considering resort facilities and friendly.

Rurrenabaque
- **(M) Hotel Oriental**
  Plaza 2 de Febrero
  Tel: (3) 892-2401
  Reasonable prices, with glorious hammocks in a garden with giant-leaf tropical plants, and at night you can hear the sounds of Bolivia's biodiversity.

Sorata
- **Residencial Sorata** (right off the central plaza)
  Funky colonial, incredible architectural artisanry with hidden patios and quirky rooms.
  Tel: (2) 811-5044

Salar de Uyuni
- **Hotel Playa Blanca**
  (Aptly named 'White Beach'), this is the only choice for those who will stay over night and give infinity a chance at the vast and eerie Uyuni Salt Lake. Contact through Hidalgo Tours in Potosí. See above.

ENVIRONMENTAL ORGANISATIONS
Bolivia is a proving grounds for ecological educators and activists, both as a victim of environmental degradation

and as a sanctuary for a incredible diversity of ecosystems, microclimates, endemic species of plants and animals and old growth forests.

Many travellers interviewed for this book were able to become deeply involved in Bolivian life thanks to participating in environmental groups.

The reader may discover that an international environmental organisation with offices in his or her home country may already be engaged in activities in Bolivia. If not, readers may wish to contact a Bolivian group. Listed below is a sampling of some of the most notable Bolivian organisations dedicated to the good fight for clean air and water, thriving forests, as well as sovereignty and biodiversity of native agriculture and food consumption against industrial models based on genetically-modified organisms. Their programme statements can be found on the listed websites.

Most of the words in the Spanish names of these organisations are easily recognised cognates. *Medio ambiente* means environment and *desarrollo* means development.

- **Asociación Ecológica del Oriente (ASEO)**
  Radial 19 Calle 7 #150, Santa Cruz
  Tel: (3) 355-6587 or (3) 355-1747
  Email: Aseoscz@cotas.com.bo

- **Foro Boliviano Medio Ambiente (FOBOMADE)**
  Av Abdon Saavedra 2370, La Paz
  Email: fobomade@fobomade.org.bo
  Website: http://www.fobomade.org.bo

- **Liga de Defensa del Medio Ambiente (LIDEMA)**
  Av Ecuador 2131, La Paz
  Tel: (2) 241-9393
  Email: lidema@lidema.org.bo
  Website: http://www.lidema.org.bo

- **Protección del Medio Ambiente Tarija (PROMETA)**
  Calle Alejandro del Carpio #E-659, Tarija
  Tel: (4) 664-5865

Email: prometa@prometa.org
Website: http://www.prometa.org

- **La Sociedad Potosína de Ecología (SOPE)**
  Calle Sucre 51, Potosí
  Tel: (4) 622-7324
  Email: sopeforo@cotapnet.com.bo

LANGUAGE STUDY

As a language teacher, I find it difficult to favour any one programme over another. In the best of schools you can get stuck with a bad teacher, and in some institutes with a bad reputation, you might be pleasantly surprised. The best strategy is to research the offerings. Contact a school and ask to speak to some former students who have taken classes there. Most important, ask about the school's methodology. The best answer would be: 'we use the best aspects from many different methods'. Rather than repeat what you'd find in the Yellow Pages, here we list two umbrella organisations that have links to many study opportunities all over Bolivia, plus an option for the study of indigenous languages.

- http://www.studyabroadlinks.com/search/Bolivia/learn_Spanish
- http://www.languageschoolsguide.com/Bolivia.cfm (Spanish)
- Instituto de Langua y Cultura Aymara (ILCA), which has connections with several universities in the USA and Britain, as well as with the Alliance Française in La Paz.
  Website: http://www.ilcanet.com
  Tel: (2) 239-6806
  Offers courses in Aymara, Quechua and Spanish.

Private or small-group classes are posted on bulletin boards, and often the price is right. Or, you may place your own classified ad, offering English-language conversation in exchange for Spanish, Aymara or Quechua instruction. Thus you will have free instruction and you may be lucky enough to find a trained teacher. It's not recommended to meet alone with an ad-answering stranger. Use a café until you get to know the person, or have a friend tag along.

FURTHER READING

The following books and articles are available in English, and are deemed as most entertaining (although not necessarily happy) reading, so that one can get a feel for the people, culture and history of this dramatic country. With Bolivia in a state of change, this bibliography also includes authors to look for right now, via word search, periodicals or bookshops.

ROOTS

This list offers a quick foundation for basic but no less exciting knowledge in history and culture.

Rebellion in the Veins: Political Struggle in Bolivia, 1952–1982 James C Dunkerley. London, UK: Verso, 1984.
- By British historian and Latin American expert James C Dunkerley. Well written, critical, with a wily sense of humour, this book has been translated into Spanish.

Let Me Speak! / Si Me Permiten Hablar... Domitila Barrios de Chungara. New York, NY: Monthly Review Press, 1978.
- This is a chronicle of the strength, endurance and generosity of the human spirit. Set in Bolivian mining communities during times of social upheaval, it is written by Domitila Barrios de Chungara, the wife of a miner. Domitila participated in the United Nations's International Women's Year Tribunal in 1975.

'Kallawaya: the Nomadic Medicine Men of Bolivia'. *Perspectives in Health Magazine.* Debbie K Becht. PanAmerican Health Organization: Vol 3, Number 1, 1998.
- You can find this one on the web.

I Am Rich Potosí: The Mountain that Eats Men. Stephen Ferry with Eduardo Galeano and Marguerite Holloway. New York, NY: The Monacelli Press, 1999.
- Deep and lyrical images of the mining life.

WHAT'S GOING ON RIGHT NOW?

The following names pop up in vital moments as active observers of current Bolivian events and their historical background.

Alvaro García Linera

This sociologist and former political prisoner was elected vice president in 2005. He coordinated the most comprehensive picture of Bolivia's social movements in *Sociología de los Movimientos Sociales en Bolivia*, along with colleagues Marxa Chavez Leon and Patricia Costas Monje, co-published by Plural in Bolivia and NGOs Oxfam and Diakonia, second updated edition 2005. Translations of and references to his articles and opinion often appear on the web.

Eduardo Galeano

A hero for many of those who seek a better world, this Uruguayan writer is the author of numerous books on history and society, which are noted for their lyrical and humoristic style.

Tom Kruse

A thorn in the side of Bechtel, Kruse specialises in issues of natural resources and fair trade.

Oscar Olivera

Cochabamba! Water War in Bolivia, published by South End Press in 2004. Cochabamba was one battle won but the war continues, and Olivera aptly goes beyond the events of 2000 and looks forward. Mr Olivera is a protagonist, an unassuming hero, and students of Bolivian reality should have his name ready for any word search concerning the struggle for natural resources.

James Petras

An iconoclast historian with a cynical but thinking view of people and events. Would-be heroes are taken apart with an intelligent slam-dunk.

FURTHER READING 295

Christian Parenti
A journalist who knows how to chase down a story, his work appears in *The Nation* and other publications.

Susan Spronk
A hands-on scholar who attacks confusion and comes out with clarity.

ADVENTURE
Bolivia Handbook: The Travel Guide. Alan Murphy. Bath, England: Footprint Books Ltd, 2002.
- Yes, this is a guidebook, but it's also a good read, with a sense of humour, by an adventurous soul who knows Bolivia! Always check the most updated edition.

Trekking in Bolivia: A Traveler's Guide. Yossi Brain, Andrew North and Isobel Stoddart. Seattle, WA: The Mountaineers Books, 1997.
- Lots of strategic advice by hikers who have blazed new trails. One reviewer has criticised the imperfection of some of the maps here. But many of these hikes are through uncharted territories. From my own experience of having to make my own maps as I go, I couldn't do half as good a job. The late Yossi Brain, a hero of trekkers and mountaineers in Bolivia, also wrote *Bolivia—A Climbing Guide* (The Mountaineers Books, 1999).

Bolivia, Lonely Planet's Travel Survival Kit. Australia: Lonely Planet Publications.
- Always check the most updated edition.

LITERATURE
The Fat Man from La Paz: Contemporary Fiction from Bolivia. Ed. Rosario Santos. New York, NY: Seven Stories Press, 2000
- This is the most extensive English-language collection of Bolivian fiction, representing a multiplicity of tones and perspectives. Bravo to Seven Stories Press and editor of the collection, Rosario Santos, for giving Bolivia's talented

but landlocked and PR-challenged writers an international audience. What better way to get a feel for the country than through its fiction.

POSTSCRIPT

Journalist Mike Ceaser is the only person I've known to have got around hilly La Paz primarily by bicycle. As a digger for good stories, he has reached people and places that are beyond the horizon of most of his colleagues. Check him out on the web.

ABOUT THE AUTHOR

As a Bolivia-based journalist, Mark Cramer covered a variety of subjects, from politics to sports, from indigenous customs to international business.

Reviewed in dozens of publications, Cramer's *Funkytowns USA: The Best Alternative, Eclectic, Irreverent & Visionary Places* scored a strange exacta when it was written up in both scholarly journals on the one hand and *Playboy* and a supermarket tabloid on the other. *Funkytowns* was featured in a 10-minute spot on CNN and several rebellious profs have used it for their university students. His Marshall Cavendish books on Cuba and Mexico have also been used in settings of higher education. His horse racing novel, *Scared Money*, will be republished in paperback in 2006.

Cramer's lifelong avocation is living the daily life of different countries. His heroes include writers Eduardo Galeano (Uruguay) and Charles Bukowski (USA), jazz pianist Thelonius Monk and the great Bolivian artist and defender of justice Walter Solón Romero.

Horrified by the receding glaciers in his favourite Bolivian hiking territory and strip-mall banality of suburban America, Cramer resolved to oppose the car-oil economy, not only politically but through the symbolic act of doing all his commuting by bicycle, rain or shine, winter or summer.

He currently lives in Paris, France with his wife and son (who has done an internship in Bolivia). The Cramers continue to maintain a second residence in La Paz.

INDEX

A
accommodation 216
Afrobolivianos 82
AIDS 71
Altiplano 16, 19, 76–77, 92, 100, 151, 163, 170, 183, 186–188, 194–195, 198, 207, 213
altitude 2, 5–7, 10–11, 14–18, 33, 53–54, 82, 113, 115–117, 127, 140–141, 178, 182, 187, 189, 193, 196, 198, 201, 204, 208, 212, 215, 219, 243, 247, 254, 260
Amazon 4, 12, 197, 205, 223, 225, 227
Apolo 206–208
architecture 95, 125, 163, 171, 181–182, 198
art 63, 72–76, 87, 96, 105, 107, 125, 164–168, 170, 171, 180–181, 191, 193, 196, 228, 241
  art galleries 72–73, 165
Aymara 9, 23, 37, 56–57, 75–78, 82, 91, 95, 150, 156, 159, 184, 186, 201, 213, 220, 222, 230, 234–235, 238, 254–255, 257

B
Bánzer Hugo 31, 38, 79
Bolivian Labour Confederation 35
  COB 35–39, 96, 258
buses 66, 121, 175, 212
business customs 241
  bribes 64, 67, 95
  cultivating contacts 243
  functions 31, 76, 98, 145, 198
  personal referrals 243

C
Cambas 77, 79–81, 194
Catholicism 92, 145, 255
caves 194
Chaco 12, 79, 81, 84–86, 95, 196, 197, 199
chagas 114
Challapampa 219–222
children 26–27, 30, 68, 70–72, 99, 104, 127–128, 138, 140, 147, 167, 169–170, 184, 190, 194, 197, 219, 224–225
Chinkana Temple 221–222
cholera 114, 133, 194, 198
Cholos 57, 93, 96, 145
cities
  Cobija 200, 247
  Cochabamba 11, 14, 17, 20–21, 30, 35, 41–42, 47, 61, 71–72, 74–75, 79, 134, 151–153, 185, 189, 192–195, 198, 234, 248, 254, 259
  Copacabana 10, 146, 150, 217, 218, 223
  El Alto 2–4, 10, 23, 25–28, 35, 43–44, 65, 71, 75, 92, 150, 158, 171, 182–187, 203, 259
  La Paz 2–27, 31, 33–34, 41–42, 47, 50–51, 54–57, 62, 67–75, 79, 82–84, 86, 93, 96, 100, 102, 106, 115–116, 118, 122, 124, 126, 128–129, 133, 136, 146, 151–153, 156–178, 182–184, 186–192, 194, 196, 198–199, 201–204, 212, 215, 222–223, 226, 229–230, 234, 243, 250, 253–254, 259, 260
  Oruro 10, 47, 75, 79, 83, 92–93, 121–122, 146–149, 152–153, 187–188, 254
  Potosí 10, 19–20, 39, 47, 54, 70, 72, 75, 79, 82, 87–88, 94, 152, 178–179, 181–182, 187–188, 193, 201, 205, 212, 234, 254
  Santa Cruz 12, 41, 45, 72, 78–79, 82, 85, 122, 130, 146, 150–151, 153, 168, 172, 195–199, 254
  Sucre 5, 11, 14, 17, 20–21, 44, 74–75, 79, 93, 123, 149–150, 152, 156, 182, 188–195, 234, 253
  Tarija 11, 21, 89, 108, 137, 140, 150–153, 189–196, 254
  Trinidad 151, 200, 226
class structure 238
coca 1, 4, 6–7, 29–34, 39, 40, 42, 60, 76, 89, 113, 138, 140, 160, 179, 208, 210–211, 221, 255, 257
cocaine 26–27, 30–31, 34, 39, 76, 97, 208
coffee 133, 138, 157, 196, 255
commerce 8–9, 48, 87, 95, 164, 172, 241, 249
conservation 207
Creole 37, 93, 95, 134, 179, 198
culture shock 92, 100, 105, 127–128, 141, 147, 150, 153, 188, 229
currency 119, 233, 255

INDEX

D
dance 52, 82, 128, 144–145, 147, 151–152, 164, 167, 191
democracy 23, 38, 45, 62, 97–98, 154, 172, 184, 260

E
ecotourism 209–211, 224
education 62, 68, 101, 127–128, 157, 219, 224, 231, 234–235, 249

F
festivals 7, 10, 92, 144–145, 150, 153, 187, 195, 220
  Carnaval 92, 121, 146–149, 151, 187
football 4, 6–7, 16–18, 51–53, 79, 81–82, 87, 106–108, 116, 128, 141, 151, 166, 172, 188, 208, 210, 214, 242–243, 256

G
Guarani 12, 199
Guevara, Che 15, 16, 73, 110, 153

H
health 18, 21, 47, 55–56, 62, 101, 115, 117–118, 129, 133, 182, 198, 247
hiking 18, 117, 200, 208, 216
human rights 35, 46, 74, 100, 154, 258
Huyustus 62, 133, 160–161, 172

I
Incas 75, 95, 135
inflation 59, 97
Island of the Sun 217–223, 225

K
Kollas 77, 79–81, 194, 198

L
Lake Titicaca 2, 10, 20, 75–77, 135, 146, 184, 201, 207, 212–213, 218–219, 234
Lozada, Sánchez de 25, 33, 36, 39–40, 60, 76, 100, 185, 256
lustrabotas 68

M
markets 30–31, 70, 77, 98, 109, 120, 137, 160–161, 172, 193, 240, 246, 247–249
medicine 54–56, 85, 117, 162, 183, 219

mestizo 75, 85, 181, 187
miners 16, 68, 87, 89
mosquito 21, 83, 92, 215, 226, 228
mountains
  Andes 6, 9, 12, 26, 93, 117, 192, 197, 202, 247, 256
  Huayna Potosí 54, 205
  Mount Illampu 207, 212
  Mount Illimani 4, 9, 158, 165, 168, 171, 201–204

N
non-governmental organisation (NGO) 61, 155–156, 207

P
penal system 34
politics 78
poverty 34, 47, 64–67, 71, 97, 99, 114, 170, 187

Q
Quechuas 9, 47, 75, 95
quinoa 77, 134, 220, 247–248, 255

R
Río Choqueyapu 157
River Beni 227
Rurrenabaque 156, 226, 228–229

S
Salar de Uyuni 182, 188
Simón Bolívar 189
Solón, Walter Romero 73, 188, 191
Spanish Conquest 92, 220
street vendor 59

T
Tiahuanaco 75, 77, 152, 171–172, 184
tourism 46, 100, 144, 151–152, 164, 172, 201, 219, 223–224
trekking 84, 216, 224–226
Tuichi River 211, 227–228

V
visa requirements 111

Y
Yungas 6, 7, 13, 21, 30, 33, 82–84, 88, 122, 151–152, 174–175, 177, 212, 216

Titles in the CULTURESHOCK! series:

Argentina	Hawaii	Pakistan
Australia	Hong Kong	Paris
Austria	Hungary	Philippines
Bahrain	India	Portugal
Barcelona	Indonesia	San Francisco
Beijing	Iran	Saudi Arabia
Belgium	Ireland	Scotland
Bolivia	Israel	Sri Lanka
Borneo	Italy	Shanghai
Brazil	Jakarta	Singapore
Britain	Japan	South Africa
Cambodia	Korea	Spain
Canada	Laos	Sweden
Chicago	London	Switzerland
Chile	Malaysia	Syria
China	Mauritius	Taiwan
Costa Rica	Mexico	Thailand
Cuba	Morocco	Tokyo
Czech Republic	Moscow	Turkey
Denmark	Munich	Ukraine
Ecuador	Myanmar	United Arab
Egypt	Nepal	Emirates
Finland	Netherlands	USA
France	New York	Vancouver
Germany	New Zealand	Venezuela
Greece	Norway	Vietnam

For more information about any of these titles, please contact any of our Marshall Cavendish offices around the world (listed on page ii) or visit our website at:

www.marshallcavendish.com/genref